RADICAL NATION

JOE BIDEN AND KAMALA HARRIS'S
DANGEROUS PLAN FOR AMERICA

SEAN SPICER

Humanix Books
www.humanixbooks.com

Humanix Books
RADICAL NATION
Copyright © 2021 by Sean Spicer
All rights reserved

Humanix Books, P.O. Box 20989, West Palm Beach, FL 33416, USA
www.humanixbooks.com | info@humanixbooks.com

Humanix Books is a division of Humanix Publishing, LLC. Its trademark, consisting of the words "Humanix Books," is registered in the Patent and Trademark Office and in other countries.

ISBN: 9-781-63006-171-5 (Hardcover)
ISBN: 9-781-63006-172-2 (E-book)

Printed in the United States of America
10 9 8 7 6 5 4 3 2 1

To my family and friends

Contents

1

Transfer of Power

MY ALARM SOUNDED AT 5:30 a.m., almost an hour earlier than normal, the morning of January 20, 2021. It was the final day of Donald Trump's presidency, and I wanted to go to Joint Base Andrews and see him off for the last time. There had been a lot of media speculation about how many people would show up and who would be there. Some prominent Trump administration figures and Republican lawmakers had indicated that they wouldn't attend, but I wanted to be there. For one thing, I wanted to be a part of that chapter of history, to be a witness to the final moments of the administration I had played a role in. For another, I knew it would be an exciting event to discuss for our daily Newsmax TV show *Spicer & Co.*

Katie Armstrong, who manages my business affairs, speaking engagements, and media opportunities, picked me up, and we drove to Joint Base Andrews (JBA) in Prince George's County, Maryland. I knew the place well. I had visited JBA many times during my 22 years in the Navy, I had attended an air show there, and I had departed and arrived at JBA many times aboard *Air Force One* during my time at the White House.

It's normally a 25-minute drive from my home to the base. But as we got within a quarter mile of the gate, it was obvious that this would be no ordinary day getting into JBA. Traffic was already backed up because the normal flow of arriving military personnel was joined by a crowd of Trump well-wishers and former administration appointees, slowing the procession through the main gate. My invitation said to arrive no later than 7:30 a.m., so by 7:25, I was getting nervous. I had my military ID ready to flash, but we were still so far back in the line of cars that I feared we'd be turned back at the gate.

I told Katie, "I can't believe we got up this early, and we still might miss the cut-off."

We finally cleared the gate and drove about a quarter mile to an overflow parking lot. After parking, we boarded a government bus that took us to an airplane hangar. There the hundreds of attendees passed through metal detectors and were cleared. We waited until a little after 8 o'clock, when an Air Force officer made the announcement that they would open the hangar doors and escort folks out to the flight line to await the president's arrival.

The crowd of Trump fans and well-wishers moved out to the flight line in front of the VIP passenger terminal. There we were greeted with the majestic sight of the blue and white Boeing VC-25—the military version of the Boeing 747 airliner—designated *Air Force One* whenever the president is aboard.

How large was the crowd? For days, the media had been speculating about whether people would show up or not. I couldn't tell you how many were there. I got out of the crowd-estimating business a long time ago. But it was smaller than any Trump rally I've attended. Some in the media claimed that the White House had tried to build a big crowd by permitting up to five guests per invitation. Maybe I'm not as cynical as the media, but I didn't think the White House was trying to inflate the crowd. Instead, I thought it was a kind gesture, as if to say, "Your family members are welcome to come and be a part of history."

There was a stage with a presidential podium set up. Beside the stage, members of the Trump family waited: Ivanka Trump and her husband Jared Kushner, Don Jr. and his girlfriend Kimberly Guilfoyle, Eric and Lara Trump, and Tiffany and her fiancé, along with a number of President Trump's grandchildren. The weather was bitterly cold and windy as we all waited, looking to the sky for the approach of the president's helicopter, *Marine One*.

As a campaign strategist, White House press secretary, and commentator, I had invested a great deal of energy in this president and his policies. Now it was about to end. He was going to fly off to Florida, and all the folks I had known from the campaign and the administration were going to go their separate ways. A new team from the opposing party was coming to town.

"I Told You So"

At around 8:30 a.m., the crowd heard the distant thrum of helicopter rotors pounding the air. Low over the horizon, three helicopters appeared—*Marine One*, carrying the president, and two identical decoy helicopters. A buzz of conversation rippled through the crowd as people speculated as to which helicopter bore the president. One of the White House advance men saw me and said, "He's on the second one. It'll pull up close to the platform." I nodded and thanked him.

Moments later, the helicopter landed and pulled up in front of *Air Force One*, greeted by a wave of cheers and applause. At that point, we had been standing on the flight line for more than 20 minutes in the wind and cold. Once *Marine One* touched down, I didn't notice the cold anymore. I don't think anyone did.

As President Trump and the first lady emerged from the helicopter, the Air Force band played "Hail to the Chief" while a line of field artillery fired a 21-gun salute. Chants of "We love you!" exploded from the crowd as the first couple climbed the steps to the platform. Trump approached the microphone with a broad smile. "Thank you," he said, "and we love *you*, and I can tell you that from the bottom of my heart."

Speaking without notes, he thanked his family, friends, and staff and talked about the accomplishments of the past four years. He praised his wife Melania as "a woman of great grace and beauty and dignity." He asked Melania to speak, and she thanked the supporters and wished God's blessing on them all and on "this beautiful nation."

President Trump then listed some of the great accomplishments of the preceding four years—rebuilding the military, founding the Space Force, reforming the Veterans Administration, cutting taxes, slashing regulations, unleashing the economy, growing the number of jobs by leaps and bounds, and on and on. In a wry aside, he added that he hoped the Democrats wouldn't raise taxes again—"but if they do, I told you so."

President Trump acknowledged that his White House was not a "regular administration," but his family and his team had worked hard for the American people. "We've left it all on the field," he said. "We had a lot of obstacles, and we went through the obstacles."

He urged his followers to be wary of the virus that had originated in Communist China—"a horrible, horrible thing." And he took a moment to remember all who had suffered, died, or lost family members because of the virus.

"You are amazing people," he said. "This is a great, great country. It is my greatest honor and privilege to have been your president." At this, the crowd erupted in cheers of "USA! USA!" and "Thank you, Trump! Thank you, Trump!"

"I will always fight for you," he continued. "I will be watching, I will be listening, and I will tell you that the future of this country has never been better. I wish the new administration great luck and great success. I think they'll have great success. They have the foundation to do something really spectacular." It was a big-hearted olive branch to his political foe. He concluded with the words, "Have a good life. We will see you soon."

And it was over.

Pomp, Circumstance, and a Disco Beat

As President Trump and the first lady stepped down from the stage, something happened that took me by surprise—though it probably shouldn't have. Up to that moment, this farewell event had been conducted with traditional presidential pomp and circumstance. But immediately after President Trump concluded his farewell speech, I heard the familiar brass riff and disco beat of the Village People's "Y.M.C.A." blaring from the loudspeakers.

On the red carpet leading to *Air Force One*, Mr. Trump went into the same fist-pumping boogie he had done at many of his rallies. So this was Donald J. Trump, making his exit from an event that was half Trump rally, half official send-off. That song, that red carpet dance, that style defied every notion of presidential and military protocol—but then so had the last four years. As odd as it felt, it was a fitting end to President Trump's disruptive, turbulent, and nontraditional administration.

The first couple climbed the steps to the door of *Air Force One*, where they waved to the crowd a final time. Then they stepped inside and were gone from view. Minutes later, the presidential aircraft taxied down the runway and roared into the air—its last flight with Donald Trump aboard as commander-in-chief.

Traditionally, of course, the outgoing president attends the inauguration of the incoming president. During the weeks before the Biden inauguration, many people told me, "Trump has to attend the inauguration. It's tradition." I would always say, "There's no way Donald Trump will attend Joe Biden's inauguration." After the past four years and the tumultuous final months, I just couldn't picture it happening.

If Donald Trump had attended the inauguration, he could have still departed Washington aboard the presidential aircraft—but it would no longer have the call sign *Air Force One*. The airplane is only designated *Air Force One* when the president is on board. All other flights are designated *special air missions* (SAMs). I don't think Donald Trump wanted to leave Washington, DC, as a former president, flying aboard a special air mission. That wouldn't fit the Trump brand. I believe he wanted to still be the president of the United States when *Air Force One* landed in Florida.

As the president's jet shrank to a distant speck in the morning sky, I turned to Katie and said, "I don't think it has sunk in yet. Today feels like my last day of college. I have good memories to look back on, the future looks uncertain, and the folks I spent the last four years with are never going to be together again the same way—and a whole new class of students has arrived on campus. It hasn't sunk in yet. It's going to take a few days."

A Peaceful Transfer of Power

I returned home from JBA, turned on the TV, and watched the inauguration of the new president unfold. I saw the people flowing into the Capitol, all the dignitaries, members of Congress, Vice President Mike Pence and his wife Karen, and three former presidents—Bill Clinton, George Bush, and Barack Obama (96-year-old Jimmy Carter couldn't travel because of ill-health).

A number of reporters and pundits claimed that because President Trump was not physically present at the inauguration, we didn't have a "peaceful transfer of power." One of them, CNN's Jake Tapper, tweeted, "Respectfully, the transfer of power has not been peaceful. That ship has sailed."[1]

It's true that Donald Trump was the first president to forgo his successor's inauguration since 1869, when Andrew Johnson skipped the inauguration of Ulysses S. Grant. John Adams also avoided the inauguration of Thomas Jefferson in 1801, and John Quincy Adams gave Andrew Jackson's inauguration a pass in 1829. Yet, in each instance, we had a peaceful transfer of power. The Republic endured.

There's great symbolic value when one administration visibly passes the torch to the next, as when Barack Obama attended the inauguration of Donald J. Trump. But after the bitterness of the 2020 election and the storming of the Capitol on January 6, it wasn't going to happen. Joe Biden was probably relieved as well. If Trump had attended, the coverage would have focused on the drama of these two adversaries on the same stage. Tradition and symbols are important, but President Trump got to end his presidency his way, and Joe Biden got to begin his presidency in a way that focused on him and his message.

"A Very Generous Letter"

President Trump did observe one White House tradition that began with Ronald Reagan in 1989—the tradition of an outgoing president leaving a note for his successor. Reagan had left a note on a sheet of humorous printed stationery. At the top were the words "DON'T LET THE TURKEYS GET YOU DOWN," and at the bottom was a cartoon elephant lying prone on the ground with a flock of turkeys perched on its back and trunk. Reagan wrote:

> Dear George:
> You'll have moments when you want to use this particular stationery. Well, go to it. George, I treasure the memories we share and wish you all the very best. You'll be in my prayers. God bless you and Barbara. I'll miss our Thursday lunches.
> Ron

That tradition has continued unbroken to the present day. I was present in the Oval Office four years earlier when President Trump read the letter President Obama had left for him on January 20, 2017. It read:

Dear Mr. President—

Congratulations on a remarkable run. Millions have placed their hopes in you, and all of us, regardless of party, should hope for expanded prosperity and security during your tenure.

This is a unique office, without a clear blueprint for success, so I don't know that any advice from me will be particularly helpful. Still, let me offer a few reflections from the past eight years.

First, we've both been blessed, in different ways, with great good fortune. Not everyone is so lucky. It's up to us to do everything we can [to] build more ladders of success for every child and family that's willing to work hard.

Second, American leadership in this world really is indispensable. It's up to us, through action and example, to sustain the international order that's expanded steadily since the end of the Cold War, and upon which our own wealth and safety depend.

Third, we are just temporary occupants of this office. That makes us guardians of those democratic institutions and traditions—like rule of law, separation of powers, equal protection and civil liberties—that our forebears fought and bled for. Regardless of the push and pull of daily politics, it's up to us to leave those instruments of our democracy at least as strong as we found them.

And finally, take time, in the rush of events and responsibilities, for friends and family. They'll get you through the inevitable rough patches.

Michelle and I wish you and Melania the very best as you
embark on this great adventure, and know that we stand
ready to help in any ways which we can.
Good luck and Godspeed,
B.O.[2]

As President Trump read those words aloud, I could see that he
was genuinely touched by his predecessor's gracious words. During
the campaign, President Obama had strongly supported Hillary
Clinton and had been very critical of Donald Trump. Yet President
Obama now wished him well and even offered him heartfelt advice
for a successful presidency. Prior to becoming president, Donald
Trump had never run for public office, so the idea of a tough political adversary treating him with such magnanimity after the race was
over—that was something Trump had never experienced before.

Donald Trump fully understood that Obama didn't wish him
political success. He wished him success in leading the nation and
doing the people's business. Donald Trump had inherited a great
tradition in which, regardless of your party or political ideology,
no matter how intensely the candidates had fought on the campaign trail, it is the majesty of the American democracy that holds
the nation together when all is said and done. Donald Trump was
moved because the outgoing president had not only wished the
country well but also wished him well.

Seeing how Donald Trump was affected by Barack Obama's
gesture, I believe Trump wanted to be a part of history in the
very same way. He wanted to convey to President Joe Biden that
he wished him success in keeping America strong and free. So he
wrote a note to President Biden in the same magnanimous spirit
as that of the letter Barack Obama had written to him.

For now, only Joe Biden and Donald Trump know what was in that letter. Biden would only say, "The president wrote a very generous letter. Because it was private I will not talk about it until I talk to him, but it was generous." My instincts tell me the letter will likely never be released. Knowing President Trump, I believe he left that note intending it to be released to the public, as all previous letters have been. Some commentators suggest that Joe Biden showed kindness in characterizing the letter as "very generous." I wonder. Maybe Joe Biden was taunting Donald Trump, in effect saying, "If you want the world to read that letter, you have to make the first move and call me."

A Seamless Transition

Despite media claims to the contrary, President Trump took part in the peaceful transfer of power. That seamless transition from one president to the next is the miracle of American self-governance. It's the foundation of our continuing democracy.

According to *The Economist*, only slightly more than half the nations in the world have had even one peaceful and orderly transfer of power in the last 100 years. In those other nations, the transfer of power has been accompanied by a coup, a civil war, or a constitutional crisis.[3]

The media had been predicting for months that Donald Trump would never leave office peacefully if he lost the election. Those of us who have known Mr. Trump always knew there would be a peaceful transfer of power if he lost. Yes, he fought hard through the courts to make his case that the election had been stolen. But when he had exhausted all legal avenues to overturning a result he thought unfair, Donald Trump told the nation on January 7, "Congress has certified the results, and the new administration will be inaugurated on January 20. My focus now turns to ensuring a smooth, orderly, and seamless transition of power."

That sounds like a peaceful transfer of power to me.

Every four years, it's important that we all step back from our respective parties and reflect on who we are as Americans. We celebrate Inauguration Day—even if our side lost. We celebrate because our democracy goes on. We celebrate not as Democrats or Republicans but as Americans. What's more, we collectively hope and pray that our president will succeed in keeping America safe and prosperous and free. We don't necessarily want the incoming president to succeed politically—and that's fair; that's as it should be. But we understand that an administration that fails utterly (the Carter years leap to mind) inflicts misery and peril on us all.

The Loudest Wake-Up Call

It's going to be a long four years with Joe Biden as president and Kamala Harris as vice president. Though I have spent decades fighting for conservative principles and to elect Republicans up and down the ticket, I'm committed to the idea that we are all Americans first and foremost. After an election, we should all unite around what is best for America and the American people.

So I believe that we need to pray for President Biden—not that he would succeed politically, not that he would implement all his misguided Progressive policies, but that he would succeed in keeping America safe and strong and secure. (Throughout this book, I've capitalized *Progressive* to distinguish the radical-left ideology from *progressive*, meaning "gradually improving.") As you will see throughout this book, I believe that the policies President Biden has proposed will do great harm to our nation, our communities, our schools, our children and grandchildren, and the future of the world. I absolutely stand up for protecting the unborn, securing the border, defending our constitutional rights, lowering taxes, and maintaining a strong national defense. So I hope Joe Biden's policies fail—but I pray that he succeeds in safeguarding the Constitution and the Republic.

You might say, "I can't pray for Joe Biden and Kamala Harris! They stand for everything I'm against!" But St. Paul urged early Christians to pray for "kings, and for all that are in high station: that we may lead a quiet and a peaceable life in all piety and chastity" (1 Timothy 2:2, Douay-Rheims American Edition). At that time, the emperor of Rome was Nero, who was notorious for torturing and mass-executing Christians. If St. Paul urged first-century Christians to pray for Nero, then shouldn't twenty-first-century Christians pray for Joe Biden and Kamala Harris?

To those of us who believe that President Trump's policies moved the country in the right direction, these are troubling times. The election of Joe Biden and Kamala Harris is the loudest wake-up call you've ever heard. Everything is at stake. Joe Biden has promised to be the most Progressive president this country has ever seen. This is not empty hyperbole. He means it. He's already proving it. Take him at his word.

For the next four years, the Biden-Harris team is in the White House. And we need to understand how wrongheaded, destructive, and dangerous the current Biden-Harris agenda is. We must present a *strong* opposition to the many deluded and divisive notions this president has put forward. It's going to take every one of us, working together, to rescue America from the Biden-Harris radical agenda. We need all hands on deck.

In the coming pages, you'll learn how *you* can make a difference.

2

A Divisive Call to Unity

T HE INAUGURATION CEREMONY FOR President Joe Biden was replete with all the traditional symbols of our democracy— the majesty of the Capitol Building, the lofty speeches and stirring patriotic music, the words of poets and celebrities, and American flags everywhere. But there was one scene that was so funny it became a viral internet meme.

I'm talking about the image of Senator Bernie Sanders sitting by himself on the Capitol Hill bleachers, waiting for the inaugural ceremony to begin. Reporters took note of the big, warm-looking mittens Bernie wore on that bitterly cold day. *Slate* online magazine later learned that Sanders's mittens were a handmade gift from a Bernie supporter, Jen Ellis, a second-grade teacher from

Essex Junction, Vermont. She had given Bernie the mittens in 2016, after he lost the Democratic nomination to Hillary Clinton.

In an interview, Ellis told *Slate,* "I don't have much of a mitten business anymore because it really wasn't worth it. Independent crafters get really taken for a ride by the federal government. We get taxed to the nth degree." In the same interview, Ellis said that she is still a big supporter of Bernie Sanders, Joe Biden, and Kamala Harris—and she wept tears of joy as she watched Biden being sworn in.[4]

How ironic is that? Bernie was wearing mittens made for him by a woman whose business was wiped out by the very overregulation and taxation policies that Sanders, Biden, and Harris promote. Yet she continues to support them and vote for them and weeps for joy when they are sworn in. She sounds like a conservative when she complains about government overreach—yet she votes for Progressives and is completely unaware of the disconnect in her thinking.

I believe this Vermont teacher typifies many Democratic voters. They live, work, and raise their families according to traditional values. They believe in the value of hard work and fair play. They love liberty, and they love their country. They support the police and the military. And every election year, they go to the polls and vote for Democratic candidates who represent the exact opposite of their values—and they don't even realize it.

The viral internet meme of Bernie and his mittens is hilarious, but what those mittens represent is no joke. Millions of people voted for Joe Biden and against their own interests. They were duped by the Biden-Harris campaign and the leftist media into voting for a radical agenda.

A Divisive Speech about Unity

Joe Biden's inaugural address was filled with lofty-sounding words designed to stir our emotions. Biden presented himself as a man of empathy and caring, a healer, and a uniter. Yet he also spent a lot of time talking about what he thinks is wrong with America. This was not a speech about jobs and economic recovery, nor was it a call for America to confront the global threats and crises of the twenty-first century. It was, in large part, a rebuke to America for the sin of electing Donald Trump four years earlier.

The speech offered no glimpse into Joe Biden's policy agenda and his plans for America. Inauguration addresses are not traditionally policy speeches, but this speech was exceptionally barren of substance. In fact, as I listened to the speech in real time, it struck me as a run-of-the-mill political speech.

Later, as I listened to commentators discuss Biden's address, I wondered, "Were we hearing the same speech?" One of the most bizarre responses came from MSNBC national affairs analyst John Heilemann, who gushed, "There was a lot about the speech that was soaring. It may have been the best speech Joe Biden has ever given. . . . It was not a political speech at all. It was a speech that had a much higher purpose than that, and I don't want to go overboard and compare to it Lincoln's second inaugural, but aspirationally that's where it wanted to live." He's comparing Joe Biden to . . . Lincoln?

I took another look at Biden's inaugural speech. As I reconsidered what I'd heard, I realized that something had been nagging me about it. Finally, it dawned on me what it was: In spite of the lofty-sounding rhetoric, it was really a very passive-aggressive speech. What do I mean by passive-aggressive? The Mayo Clinic defines *passive-aggressive behavior* as "a pattern of indirectly expressing negative feelings instead of openly addressing them. There's a disconnect between what a passive-aggressive person says and what he or she does."[5] We see that disconnect when Biden uses the word *unity* eight times, and yet the net effect of the speech is divisive.

He was quick to remind his audience that "on this hallowed ground . . . just days ago, violence sought to shake this Capitol's very foundation." Yet there was not one word in Biden's speech about the far-left riots that began in May 2020 and continued for months in cities across the nation. Biden said nothing about the nights of leftist rioting in front of the White House. He didn't mention the defacing of the Lincoln Memorial, the World War II Memorial, the statue of Andrew Jackson in Lafayette Square, or other statues. He didn't mention the attempt by rioters to burn down "the Church of the Presidents," St. John's Episcopal Church at Lafayette Square.

The Capitol is unquestionably in a league of its own, but weren't all those sites in Washington, DC, "hallowed ground" as well?

Lecturing Americans

Further into the speech, President Biden said, "This is a great nation, and we are a good people." When I heard that line the first time, I thought I actually agreed. But later in the speech he accused his fellow Americans of "distrusting those who don't look like you do, or worship the way you do, or don't get their news from the same sources you do." This is what Progressives do. They lecture their fellow Americans about what terrible people they are.

When I was a budding conservative in my college days, I saw how horrendously conservatives were treated by leftist professors and students on campus. We see that same condescending attitude toward conservatives throughout academia, in the Hollywood media, the news media, and the leftist political establishment. In his speech, Joe Biden called for unity—but he didn't call out his own side, the cancel culture, the mockers in the news media, the rioters or the looters in the streets. He reserved all his scolding for those of us on the right.

So Biden's words rang hollow as he said, "Today, on this January day, my whole soul is in this: Bringing America together. Uniting our people. And uniting our nation. I ask every American to join me in this cause. Uniting to fight the common foes we face: anger, resentment, hatred. Extremism, lawlessness, violence. Disease, joblessness, hopelessness. With unity we can do great things. Important things."

Joe Biden didn't have to put this call for unity in his inauguration speech. He could have kicked off his administration in any way he liked. He could have simply stated, "Here's our legislative agenda, this is what we are going to do whether you like it or not, so if you don't want to get trampled, stay out of our way." Instead, he chose to call for unity. But if he is going to call for unity, then he must do something that *brings people together*. Just saying the word over and over like a magic incantation will not produce unity.

Words Ring Hollow

While hypocrisy is the chief export of Washington, DC, Joe Biden excels at it. His words and his actions are constantly out of alignment. He wraps himself in his Catholicism while pushing a radical pro-abortion agenda. He moves a bust of union hero Cesar Chavez into the Oval Office right before killing the Keystone XL Pipeline and thousands of good union jobs.

During the 2018 Brett Kavanaugh Supreme Court confirmation hearings, Biden said that a woman accusing Kavanaugh of sexual assault should be granted "the presumption that at least the essence of what she is talking about is real." But two years later, when former Biden aide Tara Reade made similar accusations against Biden, he angrily denounced her claims as "not true."

Joe Biden's call to unity in the midst of a divisive speech is equally hypocritical. Words mean nothing if they are not aligned with actions. Before President Biden preaches unity to the right, he should rebuke Maxine Waters, who said, "If you see anybody from that Cabinet in a restaurant, in a department store, at a gasoline station, you get out and you create a crowd. And you push back on them. And you tell them they're not welcome anymore, anywhere."[6]

And Biden should rebuke Senator Cory Booker, who said, "That's my call to action here. Go to the Hill today. Get up and please get up in the face of some congresspeople."[7]

And he should rebuke Speaker of the House Nancy Pelosi, who said, "I just don't even know why there aren't uprisings all over the country, and maybe there will be."[8]

And he should rebuke former Attorney General Eric Holder, who said of Republicans, "If they go low, we kick them."[9]

And he should rebuke Missouri state legislator Maria Chappelle-Nadal, who said, "I hope Trump is assassinated!"[10]

And Joe Biden should even rebuke Joe Biden, who said of President Trump in March 2018, "If we were in high school, I'd take him behind the gym and beat the hell out of him."[11]

Has Joe Biden called out the anger and hatred from his own party? Has he called out the extremism and lawlessness of leftist radicals in American streets during the "Summer of Rage" in

2020? No, he only condemns us on the right—so his words of unity ring hollow.

Forty-Seven Lost Years

In his inaugural address, Biden said, "We can deliver racial justice," apparently forgetting that he's already spent 47 years in the government—more than enough time to "deliver racial justice." What was he doing during those 47 lost years? When he chaired the Senate Judiciary Committee in 1994, why did he push so hard for a crime bill that sent a disproportionate number of black people to hard time in prison for minor offenses? Yet here he is, riding into town to save us all, promising to do what he should have been doing over the past half century.

The black community is beginning to see how hollow Democratic Party rhetoric is—and how effective President Trump's policies have been. According to NBC News, "Trump won 12 percent of the black vote, which is the highest share for a Republican candidate in the past twenty years."[12] During the first three years of the Trump administration, black and Hispanic unemployment plummeted. President Trump permanently funded historically black colleges and universities, created "opportunity zones" that brought $75 billion of investment into distressed communities, and fought for school choice (which especially benefits black children). He also fought for and signed the First Step Act, which gave many people in prison a second chance.

Biden went on to say, "We can make America, once again, the leading force for good in the world." As if America wasn't *already* the leading force for good in the world. During the previous four years, America defeated ISIS, moved the U.S. Embassy in Israel from Tel Aviv to Jerusalem, killed the murderous Iranian general

Qasem Soleimani, brokered a cooperative agreement between Israel and Saudi Arabia, brokered a broad Middle East peace deal, forged a new alliance with Brazil, persuaded North Korea to stop its missile tests, forced NATO nations to pay their fair share, confronted Communist China's expansionism and unfair trade practices, and exposed the corruption in the World Health Organization. How does President Biden plan to improve on that?

Biden went on to say, "This is our historic moment of crisis and challenge, and unity is the path forward." That statement is simply wrong. He is trying to *demand* unity by executive fiat. He thinks he can say the word *unity* and we'll all say, "Oh, what a great idea! Unity! Why didn't we think of that?" But that's not the way the world works.

A Thumb in the Eye

Unity is not a path. Unity is a goal. Unity is a difficult and hard-won achievement. And it takes more than empty words to bring divided people together in unity. To achieve unity, people must practice civility, compromise, tolerance, and a willingness to listen to each other. There's scant evidence of those qualities in the actions and rhetoric of Joe Biden, Kamala Harris, and the rest of the Democratic Party. In the days and weeks following Biden's call for national unity, all we heard from his party were calls to cancel and deplatform Republicans—and Biden has made no effort to rein in the cancel culture within his own party.

So it's clear what Joe Biden meant when he said unity again and again in his speech. Unity, to Progressive Democrats, means, "You can come along with me as long as you agree with everything I do and say. You're welcome to join the left and support our radical policies. If you conform to our Progressive agenda, we'll have unity."

President Biden went on to add, "I pledge this to you: I will be a president for all Americans. I will fight as hard for those who did not support me as for those who did." But what does that mean? Does that mean he will listen to the 74 million people who voted for Donald Trump? Will he try to understand their concerns and convictions? Will he reach out to them and truly listen to them? Will he encourage his party to make compromises and accommodations with conservatives in the Democratic legislative agenda?

No. He will "fight for" conservatives by forcing them to accept the Progressive policies and programs that *he* thinks are best for them. He doesn't care what conservative Americans think. He doesn't care about their pro-life convictions or the jobs that his immigration and energy policies will destroy or their children who are harmed by school closures and leftist indoctrination. He demonstrated his true intentions later the same day when he signed a stack of executive actions that poked a thumb in the eye of all the American voters who did not vote for him.

Joe Biden Is No Jack Kennedy

One of the most strikingly passive-aggressive moments of Biden's speech came when he said, "Recent weeks and months have taught us a painful lesson. There is truth, and there are lies. Lies told for power and for profit." Here we see Joe Biden indirectly indicting Donald Trump without openly naming him. When we hear the word *lies*, we're supposed to mentally fill in the name *Trump*.

This lecture on lies comes from the man who claimed he graduated first in his law school with a full academic scholarship, that he was arrested in South Africa with Nelson Mandela, that he was repeatedly endorsed by the NAACP, that he opposed the Iraq War from the beginning—all lies. Perhaps his slickest lie of all was his "nondenial denial" of his involvement with his son Hunter's corrupt dealings in Ukraine and Communist China (he called the charges "smears" but never said they were untrue).

As I listened to the inaugural address of America's second Catholic president, I found myself comparing his words against those of America's first Catholic president, John F. Kennedy. In January 1961, JFK delivered a resoundingly pro-America speech—a speech that sounded a call to active citizenship, to the hard work of keeping America strong and free. Kennedy said, "Let every nation know, whether it wishes us well or ill, that we shall pay any price, bear any burden, meet any hardship, support any friend, oppose any foe to assure the survival and the success of liberty."

At the close of his inaugural address, JFK issued a strong challenge: "And so, my fellow Americans: ask not what your country can do for you—ask what you can do for your country." Joe Biden turned Kennedy's challenge on its head, saying in essence, "Here's what's wrong with America. Here's how America has wronged you. Here's what your country owes you." What a contrast between the first and second Catholic presidents, inaugurated 60 years apart.

President Biden closed by promising that "together, we shall write an American story of hope, not fear. Of unity, not division. Of light, not darkness. An American story of decency and dignity. Of love and of healing. Of greatness and of goodness. May this be the story that guides us. The story that inspires us. The story that tells ages yet to come that we answered the call of history. We met the moment. That democracy and hope, truth, and justice did not die on our watch but thrived."[13]

And then, within hours, he signed 17 documents, 17 executive actions that began the process of dividing America, of rubbing salt in America's wounds, of killing well-paying jobs, of discarding hope and truth while undermining justice.

Executive actions speak much louder than words. By the time the sun went down on Joe Biden's first day in office, he was well on his way to fulfilling his pledge to become the most Progressive president in American history.

3

Executive Action Frenzy

A T A LITTLE AFTER 5 p.m. on Inauguration Day, President Biden entered the Oval Office for the first time as president and seated himself behind the Resolute Desk. There, in the space of about 20 minutes, he destroyed women's sports, slammed the brakes on America's economic recovery, eliminated thousands of jobs, made American families poorer, opened America's borders, angered our ally Canada, and gave a huge gift to America's worst international foes, including Russia and Communist China.

All in a day's work for the president who, a few hours earlier, had pledged, "I will be a president for all Americans." By placing his signature on 17 executive actions, he had sent America careening far to the left.

Millions of voters had signed on to Joe Biden's presidency without knowing what his policies would be. But on Biden's first day in office, they finally had a chance to find out.

For four years, President Trump's policies had been moving America in the right direction, strengthening national security, fueling economic recovery, reducing unemployment to historic lows, lifting minority families out of poverty, and launching an all-out assault on the COVID-19 virus through Operation Warp Speed. Armed with a fountain pen and a delusional ideology, President Joe Biden devastated American growth, sovereignty, and national security. Ironically, the ideology Democrats call "Progressivism" has radically reversed the *real* progress of the preceding four years.

Progressives themselves would tell you that Progressivism is a political philosophy that seeks to reform society for the good of ordinary people, the middle class, the poor, the marginalized, and the oppressed. They want to use the power of "big government" to tax the rich, redistribute wealth, promote equal economic and social outcomes for all people, promote an extreme environmental agenda, and throw America's borders wide open. Progressives support massive government programs and seem unconcerned about our mounting national debt. Above all, Progressives are proud of their extremism. As Bernie Sanders tweeted in 2016, "You can be a moderate. You can be a progressive. But you cannot be a moderate and a progressive."[14]

If Joseph R. Biden never accomplishes anything else in the rest of his presidency, those 17 executive actions he signed on day one of his presidency will have made him the most Progressive president in American history.

Let's look at a few of President Biden's day one executive actions and see what they portend for the rest of his presidency.

Advancing Racial Equity

First, we'll examine President Biden's Executive Order 13985: "Advancing Racial Equity and Support for Underserved Communities Through the Federal Government." The order begins by condemning America as home to "systemic racism" that has created "inequities" for people who have been "historically underserved, marginalized, and adversely affected by persistent poverty and inequality." The order states that today's "economic, health, and climate crises" have "exposed and exacerbated inequities, while a historic movement for justice has highlighted the unbearable human costs of systemic racism."

Always pay close attention when Progressives use terms like *equity* and *justice*. The word *equity* has traditionally been defined as "the quality of being fair and impartial." The word *justice* has been defined as "fair and equal treatment." Progressives have co-opted and redefined these words so that they mean the opposite of what they once meant. One Progressive website explained the difference between *equality* and *equity* this way:

> Although both promote fairness, equality achieves this
> through treating everyone the same regardless of need,
> while equity achieves this through treating people differently
> dependent on need. However, this different treatment may be
> the key to reaching equality.[15]

This is the rationale behind the famous slogan of Karl Marx, "From each according to his ability, to each according to his needs."[16] The problem is that Progressives don't treat people as individuals. They see people only as a skin color, a gender, or a sexual orientation. Bari Weiss, an opinion editor at the *New York Times* until July 2020, when she resigned after being bullied by woke activist colleagues, explains woke Progressivism this way:

> In this ideology, you are guilty for the sins of your father. In other words: you are not you. You are only a mere avatar of your race or your religion. And racism is no longer about discrimination based on the color of someone's skin. Racism is any system that allows for disparate outcomes between racial groups. That is why the cities of Seattle and San Francisco have recast algebra as racist. Or why a Smithsonian institution this summer declared that hard work, individualism and the nuclear family are "white" characteristics.[17]

So when President Biden issues an executive order called "Advancing Racial Equity," he's not advancing equality but the *opposite* of equality. He is favoring one racial group over another—and he's quite open about it. For example, on January 8, 2021, President-elect Joe Biden said, "Our focus will be on small businesses on Main Street that aren't wealthy and well connected, that are facing real economic hardships through no fault of their own. Our priority will be black, Latino, Asian, and Native American–owned small businesses, women-owned businesses, and finally having equal access to resources needed to reopen and rebuild."[18] That's what it means to advance equity (as Progressives now define it) instead of equality.

Wouldn't it make more sense to prioritize sending aid to struggling businesses according to their individual need rather than according to race or gender? Of course, it would. Here's why.

Picture a small-business owner who doesn't meet Joe Biden's priorities. Let's say he's a white male small-business owner who employs a large number of blacks, Latinos, Asians, Native Americans, and women. In Joe Biden's America, all these minorities are now in the back of the bus because they work for a white male employer. Why? Because Joe Biden bases his equity priorities on the race or gender identity of the business owner rather than focusing on the needs of all Americans. In his misguided attempt to create equity, as defined by Progressives, he has created massive inequity, inequality, injustice, and hardship for people who need government help.

This is no way to run a country. Joe Biden's announcement may be a good way to signal his virtue, but it's not a good way to help people in need. Instead of picking winners and losers according to the color of people's skin, we should simply help those who need help, equally and impartially. If we do that, we will end up helping minorities and women who have been truly disadvantaged and who need government help the most.

Just remember that when a Democrat says "equity," it doesn't mean equality. It means the opposite. And when a Democrat says "justice," it doesn't mean "fair and equal treatment." It means the opposite. And when a Democrat talks about "economic justice" or "racial justice," the policy prescription is going to make the problem worse, not better.

Abandoning Science for Climate Equity

On day one, President Biden signed two executive actions that focused on climate change. The first was an order titled, "Paris Climate Agreement." Though the press has referred to it as an "executive order," it is not entered in the *Federal Register* with an EO number. It is a very brief statement that reads, "I, Joseph R. Biden, Jr., President of the United States of America, having seen and considered the Paris Agreement, done at Paris on December 12, 2015, do hereby accept the said Agreement and every article and clause thereof on behalf of the United States of America."

President Trump withdrew the United States from the Paris Agreement in May 2017 because he knew it was all downside and no upside for the United States. In fact, the Paris Agreement would impose such burdens on the U.S. economy that it would harm our ability to reduce greenhouse gas emissions.

President Biden recommitted the United States to the Paris Agreement through this statement, which has been sent to United Nations Secretary-General António Guterres. Thirty days after the UN receives this notification, the United States officially rejoins the Paris Agreement. The United States is then required to submit a number of "nationally determined contributions," including the U.S. goals for reducing greenhouse gas emissions and the U.S. plan to contribute hundreds of billions of dollars to a fund that would supposedly be used by other member nations to reduce greenhouse gas emissions.

When the United States joined the Paris Agreement in 2015, President Obama committed the nation to a fanciful goal of a 26 to 28 percent emissions reduction by 2025. To meet this goal, the United States would have had to impose suffocating regulations (and a possible carbon tax) on the energy industry, which would send energy prices skyward. High energy prices are regressive, doing the most harm to those who can least afford it. The Obama administration placed the American economy and American families on the sacrificial altar of climate change.

A Heritage Foundation analysis projected an array of devastating costs the Paris Agreement would impose on the United States and American families by 2035: soaring energy and consumer goods costs, 400,000 jobs lost (half in manufacturing), an average total income loss of more than $20,000 for a family of four, and a $2.5 trillion loss in gross domestic product for the United States.[19]

Why should the American economy and American families be punished when the United States is already more successful than any other nation on earth in controlling greenhouse gas emissions? According to *Our World in Data*, in 2000, the United States produced 23.88 percent of the world's annual carbon dioxide (CO_2) emissions. By 2010, that percentage had fallen to 17.20 percent. By 2017, it was 14.72 percent.[20]

The International Energy Agency (IEA), an autonomous intergovernmental organization headquartered in Paris, recently reported, "The United States saw the largest decline in energy-related CO_2 emissions in 2019 on a country basis," adding that U.S. emissions had declined 2.9 percent from a peak in the year 2000—"the largest absolute decline by any country over that period." Two years after withdrawing from the Paris Agreement, the United States led the world in CO_2 reduction.

"Woke" Marxist Science

Joe Biden's decision to submit the United States to the Paris Agreement is not driven by science but by ideology. The scientific data show that America is already doing more than any other nation to reduce greenhouse gas emissions. But the Biden-Harris administration now speaks about climate change in the woke terminology of radical social justice warriors, using terms like *justice* and *equity*. According to the *Washington Post*, on January 27, 2021, "Biden signed an executive order establishing a White House interagency council on environmental justice, create an office of health and climate equity at the Health and Human Services Department, and form a separate environmental justice office at the Justice Department."[21]

The Biden-Harris administration is in the thrall of a far-left Marxist-influenced ideology that has infected the entire Progressive spectrum, including its environmental activism wing. They speak a cultlike Progressive jargon because terms like *environmental justice* and *climate equity* sound much more noble than *killing jobs* and *driving the American economy off a cliff.*

If we cripple our economy to reduce emissions even further while other nations continue to spew CO_2 without restraint, the air won't get cleaner, the planet won't get cooler—but America will become poorer and less competitive. To continue cleaning up the planet, we must keep the American economy free.

The second environmental executive action President Biden signed on day one was equally disastrous: Executive Order 13990: "Protecting Public Health and the Environment and Restoring Science to Tackle the Climate Crisis." The centerpiece of this order is Section 6, "Revoking the March 2019 Permit for the Keystone XL Pipeline."

By yanking the Keystone XL permit, President Biden knowingly killed a minimum of 11,000 well-paying pipeline jobs, plus an unknown number of ancillary jobs all along the pipeline route. This action makes no scientific sense and will make environmental and climate problems worse. By hampering the ability of the United States and Canada to bring this oil to market, Biden gave a huge gift to such adversaries as Russia, China, and socialist Venezuela. Biden paid lip service to building America's infrastructure, claiming his Build Back Better program would create well-paying jobs without increasing carbon emissions. Continuing the Keystone XL project would have been in line with that promise. Instead, he killed well-paying jobs and forced oil producers to ship their product aboard carbon-spewing trains and trucks.

We'll take a closer look at these and other Biden climate-change policies in Chapter 13.

The Muslim Travel Ban Lie

Another executive action on day one was Proclamation 10141: "Ending Discriminatory Bans on Entry to the United States." This proclamation overturned the Trump travel ban of January 2017. It opens with a true but irrelevant statement: "The United States was built on a foundation of religious freedom and tolerance, a principle enshrined in the United States Constitution." Why does President Biden bring religion into it? The Trump travel ban was never a Muslim travel ban, as the Democrats repeatedly claim. But that lie is now enshrined in a presidential proclamation.

The proclamation continues:

Nevertheless, the previous administration enacted a number of Executive Orders and Presidential Proclamations that prevented certain individuals from entering the United

States—first from primarily Muslim countries, and later, from largely African countries. Those actions are a stain on our national conscience and are inconsistent with our long history of welcoming people of all faiths and no faith at all.

President Biden would have us believe that President Trump banned people from entering the United States because of their Islamic faith, that he did so because he is a bigot, and that the ban was discriminatory and a violation of American law—none of which is true. The travel ban was based not on religion but on national security. It was directed at nations that lacked the ability to certify that their citizens would not threaten our national security.

The ban barred travel from seven countries that the Obama State Department had identified as failed states that could not provide reliable background checks: Syria, Iraq, Iran, Libya, Somalia, Sudan, and Yemen. The list was later amended to remove Iraq while adding North Korea and Venezuela. From beginning to end, the travel ban was always about national security, never about religion.

Nearly 90 percent of the world's Muslims were unaffected by the ban. Those who were affected could apply for waivers. The Supreme Court ruled that the ban passed constitutional muster. It was lawful, and it protected America from its adversaries. It was certainly *not* a "stain on our national conscience."

In his inaugural address, Joe Biden said, "There is truth and there are lies. Lies told for power and for profit." One of Biden's first official proclamations is a lie told for power.

The 100-Day Mask Challenge

President Biden also enacted a so-called 100-day mask challenge, consisting of two executive orders, one mandating social distancing and masks on all federal properties and the other mandating masks on interstate public transportation. He also tweeted, "Wearing masks isn't a partisan issue—it's a patriotic act that can save countless lives. That's why I signed an executive order today issuing a mask mandate on federal property. It's time to mask up, America."

A few hours after signing those orders and sending that tweet, he delivered a televised speech from the Lincoln Memorial—that is, from federal property—*without* wearing a mask. Biden family members were also photographed unmasked at the Lincoln Memorial.

Is this a display of hypocrisy on Biden's part? Is it a big deal? Should those who make the rules for us have to obey the rules themselves? I'll let you decide.

During a briefing the following day, Fox News reporter Peter Doocy asked White House Press Secretary Jen Psaki about President Biden's barefaced appearance at the Lincoln Memorial. Psaki replied that the president and his family were celebrating a "historic day in our country," adding that the mask order he had signed "sent a message" to the American people. "We take a number of COVID precautions here, as you know. I don't know that I have more for you on it than that."

Doocy followed up, noting that President Biden had said in his inaugural address that leaders lead "not merely by the example of our power but by the power of our example." Then Doocy asked, "Was that a good example for people watching?"

Psaki replied, "I think we have bigger issues to worry about at this moment in time."[22]

A lot of Americans at home undoubtedly heard that and thought, "Just like President Biden, I have bigger issues to worry about than his mask mandate." One of the first obligations of the presidency is to be a role model to the nation. President Biden failed that test on day one.

Killing Women's Sports and Opening the Border

President Biden also signed an executive order titled, "Preventing and Combating Discrimination on the Basis of Gender Identity or Sexual Orientation." With the stroke of a pen, he took a wrecking ball to women's and girls' sports. The order claims to be based on the Supreme Court's *Bostock v. Clayton County*, Georgia, decision in 2020. In that decision, Justice Neil Gorsuch, writing for the majority, specifically stated that the ruling had no bearing on "sex-segregated bathrooms, locker rooms, and dress codes."

But Biden's order *is* specifically about bathrooms and locker rooms: "Children should be able to learn without worrying about whether they will be denied access to the rest room, the locker room, or school sports. . . . All persons should receive equal treatment under the law, no matter their gender identity or sexual orientation." Schools will be forced to allow biologically male individuals who claim to be transgendered to have access to the girls' bathroom, the girls' locker room, and girls' sports.

The issue of transgender athletes came to the fore in Connecticut at the 2019 state indoor track championships. Two transgender sprinters finished first and second in the 55-meter dash, shattering the hopes of the biologically female sprinters at the meet. As Abigail Shrier explained in the *Wall Street Journal*:

Once male puberty is complete, testosterone suppression doesn't undo the biological advantages men possess. . . . It should be no surprise, then, that the two trans-identified biological males permitted to compete in Connecticut state track finals against girls—neither of whom was a top sprinter as a boy—consistently claimed top spots competing as girls. They eliminated girls from advancement to regional championships, scouting and scholarship opportunities and trophies, and they set records no girl may ever equal.[23]

Biden's order is also a huge gift to the trial attorneys. Whenever a transgender student tries out for the girls' basketball or volleyball team and doesn't make the cut, the school can expect to be slapped with a costly discrimination lawsuit—and greedy attorneys will collect fat fees at the expense of our children's education.

President Biden also signed a proclamation titled, "Termination of Emergency with Respect to the Southern Border of the United States and Redirection of Funds Diverted to Border Wall Construction." The Democratic Party has become the party of open borders. Even while American schools, churches, and small businesses remained shut down due to COVID-19, President Biden opened the border. Never in American history has a president's priorities been so completely upside down. He placed the irrational demands of his radical base above the safety, security, and jobs of Americans.

By halting construction of the border wall, President Biden knowingly leaves large stretches of our southern border undefended. The word goes out, the illegal immigrants flood in, and the lives of border agents and citizens are put at risk. The fact that President Trump had to use an executive action to secure the southern border and that President Biden could use executive action to suddenly reverse course demonstrates that Congress—the institution that is supposed to pass immigration laws and secure our borders—has failed to do its job.

We'll take a closer look at President Biden's open borders policy in Chapter 14.

Ease Up, Joe!

We've looked at just a handful of the many executive actions President Biden took in the opening days of his administration. Even the radical-left *New York Times* was dismayed by the recklessness of Joe Biden's executive penmanship. A week after the inauguration, the Editorial Board of the *Times* published an editorial headlined, "Ease Up on the Executive Actions, Joe." With uncharacteristic wisdom, the *Times* opined:

> This is no way to make law. A polarized, narrowly divided Congress may offer Mr. Biden little choice but to employ executive actions or see his entire agenda held hostage. These directives, however, are a flawed substitute for legislation. . . .
>
> Executive actions are far more ephemeral and easily discarded than legislation, which can set up a whipsaw effect, as each president scrambles to undo the work of his predecessor. Just as Mr. Trump set about reversing as many of President Barack Obama's directives as possible, Mr. Biden is now working to reverse many of Mr. Trump's reversals. With executive orders, there is always another presidential election just a few years off, threatening to upend everything.[24]

This frenzy of executive actions by the newly inaugurated president shows us exactly where Joe Biden intends to take the nation. His opening salvo of executive orders, proclamations, and memoranda should trouble and frighten every clear-thinking American.

Even more important, it should energize us and move us to action.

4

The Most Progressive
President in History

I n one of Joe Biden's last stops of the 2020 campaign, exactly one week before Election Day, he spoke at Franklin Delano Roosevelt's "Little White House" in Warm Springs, Georgia. There, at the place where FDR died in April 1945, Biden told a gathering of supporters, "I say to you today, if you give me the honor of serving as your president, clear the decks for action, for we will act!"

Throughout his political life, Joe Biden looked to Roosevelt as a hero and a role model. FDR was an activist Progressive president. His administration was perhaps the closest America has ever come to an imperial presidency. After FDR took office during the depths of the Great Depression, he coined the notion of "the first 100 days." He issued a flurry of policy initiatives during his first three months that sent the United States veering leftward toward big-government Progressivism. Presidents have been judged by their first 100 days ever since.

Biden's 100-Day Agenda

Biden has spoken often about his plans for his first 100 days. By April 30, his one-hundredth day in office, the new president planned to:

- Completely undo the legacy of his predecessor (Kenneth Mayer, author of *With the Stroke of a Pen: Executive Orders and Presidential Power,* said that by the end of his second day in office, Biden had reversed 28 Trump executive orders, memos, and proclamations and reinstated a dozen regulations Trump had rescinded).
- Immediately halt construction of the border wall.
- Pass a radical immigration overhaul, providing a path to citizenship for an estimated 12 million illegal immigrants who arrived in the United States as recently as January 1, 2021—a position far to the left of the Democratic Party of just a year or two earlier.
- Rescind the Trump-era travel bans that had been so effective in protecting the United States from terrorist attacks.
- Vaccinate 100 million Americans against COVID-19 (incidentally, 1 million vaccinations a day is exactly the same rate the Trump administration achieved).
- Reopen half the public elementary and middle schools (we later learned that holding classes *just one day a week* counts as "reopening" a school).

- Pass a $1.9 trillion COVID-19 relief and stimulus package, including $1,400 for each eligible person, a $15 an hour federal minimum wage, expanded unemployment payouts, rent relief, child care assistance, and more (Larry Summers, secretary of the treasury in the Clinton administration, warned in the *Washington Post* that Biden's massive stimulus scheme could "set off inflationary pressures of a kind we have not seen in a generation, with consequences for the value of the dollar and financial stability. . . . Stimulus measures of the magnitude contemplated are steps into the unknown").[25]
- Complete a criminal justice overhaul, including the creation of a national police oversight commission—a concession to the 2020 Black Lives Matter protests.
- Overhaul the tax code, saddling COVID-strapped small businesses with a new corporate tax hike to 28 percent.
- Toss an array of sops to the far-left environmentalist fringe that will do nothing to "save the planet" but will destroy American jobs, businesses, and competitiveness (these actions range from rejoining the Paris Climate Agreement to killing the Keystone XL pipeline to imposing new regulations on oil and gas operations and automobile fuel economy standards).

It's not surprising, then, that Barack Obama called President Biden's agenda "the most progressive platform of any major-party nominee in history."

Biden has cast himself in FDR's mold—and the mainstream media agree. *Time* magazine headlined a story, "How Joe Biden Is Positioning Himself as a Modern FDR." *New York* magazine announced, "Joe Biden Is Planning an FDR-Size Presidency." *Foreign Policy* ran the headline, "The Biden-FDR Connection Runs Deeper Than You Think." And the *New York Times* proclaimed, "Biden's Fast Start Echoes FDR's."

To anyone who understands history, the Biden-FDR comparisons are troubling.

The Job-Killing $15 Minimum Wage

A federal minimum wage was first enacted in 1933, when Franklin D. Roosevelt signed the National Industrial Recovery Act as part of his New Deal agenda. The Supreme Court struck down FDR's minimum wage in a 1935 ruling. FDR's anger over this and other high court decisions prompted his 1937 court-packing scheme.

The federal minimum wage FDR signed into law in 1933 was 25 cents an hour—or about $5.03 in 2021 dollars. Joe Biden and the Democratic Party are pushing to more than double the national minimum wage in phases from $7.25 an hour to $15 an hour by 2025. In an interview with Norah O'Donnell of CBS News, February 5, 2021, President Biden said, "I do think that we should have a minimum wage, stand by itself, $15 an hour. . . . All the economics show, if you do that, the whole economy rises."

Who or what are "all the economics"? Does he mean liberal economists? Whatever that sentence is supposed to mean, it defies common sense.

Three days after President Biden made that statement, the Congressional Budget Office (CBO) released its scorecard on the $15 federal minimum wage. According to the CBO, the wage hike would eliminate 1.4 million jobs by 2025, increase the federal budget deficit, raise the cost of goods and services, and increase inflationary pressure on the economy.[26]

Whenever you raise the minimum wage on a national basis, you destroy jobs. You eliminate the employment opportunities for entry-level and low-skilled workers.

Let's say I'm a small-business owner who needs someone to stock shelves. Times are tough and I'm barely making it, but I can afford to pay $10 an hour. Let's say you're fresh out of high school, with very few skills but very few expenses. You need to get one foot into the job market, and you're willing to take the shelf-stocking job for $10 an hour.

But President Biden won't let you have that job. He has declared your $10-an-hour job illegal. The "logic" of a $15 minimum wage is that you are better off broke and unemployed than to be working for $10 an hour.

Why does President Biden think this way? It's because he's never been an employer and he hasn't held a regular job in almost 50 years. He was elected to the Senate at age 29 and has no concept of business economics. He has never been a small-business person, worrying about paying rent, accounts payable, insurance, utilities, taxes, and payroll. He has no concept of how the cost of labor impacts the viability of a business—especially in the wake of a global pandemic.

A Small-Business Killer

Progressive prescriptions for the economy are inevitably toxic. Federal policymakers in Washington, DC, have no idea what a fair wage would be in the rest of the country. They live in one of the most expensive cities in the nation. Is it rational to mandate the same wage in a city where the cost of living is significantly lower? After all, a $15-an-hour wage in Harlingen, Texas, or Kalamazoo,

Michigan, is the equivalent of earning from $32 to $51 an hour in San Francisco, New York, or Washington, DC.[27]

If a minimum wage of $32 to $51 an hour sounds outrageous to you, remember, that's exactly how outrageous a wage of $15 an hour sounds to a small-business owner in Harlingen or Kalamazoo. The law of supply and demand in a free market always produces the fairest hourly wage—not the dictates of politicians who live 2,000 or 3,000 miles away. Without question, the Biden minimum wage will kill jobs and force thousands of businesses to close forever. It will also motivate many companies to seek ways to replace employees with technology (e.g., fast-food chains replacing entry-level fry cooks with machines that flip burgers).

These are the realities behind a 2019 CBO report that predicted that a $15 minimum wage would likely put 1.4 million workers out of work and possibly as many as 3.7 million.[28] Many big corporations such as Amazon and McDonald's support the $15 minimum wage—but that's hardly a surprise. Big corporations can absorb the additional labor cost. Small businesses can't. By lobbying for a higher minimum wage, big corporations are using the blunt force of the federal government to drive their competition into bankruptcy. As Marc Freedman of the U.S. Chamber of Commerce observed, "Small businesses do not have the resources to absorb such a dramatic increase in costs."[29]

Progressives often talk about a "living wage" and say that people can't raise a family on the current minimum wage. That's true. But the minimum wage was never intended to support a family. It's intended to create a wage floor for people who are just entering the job market and have few skills to offer. You can't structure a thriving economy so that teenagers stocking shelves can afford to support a family.

In a free market, a job is worth what a willing employer will pay and a willing employee will accept—no more, no less. Nothing good happens when the federal government imposes its will on the labor market. In Joe Biden's centrally planned economy, many perfectly good jobs that exist today will soon be against the law.

Democrats had included the $15 minimum wage in the House version of the $1.9 trillion American Rescue Plan Act of 2021, which was supposedly aimed at providing "COVID relief" to Americans hard hit by the pandemic. The $15 minimum wage was cut from the Senate version after the Senate parliamentarian ruled that it violated Senate rules for legislation passed by the "reconciliation" simple-majority process. President Biden and other leading Democrats vow to enact the minimum wage in the near future.

So Much for Bipartisanship and Unity

On February 1, 2021, President Biden and Vice President Kamala Harris welcomed 10 Republican senators, led by Susan Collins of Maine, to the Oval Office to discuss the COVID relief bill. The Republican senators had written a letter to Biden that read, in part:

> In the spirit of bipartisanship and unity, we have developed a COVID-19 relief framework that builds on prior COVID assistance laws, all of which passed with bipartisan support. Our proposal reflects many of your stated priorities, and with your support, we believe that this plan could be approved quickly by Congress with bipartisan support.[30]

The group met with President Biden for about two hours, and both sides called the meeting "productive." The Republicans offered a $600 billion counterproposal to the Biden's $1.9 trillion stimulus plan.

The Republican plan offered no bailouts for state and local governments, proposed a $1,000 direct payment to Americans (the Biden plan offered $1,400), and did not include Biden's $15 federal minimum wage increase. The Republican plan was focused on genuine targeted COVID relief—$160 billion for vaccine distribution, testing, and protective gear for healthcare workers, $20 billion toward reopening schools, relief for small businesses, aid to individuals who were economically harmed by the pandemic, and an extension of unemployment benefits.

White House Press Secretary Jen Psaki summed up the meeting, saying that President Biden "reiterated that while he is hopeful that the [Biden] Rescue Plan can pass with bipartisan support, a reconciliation package is a path to achieve that end."[31] In other words, Biden told the senators that they were welcome to support his $1.9 trillion bill as written—or the Democrats would use reconciliation to pass the bill on straight party lines. So much for the spirit of bipartisanship and unity.

Yet it wasn't clear to the GOP senators in that room whether they were negotiating with President Biden—or with Biden's chief of staff, Ron Klain (known to many Republicans as "Prime Minister Klain"). Susan Collins said that she believed it might have been possible to reach a compromise with President Biden if he wasn't being quietly countermanded by Klain. "Ron was shaking his head in the back of the room the whole time," she recalled, "which is not exactly an encouraging sign."[32]

It's impossible to know if Joe Biden is making his own decisions—or if he's being pushed to the extreme left by the people around him. We do know that Ron Klain is determined to see this $1.9 trillion Progressive wish list enacted by any means necessary. As he told Joy Reid on MSNBC on February 27, 2021, "We are hopefully just weeks away from final passage of the most progressive domestic legislation in a generation."[33]

He Means What He Says

Under the leadership of Joe Biden, our government is borrowing and spending at a rate that shocks the conscience—and the Democrats are sending the invoice to future generations. Americans who support this reckless legislation are probably only thinking about cashing that $1,400 government check. We need to start thinking about how our children and grandchildren will one day have to pay it all back—with interest.

Early in his primary campaign for the Democratic nomination, Joe Biden was interviewed by Chuck Todd on NBC's *Meet the Press*. "The ideas I have, Chuck," he said, "are big and bold. I mean, this idea that I'm not the progressive in the race—I mean, my Lord, if I get elected president of the United States, with my position on healthcare, my position on global warming, my position on foreign policy, my position on the middle class—this will go down as one of the most progressive administrations in history."[34]

Joe Biden meant what he said. Since his first day in office, he's been proving it. He's been transforming the America you and I love into a radical nation.

5

Kamala Harris, the President-in-Waiting

O N NOVEMBER 15, 2018, Senator Kamala Harris was in a committee hearing, grilling Ronald Vitiello, President Trump's nominee to lead the U.S. Immigration and Customs Enforcement agency (ICE). During her questioning, Harris raised the specter of the Ku Klux Klan, asking Vitiello, "Why would we call [the KKK] a domestic terrorist group?"

Vitiello replied, "Because they tried to use fear and force to change the political environment."

"And what was the motivation for the use of fear and force?"

"It's based on race and ethnicity."

"Right. Are you aware of the perception of many about how the power and discretion at ICE is being used to enforce the laws, and do you see any parallels [with the Ku Klux Klan]?"

"I do not see any parallels between officers and agents . . ."

"I'm talking about perception. I'm talking about perception."

"I do not see a parallel between what is constitutionally mandated as it relates to enforcing the law . . ."

"Are you aware that there's a perception . . ."

"I see no perception that puts ICE in the same category as the KKK. Is that what you're asking me?"[35]

That disgusting insinuation is exactly what Kamala Harris was asking Mr. Vitiello—and Kamala Harris framed it in an especially offensive way. This is a common tactic used by Progressives whenever they don't have the facts on their side: "People are saying . . ." Or, "I've heard talk. . . ." Or, "There's a perception among many. . . ." That's the tactic Kamala Harris used to smear Ronald Vitiello and the hard-working agents of ICE.

On March 24, 2021, President Biden announced that he was appointing Kamala Harris—who compared border agents to the KKK—as the administration's point person on border issues. With Harris at his side, Biden said, "I can think of nobody who is better qualified to do this."[36]

You can't make this stuff up.

Days passed. Kamala Harris held no press conferences, issued no statements, and was nowhere to be seen. Jen Psaki fielded questions about the vice president's role in border policy—and her mysterious whereabouts. On April 10, two-and-a-half weeks after the big announcement, NBC News posted an article headlined, "Confusion Clouds Harris Immigration Role."[37]

I think I can explain Kamala Harris's vanishing act. This has been her political MO throughout her career. She avoids getting her fingerprints on any issue that might damage her political future. When Kamala Harris realized she was about to become the visible face of the border crisis, she became the "Invisible Woman."

The Inauthentic Self of Kamala Harris

On June 1, 2020, then-candidate Kamala Harris tweeted, "If you're able to, chip in now to the @MNFreedomFund to help post bail for those protesting on the ground in Minnesota." That tweet for the Minnesota Freedom Fund (MFF) was part of Harris's effort to win the woke Progressive vote during the Black Lives Matter protests of 2020.

One of the protesters helped by Kamala Harris's support was Thomas Moseley, who was arrested in October 2020 for causing damage to the Minneapolis Police Department's Fifth Precinct during the summer protests. Arresting officers found him with a handgun in his waistband. The MFF freed him by posting $5,000 bail. Mosely was arrested again in December, and the MFF posted $60,000 bail.

In February 2021, Mosely was arrested a third time because police found a cache of weapons in his possession (three handguns, a shotgun, and a semiautomatic rifle) plus an assortment of drugs. Bail was set at $250,000, and this time, Mosely remained in jail.[38]

Here's the point: Kamala Harris made her reputation as a tough-on-crime district attorney in San Francisco from 2004 to 2011 and as the tough-on-crime attorney general of California from 2011 to 2017. But in the summer of 2020, she did an abrupt about-face and became an advocate for rioters and looters, wanting them released on bail. *Prosecutor* Kamala Harris wouldn't recognize *candidate* Kamala Harris, the rioter's best friend.

Who is Kamala Harris? Does *she* even know?

Sacramento Bee columnist Gil Duran, who was Harris's communications director in 2013, observes that her biggest hurdle as a political candidate has been the widespread perception that she is always "trying to project an inauthentic self."[39] According to Politico, it was Harris's chameleon-like ability to adopt any position to get elected that sank her 2020 presidential bid before she even reached the Iowa caucuses:

> Harris's shifting positions on key policy matters undermined her short-lived run for the presidency. A former California attorney general and district attorney, Harris faced criticism over a prosecutorial record that doesn't always match with the progressive positions she espouses today. On health care, her waffling on "Medicare for All" during the presidential primary revealed a candidate torn between appealing to progressives demanding structural change and moderates favoring incrementalism—and satisfying none in the process.[40]

The mainstream media tried to define Kamala Harris as a pragmatic moderate, but GovTrack, a nonpartisan website, analyzed her voting record and concluded that she is the most far-left socialist-leaning legislator of all 100 senators.[41]

In view of President Joe Biden's age and ongoing questions about his health, Kamala Harris is the president-in-waiting. During the next four years, she stands a good chance of becoming president and imposing her agenda on the nation. And her agenda is even more radical than Joe Biden's.

The Progressive Prosecutor

Kamala Harris, like the rest of her party, claims that law enforcement in America is riddled with "systemic racism." She told CNN, "The reality of America today is what we have seen over generations and frankly since our inception, which is we do have two systems of justice in America. . . . There are huge disparities in our country based on race."[42] Though some of her Democratic colleagues have demanded "defunding the police," Harris talks about "reimagining how we do public safety in America."[43]

Steven Greenhut, writing in the *Orange County Register,* notes that while Harris has "reimagined" herself as a "Progressive Prosecutor," her "past actions bear no resemblance to her new persona."[44]

Though Harris now advocates for criminal justice reform, she has spent most of her career opposing real reform. Law professor Lara Bazelon wrote in the *New York Times*:

> Time after time, when progressives urged her to embrace criminal justice reforms as a district attorney and then the state's attorney general, Ms. Harris opposed them or stayed silent. Most troubling, Ms. Harris fought tooth and nail to uphold wrongful convictions that had been secured through official misconduct that included evidence tampering, false testimony and the suppression of crucial information by prosecutors.[45]

For example, while serving as San Francisco's district attorney, she withheld information from the court about a corrupt police drug lab technician who was skimming cocaine, tampering with lab results, and giving unreliable testimony in court. A judge castigated Harris for her indifference to the constitutional rights of defendants. More than 600 drug cases in which the technician gave testimony had to be dismissed.

Harris personally fought for a 2011 California state law that made it a criminal misdemeanor, punishable by a fine of up to $2,500 and a year in jail, for parents to allow children in kindergarten through eighth grade to miss more than one-tenth of their school year.

One victim of Harris's overzealous anti-truancy law was a black mother named Cheree Peoples, whose 11-year-old daughter, Shayla, had suffered from sickle cell anemia. Shayla's painful illness required frequent hospitalization, making regular school attendance impossible. The school and Peoples were working on a plan to permit the girl to learn at home during flare-ups of the disease. Yet, in April 2013, police handcuffed Peoples, perp-walked her in front of neighbors and news cameras, and booked her into jail. She spent two exhausting years fighting the charge in the courts.[46]

A "Reimagined" Career

On February 11, 2019, Harris appeared on *The Breakfast Club* on New York's Power 105.1. The host said he'd heard that Harris opposed legalizing marijuana. "That's not true!" Harris retorted. "And look, I joke about it, half joking, but half my family is from Jamaica! Are you kidding me?" And she laughed uproariously. The host asked if she smoked weed. "I have!" she said proudly. "And I inhaled! I did inhale." She giggled again.[47]

As district attorney, Harris jailed 1,500 people for minor marijuana offenses and fought attempts to have those sentences commuted. I wonder: Did the people she locked up for weed-related offenses find her weed confession as hilarious as she did?

Soon after that interview, Harris's father, Donald Harris, a Stanford University economics professor emeritus, released a statement that read in part, "My dear departed grandmothers . . . as well as my deceased parents, must be turning in their grave right now to see their family's name, reputation, and proud Jamaican identity being connected, in any way, jokingly or not, with the fraudulent stereotype of a pot-smoking joy seeker and in the pursuit of identity politics."[48]

The self-proclaimed Progressive prosecutor never talked about her *real* record during the campaign. She fought for higher cash minimums for posting bail, which disproportionately impacts the poor. She advocated for expanded asset forfeiture, in which police confiscate property even when the defendant isn't convicted of a crime. She fought to keep people in prison whom she knew had been wrongfully convicted.

When being tough on crime was popular, she was brutally tough. In 2020, when being woke was all the rage, she became the wokest of the woke. Kamala Harris "reimagined" her entire career as a prosecutor—and she got away with it.

Government-Enforced Equality of Outcomes

Two days before Election Day 2020, Kamala Harris tweeted an animated video she had narrated called *Equality vs. Equity.*

"So there's a big difference between equality and equity," Harris said in the narration. "Equality suggests, 'Oh, everyone should get the same amount.' The problem with that, not everybody's starting out from the same place. So if we're all getting the same amount but you started out back there and I started out over here—we can get the same amount but you're still going to be that far back behind me. It's about giving people the resources and the support

they need so that everyone can be on equal footing and then compete on equal footing. Equitable treatment means we all end up
at the same place."

Congresswoman Liz Cheney of Wyoming retweeted Harris's
tweet, adding her comment: "Sounds just like Karl Marx. A century
of history has shown where that path leads. We all embrace equal
opportunity, but government-enforced equality of outcomes is
Marxism." And Tom Fitton, president of Judicial Watch, tweeted,
"Major party candidate promotes communism."[49]

It's true. Kamala Harris's little video is pure, distilled Marxism.
The idea of equal outcomes for all was tried in the Soviet Union.
Whether you worked hard or slacked off, whether you were effi-
cient or wasteful, everybody got the same reward. Soon, Soviet
citizens realized that there was no reward for extra effort and no
punishment for inefficiency. People stopped being productive,
and the Soviet economy stagnated. Kamala Harris's lecture on
equality versus equity is a recipe for turning the USA in the USSR
and rerunning the same failed experiment.

In January 2019, Harris said:

> I support a Green New Deal. And I will tell you why. Climate
> change is an existential threat to us, and we have got to deal
> with the reality of it. . . . I think that the fact that we have
> policymakers who are in the pockets of Big Oil and Big Coal
> don't fully appreciate the fact that we are looking at some-
> thing that is presenting an existential threat to our country.[50]

Kamala Harris knew when she made this statement that the
Green New Deal, popularized by Alexandria Ocasio-Cortez,
is not just an environmental agenda. As we will see in Chapter

13, the Green New Deal has been, since its inception, a plan to impose radical Marxist-style socialism on all Americans. It's a plan for imposing equal outcomes on all Americans, just as Harris explained in her Twitter video.

The Green New Deal includes a government guarantee of a "family-sustaining wage," "safe, affordable, adequate housing," and "economic security for all who are unable or unwilling to work." Note that last phrase, "or unwilling to work." That wording is straight from the official Green New Deal document.[51]

Follow the Wokeness

On August 6, 2020, Harris teamed up with Alexandria Ocasio-Cortez on a so-called climate equity bill. The legislation was a radical-left attempt to fuse the environmental issue with the racial justice issue. Harris said:

> For generations, communities of color have faced environmental injustice that has compounded the systemic disparities—educational, income, wealth, voting participation, and health. . . . Meanwhile, there is the ongoing crisis of systemic racism in America that people of color have known and experienced for generations. All of these things intersect, and as we address the climate crisis, we must center the fight for environmental and climate justice in the broader conversation.[52]

Do you see what she did there? Harris took core issues of two different constituent groups of the Democratic Party—climate change and woke social justice—and merged them together into one big Progressive "intersectional" issue called "climate equity."

According to this bill, environmental policy doesn't have to "follow the science"—it follows the wokeness.

Harris's cosponsor, Alexandria Ocasio-Cortez, put it this way: "Major environmental policies must be written by the black, brown, and low-income people who have been and will be disproportionately impacted by it." That's right—Harris and AOC think our environmental policy should not be informed by science but should be written by low-income people.[53]

The Biden-Harris Gun Confiscation Plan

Joe Biden and Kamala Harris both support radical gun control legislation, including the mandatory buyback of 20 million so-called assault weapons. This is another example of Progressive torture of the English language. The government cannot buy back guns that it never owned. The correct word is *confiscation*.

What happens when a government confiscates weapons from law-abiding citizens? The island nation of New Zealand conducted that experiment. After a horrifying mass shooting at two mosques in Christchurch, New Zealand, on March 15, 2019, in which 51 people died, the government ordered owners of so-called assault weapons to turn their guns in and be reimbursed by the government. This is the same "mandatory buyback" program Biden and Harris support. About 56,000 of the outlawed guns were turned in, while an estimated 100,000 New Zealanders refused to surrender their guns.

Though the "buyback" wasn't as successful as the government had hoped, it succeeded in disarming many law-abiding citizens. Did the "buyback" result in fewer gun deaths? No, the number of gun deaths went up. Radio New Zealand said that over the remaining months of 2019, the nation experienced "the highest rates of gun crime and deaths involving firearms" in nearly a decade.[54]

The problem with taking guns away from law-abiding citizens is that the criminals have their guns. Knowing their victims were largely disarmed, criminals were emboldened to commit *more* gun crimes than ever before. So if you are unarmed and someone is breaking into your home, you have to call 911 and wait. As someone once said, "When seconds count, the police are only minutes away."

Sanitizing Her Image

The July 23, 2019, edition of the *Washington Post* carried a feature by left-wing columnist Ben Terris profiling Kamala Harris's close relationship with her sister Maya. The story opened with an anecdote in which Kamala Harris likened the campaign trail to imprisonment. She called a three-day break from campaigning "a treat." Ben Terris explains what came next:

> It's a treat that a prisoner gets when they ask for, "A morsel of food please," Kamala said shoving her hands forward as if clutching a metal plate, her voice now trembling like an old British man locked in a Dickensian jail cell. "And water! I just want wahtahhh ." . . . Your standards really go out the f—ing window.

Then Kamala burst into laughter.[55] This anecdote is all the more distasteful when you remember that Kamala Harris fought to keep wrongly convicted people in prison.

Fast-forward to January 2021, 18 months after this story appeared in the *Washington Post*. Shortly before Inauguration Day, the original version of this story disappeared from the *Washington Post* website. In its place was the same story, but with Kamala Harris's starving prisoner joke deleted and replaced by a new opening anecdote—and no notice that the story had been altered.

The *Post* had quietly sanitized the piece to polish up Kamala Harris's image—but the *Post* got caught. Two days after the inauguration, *Reason* magazine ran a story on the *Post*'s attempt to make Kamala Harris's unfunny joke disappear from the internet. *Reason* compared both versions of the *Post* story and concluded that the *Washington Post* was "willing to pave over its own good journalism to protect a powerful politician from *her own words*"[56] (emphasis in the original).

The *Post* and the rest of the media need to stop covering for Kamala Harris and start digging into who she really is. The American people deserve to know, especially as the White House has been elevating her stature in the administration.

In March 2021, an email from the White House Communications Office was leaked by a federal employee. The email reads, in part, "Please be sure to reference the current administration as the 'Biden-Harris administration' in official public communications." At around the same time, the White House website and the websites of all executive departments started referring to the "Biden-Harris administration."[57] Listing the president and vice president as near coequals in the administration is unprecedented.

Clearly, Kamala Harris is more than a vice president in the traditional sense. She is truly the president-in-waiting.

6

Team Biden

D URING THE TRANSITION FROM the outgoing Obama administration to the new Trump administration, I was invited
to meet with the White House press team in the West Wing of
the White House. There I met White House Press Secretary Josh
Earnest and Communications Director Jen Psaki. Both were very
generous with their time. They explained the resources available
and how they set up their press shop and some of the protocols
they observed.

After our meeting, I stepped into the hallway outside the Oval
Office and I bumped into—literally—Vice President Joe Biden.
He was very friendly and engaging. "C'mon over, Sean," he said.
"Let's chat in my office."

He led me to his office at the other end of the West Wing, and we sat and chatted about White House operations. Our talk lasted for about 15 minutes, and he was gracious and supportive, and he wished me success in my new role as press secretary.

I have a hard time reconciling the relaxed, genial Vice President Biden I met that day with the dour and divisive President Biden of today. Joe Biden has surrounded himself with two kinds of people: (1) loyalists—people who have worked with him before—and (2) people who check racial, ethnic, sexual orientation, and gender boxes—people who (as Progressives like to say) "look like America." The question "Is he or she the most qualified person for the job?" is just not an urgent priority.

Anti-Americans Representing America?

Take, for example, Jalina Porter, Biden's pick for deputy spokesperson for the U.S. State Department. In a 2016 Facebook post, Porter wrote, "The largest threat to U.S. national security are U.S. cops. Not ISIS, not Russian hackers, not anyone or anything else. If ya'll don't wake up and rise up to this truth, the genocide against blacks in America will continue until we are near extinct."[58]

She later tried to walk that back, saying

Comments I made five years ago on my personal Facebook account as a private citizen were in response to the uncomfortable—and deeply painful—truth of race-based violence in America that has continued ever since. The pain I expressed was real. Nevertheless, I should've chosen words that were less passionate and spur-of-the moment, as well as more constructive.[59]

Notice that she didn't retract anything. In fact, she doubled down on her statement.

Those remarks should be a deal breaker, proving that she's completely unqualified for the job. Yet she now speaks for the State Department and the United States of America. This is a serious problem because her unrepentant attack on her country as home to "genocide against blacks" undermines her authority to represent the United States vis-à-vis Communist China, which is right now conducting mass-scale genocide against the Uighurs.

Granted, we can and should have an honest, thoughtful, fact-based discussion about racial justice and the treatment of black Americans by law enforcement. That would be a worthy discussion. But Jalina Porter cannot be a credible spokesperson for the United States—and I'll show you why.

On March 18–19, 2021, when Secretary of State Tony Blinken's team faced off against Chinese officials at the Anchorage summit, Blinken raised a series of complaints against China's government—persecution of the Uighurs in Xinjiang, brutal oppression in Hong Kong, threats against Taiwan, and more. Yet Blinken seemed stunned by the Communists' counterargument.

Chinese diplomat Yang Jiechi lectured Blinken and National Security Advisor Jake Sullivan on American hypocrisy on human rights:

> The United States does not have the qualification to say that it wants to speak to China from a position of strength. We hope that the United States will do better on human rights. . . . There are many problems within the United States regarding human rights, which is admitted by the U.S. itself. . . . The challenges

facing the United States in human rights are deep seated. They did not just emerge over the past four years, such as Black Lives Matter.[60]

The Chinese delegation was probably aware of Jalina Porter's tweet—the People's Republic of China is very thorough. Its response to Tony Blinken was essentially a diplomatic restatement of Jalina Porter's talking points.

Back in Washington on the last day of the Anchorage summit, Jalina Porter gave a State Department press briefing in which she called for China "to end the arbitrary and unacceptable detentions of the Canadians citizens Michael Spavor and Michael Kovrig,"[61] who apparently were detained to punish Canada for its arrest of a suspected Chinese spy.

If you were Communist China, would you take Jalina Porter seriously? Of course not. You'd say, "Don't lecture us. We've read your Twitter feed."

Jalina Porter is just one example of the unqualified people Joe Biden has recruited to his team—and why Team Biden spells trouble ahead for America. Here's a quick rundown on other members of the team.

Apologizing for America:
Antony Blinken, Secretary of State

While we're on the subject, let's look at Tony Blinken's background. He has held foreign policy–related positions in the Clinton and Obama administrations and helped shape policy on Pakistan, Afghanistan, and the fatally flawed nuclear deal with Iran. After leaving the White House at the end of the Obama administration, Blinken cofounded (with other former Obama officials) a consulting firm, WestExec Advisors. (Biden appointed another former WestExec consultant, Avril Haines, as director of national intelligence.)

WestExec's website boasted of helping universities attract China's donations and Chinese students for their science, technology, engineering, and mathematics programs without jeopardizing their Department of Defense–sponsored research grants. We now know that Chinese funding and students have been used to infiltrate and spy on American research universities. WestExec also claimed to help American corporations gain access to Communist China's economic marketplace. In August 2020, shortly before Joe Biden accepted the Democratic nomination for president, those claims were scrubbed from the WestExec website.[62]

Though WestExec tried to erase its China ties from the record, Communist Chinese officials undoubtedly knew all about WestExec and Antony Blinken when they sat across the table from the U.S. delegation in Anchorage on March 18, 2021. They knew exactly what to say to put Blinken on his heels. Director Yang Jiechi told Blinken that the United States has human rights problems of its own. What right does Blinken have to lecture China about human rights when Black Lives Matter accuses the United States of wanton disregard for black lives? Yang added, "It's important that we manage our respective affairs well instead of deflecting the blame on somebody else in this world." In short, mind your own business.

Blinken responded defensively, saying that American leadership

acknowledges our imperfections, acknowledges that we're
not perfect, we make mistakes, we have reversals, we take
steps back. But what we've done throughout our history is to

confront those challenges openly, publicly, transparently, not trying to ignore them, not trying to pretend they don't exist, not trying to sweep them under a rug. And sometimes it's painful, sometimes it's ugly, but each and every time, we have come out stronger, better, more united as a country.[63]

In effect, Blinken accepted the Communist accusations as true but pleaded that we're trying to do better.

Can you imagine Blinken's predecessor, Mike Pompeo, offering such a weak comeback? Hardly. I imagine Pompeo would have said something like "Not one slave has picked cotton on American soil since 1865 because we fought a Civil War to end slavery. Your government has half a million slaves picking cotton in Xinjiang *right now*, and you're trying to pressure American companies to buy slave-picked cotton. So don't pretend there's a moral equivalence between China's human rights abuses and anything happening in America today. That won't fly."

That kind of foreign policy backbone is sorely missing in Tony Blinken and the Biden Department of State.

Radical on Abortion:

Xavier Becerra, Secretary of Health and Human Services

To me, President Biden's worst cabinet pick of all is Xavier Becerra. He somehow survived his confirmation hearings despite his radical views and a truly horrible record as California state attorney general. If Senate Republicans could knock out only one Biden nominee, they should have focused on Becerra. Instead, they spent their political capital on Hillary Clinton advisor Neera Tanden (nominee for Office of Management and Budget director) and her "mean tweets" against senators from both parties. Was Tanden a "stalking horse," a deliberate distraction to take the heat off more radical nominees like Becerra?

Joe Biden's choice of Becerra—who has a legal background, not a healthcare background—sends a strong signal about Biden's priorities. Even with the COVID-19 pandemic still raging, Biden didn't choose a doctor, a strong advocate for health issues. Biden chose a lawyer, a strong advocate for unrestricted abortion.

According to OnTheIssues.org, as a congressman from 2003 to 2017, Becerra voted to expand human embryonic stem cell research, fund abortions globally through foreign aid, and permit unrestricted interstate transport of minors to get abortions. His voting record is rated 100 percent by the National Abortion Rights Action League.

Becerra now runs the largest budget of any government department—more than $2 trillion in fiscal year 2021. Expect Becerra's HHS to pursue a pattern of restricting free speech and religious freedom in order to promote abortion. We'll take a closer look at Xavier Becerra's assault on liberty and pro-life values in Chapter 11.

The "Recyclable Boogeyman":
Susan Rice, Director of the Domestic Policy Council

President Biden chose Susan Rice to run the White House Domestic Policy Council, which has enormous influence over White House policy on immigration, healthcare, job creation, and education. At first glance, this is a perplexing choice. She was U.S. ambassador to the United Nations and national security advisor under President Obama and a foreign policy fellow at the Brookings Institution. Her portfolio is foreign affairs, not domestic policy. "At no point in Rice's career," observed Tristan Justice of *The Federalist*, has she "ever had to cast a vote in an American legislative chamber or issue an outline of her own domestic policy platform."[64]

Why didn't Biden choose Susan Rice for a post that better fits her experience? Rice acknowledges that she had a problematic past in the Obama administration, and she calls herself the "recyclable boogeyman" of the right. Accordingly, the *New York Times* reported that the Biden transition team would only consider Rice for "roles that would not require Senate confirmation,"[65] such as the Domestic Policy Council.

Susan Rice was the deceptive face of the Obama administration, going out in interview after interview, making the ludicrous claim that the 2012 attack on our embassy in Benghazi was a "spontaneous" uprising provoked by an obscure YouTube video. In fact, it was a highly coordinated attack by the Islamic militant group Ansar al-Sharia. The Obama White House had ignored intelligence reports and the ambassador's pleas for stronger security measures, resulting in the murder of four Americans, including U.S. Ambassador to Libya J. Christopher Stevens. It was a massive foreign policy failure for the Obama administration just two months before the 2012 election. So Susan Rice was sent out to lie to the American people.

For all the accusations lobbed my way about lying for President Trump, no one in the Democratic Party or the mainstream media raised the issue of Rice's Benghazi cover-up when she was appointed to the Domestic Policy Council. There's a double standard when it comes to telling the truth—and the far-left media always gives a pass to its own.

In April 2017, Judy Woodruff of PBS asked Susan Rice if she knew about government surveillance against the Trump campaign. Rice replied, "I know nothing about this. I was surprised to see the reports." Not only did Rice know all about it, but she was a key player in the spying effort and the unmasking of members of the Trump campaign and transition team.[66] (*Unmasking* is the act of revealing the redacted names of U.S. persons contained in raw intelligence reports.) Once again, Susan Rice boldly lied to the American people.

Susan Rice's biggest lie may be the one she emailed to herself. On January 5, 2017, after a briefing on Russian hacking, President Obama convened a high-level meeting with Vice President Biden, Susan Rice, FBI Director James Comey, and Deputy Attorney General Sally Yates. Fifteen days later, on Inauguration Day, at the very same hour that Donald Trump was taking the oath as president, Rice composed an email to herself—apparently her last official act as national security advisor. She described the January 5 meeting:

> President Obama began the conversation by stressing his continued commitment to ensuring that every aspect of this issue [the FBI investigation of the Trump campaign] is handled by the intelligence and law enforcement communities "by the book." The president stressed that he is not asking about, initiating, or instructing anything from a law enforcement perspective. He reiterated that our law enforcement team needs to proceed as it normally would by the book.[67]

Rice claimed through her attorney that she wrote the email on "advice of the White House Counsel's Office." Why did Rice memorialize the January 5 Oval Office meeting with the repeated phrase "by the book"? Nothing the Obama White House was doing was "by the book"—unless the book was written by Niccolò Machiavelli.

Ric Grenell, acting director of national intelligence in the Trump administration, warned, "You need to watch Susan Rice very closely. She will be the shadow president. . . . She's going to be running foreign policy [and] domestic policy."[68] Biden's selection of Susan Rice as his "shadow president" suggests that he may need someone skilled in political deception at his side.

Checking a Box:
Pete Buttigieg, Secretary of Transportation

Currently 38 years old, Pete Buttigieg was the two-term mayor of South Bend, Indiana, from 2012 to 2020. South Bend is a city of 100,000 people with a strong mayoral government, so "Mayor Pete" can claim *some* hands-on managerial experience. But the South Bend Public Transportation Corporation's fleet of 66 buses carries a daily average of only 4,300 people, according to the Indiana Department of Transportation.[69] It's quite a leap from managing 66 buses to overseeing the U.S. Department of Transportation (DOT). The various administrations of the DOT oversee aviation, railroads, highways, mass transit, shipping, pipelines, hazardous materials transport, seaways, public safety, and our national defense infrastructure.

Was Buttigieg the most qualified for the job because of his depth of knowledge and experience managing transportation systems? C'mon, man! Of course, he wasn't. In fact, after Buttigieg won the Iowa caucuses (and Biden finished fourth), the Biden campaign ran an ad on YouTube and Facebook attacking Mayor Pete for his inexperience. "What you've done matters," the ad concluded with drop-the-mike finality. After Biden chose Buttigieg for the cabinet post, the ad was quietly scrubbed from the internet.[70]

Biden and Buttigieg both admitted that Mayor Pete was chosen to check the LGBTQ box on the cabinet roster. Biden said, "Our cabinet doesn't have just one first, or just two of these firsts, but eight precedent-busting appointments. And today a ninth—the first openly gay nominee to lead a cabinet department and one of the youngest cabinet members ever." In response, Buttigieg thanked Biden "for honoring your commitment to diversity."

Buttigieg should be insulted by, not grateful for, the appointment. His response should be, "Don't talk about my sexual orientation. Don't make me your token gay and young cabinet member. Put me in a job that matches my qualifications, and then tell the world how highly qualified I am." Biden's anti-Buttigieg ads were right: What you've done matters. Mayor Pete was clearly not the most qualified person to run the DOT—but at least he checks the LGBTQ and youth boxes.

By the way, thirty-six Republican senators voted to confirm Pete Buttigieg, and a thirty-seventh, Pat Toomey of Pennsylvania, would have voted to confirm but was unable to attend the vote, according to the *Congressional Record*.[71] So much for the old canard about homophobic Republicans.

Buttigieg has tried to use his position to promote green transportation, such as bicycling. On February 25, 2021, Politico reporter Michael Stratford tweeted a video of Buttigieg riding a Capital Bikeshare bicycle with the message, "Cabinet secretaries @ bikeshare home from work, too." On April 1, CNN reporter D. J. Judd tweeted a video of Buttigieg climbing aboard a bicycle next to a black government SUV, surrounded by several men. As Buttigieg rode off, the SUV followed him. Judd wrote, "Transportation Secretary Pete Buttigieg biked to the White House for today's Cabinet Meeting, it would appear."

Conservative news sites and tweeters spotted what Judd missed: Buttigieg had faked his bike ride. He had ridden aboard the SUV to a secluded point near the White House. There his bodyguards helped him remove the bike from the bumper rack. Then he pedaled the short distance to the White House, making a performative display of using green transportation when he had made most of the trip in a gas-guzzling SUV.

The left-leaning Snopes fact-checking site labeled conservative interpretations of that video as "FALSE."[72] But you can view the video yourself at Snopes—search for "Did Pete Buttigieg Stage a Bike Ride After Riding in SUV?" You'll see Buttigieg's bodyguards tightening the straps on the bike rack as Buttigieg climbs onto the bike. It's obvious that they had just removed the bike from the rack moments before." Buttigieg's bike rides are a PR stunt, nothing more.

Dangerously Unqualified, Dangerously Radical: Other Key Members of Team Biden

John Kerry, President Biden's special presidential envoy for climate, was secretary of state from 2013 to 2017 and a key backer of the Joint Comprehensive Plan of Action (JCPOA, "the Iran nuclear deal"). After President Trump withdrew the United States from the JCPOA in May 2018, Kerry held secret talks with Iranian Foreign Minister Javad Zarif, discussing ways to reinstate the agreement. In media appearances in 2018, Kerry openly admitted meeting with Zarif "three or four times" since leaving office, indicating he had encouraged Iran to wait until Trump was out of office.[73] It's a felony under the Logan Act for a private citizen to undermine government policy through backdoor negotiations with foreign powers.

On climate issues, Kerry claims that the rules he inflicts on us don't apply to him. He opposed a wind-power project on Nantucket Sound because it would spoil the view from his seaside mansion. In 2019, he flew his private jet to Iceland to accept an award for environmental activism, explaining that a private jet was "the only choice for somebody like me, who is traveling the world to win this battle."[74] His Gulfstream GIV-SP spews an estimated 116 metric tons of carbon in a single year.[75] Whatever Kerry "accomplishes" as Biden's climate czar will almost certainly be a complete disaster—for which Kerry will claim victory.

President Biden named Denis McDonough, White House chief of staff under President Obama, to lead the Department of Veterans Affairs. McDonough has no medical background, has never served in the military, and has no experience working with veterans' service organizations (VSOs). Jeremy Butler, head of Iraq and Afghanistan Veterans of America, told the *Washington Post*, "He'll have to go a long way to prove himself to a very skeptical population who would prefer someone with more direct veteran and VA experience." An unnamed official of a veterans' organization told the *Post*, "Is this just a crony pick, or an afterthought? He [McDonough] has zero affiliation with veterans. . . . [McDonough] is not a vet . . . [and] doesn't understand the culture of the only cabinet-level agency with a built-in constituency that's actually engaged and vocal." Is Denis McDonough the most highly qualified person Biden could have picked for this critically important post?

We'll look at Biden's Secretary of Education Miguel Cardona in Chapter 12 and Secretary of Homeland Security Alejandro Mayorkas in Chapter 14.

This brief survey shows that Biden has assembled a team of people who, for the most part, have very little experience (like Mayor Pete) or the wrong experience (like Denis McDonough) or glaring character defects (like Susan Rice) or an unwillingness to speak up for America (like Antony Blinken). Team Biden is a collection of some of the worst Obama-era retreads plus a number of appointments that serve only to check a box.

America deserves better. This is no way to run a country.

7

Biden, Inc.

I N 2017, JOE BIDEN mused to *Vanity Fair* writer David Kamp, "I should have raised one Republican kid." Surprised, Kamp asked Biden what he meant. Biden explained that he sometimes wished that one of his children had made a lot of money to provide for him in his old age. That way, "when they put me in a home, I'd have a window with a view, you know what I mean?"[76]

What an odd thing to say. At that time, Joe Biden was certainly aware that his son Hunter was raking in megabucks from international business dealings. Four years earlier, in December 2013, Joe Biden, then the sitting vice president, took *Air Force Two* to Beijing for a meeting with Xi Jinping—and Hunter tagged along. During their stay, Hunter arranged for his father to meet his Chinese business partner, Jonathan Li.[77]

According to an April 2015 email, Hunter also arranged for his Ukrainian business associate, Vadym Pozharskyi, to meet with Vice President Biden in Washington (the Biden team says no such meeting was on Biden's schedule but has not denied that it took place).[78] So Joe Biden was clearly aware of Hunter's lucrative dealings when he made his Republican kid remark. Here are some of Hunter's international dealings:

- Beginning in 2013, Hunter was a partner in a China-based private equity fund BHR Partners, holding a 10 percent stake.
- Beginning in 2014, Hunter had a seat on the board of Ukraine's Burisma Holdings, for which he was paid $83,333 a month to serve as a "ceremonial figure" with a "powerful name."
- In early 2014, Hunter received a wire transfer of $3.5 million from billionaire Elena Baturina, widow of the former mayor of Moscow, for unknown reasons (according to an 87-page report produced by Senate Republicans).
- In 2017, Hunter signed a consulting contract with China's largest private energy company, CEFC China Energy, guaranteeing Hunter $10 million a year plus a 50 percent stake in the company "for introductions alone," according to leaked emails.[79]

Hunter Biden has made quite a haul by trading on the Biden family name. So have other members of Joe Biden's family. In fact, the media have nicknamed Joe Biden's clan "Biden, Inc." There are troubling questions about whether or not Joe Biden himself might have received a share of the proceeds—and whether his involvement might compromise his ability to deal effectively with Communist China and other nations.

The Origin of Biden, Inc.

Joe Biden's younger brother Jim was in his senior year at the University of Delaware when he served as finance chairman of Joe's 1972 Senate campaign.[80] After Joe was elected to his first term, Jim became an entrepreneur.

During the 1970s, Joe Biden served on the Banking Committee. Somehow, Jim—a young man in his twenties with no business track record—obtained generous business loans on unusually favorable terms from more than one lender.

One bank that took a risk on Jim Biden was Farmers Bank of Wilmington. In early 1973, Jim and a business partner took out a series of loans from Farmers Bank, at least one of which was unsecured. Jim and his friend opened a nightclub called "Seasons Change" near the Delaware–Pennsylvania state line. Within two years, the nightclub was failing, and Jim was missing loan payments and nearing default.

Jim's big brother, Senator Joe Biden, blamed the bank. "What I'd like to know," Joe told the *News Journal* of Wilmington, "is how the guy in charge of loans let it get this far." The newspaper found that Farmers Bank had extended Jim credit based on the Biden name.

After the bank tried to collect the debt, Senator Biden called the chairman of Farmers Bank, complaining that the bank was harassing his brother. Apparently, the bank had told Jim that if he defaulted on the loan, it would reflect badly on Senator Biden. As Joe complained to the *News Journal*, "They were trying to use me as a bludgeon."

In 1975, Jim and his partner approached First Pennsylvania Bank, even as Jim was in default to Farmers Bank. First Pennsylvania lent Jim Biden $500,000 (the equivalent of about $2.4 million today) to expand the nightclub. According to the *News Journal*, Democratic Pennsylvania Governor Milton Shapp had urged First Pennsylvania to give Jim Biden the loan. One of Governor Shapp's former aides was John T. Owens, who was married to Joe and Jim's sister, Valerie. John Owens would later join the ownership group of the nightclub.

In 1977, Jim Biden got out of the nightclub business when First Pennsylvania found a buyer to take it over. In 1981, the FDIC took Jim and his partners to court over the defaulted loans to Farmers Bank.[81] There's no evidence that Senator Joe Biden pulled any strings to help Jim get the loans, but we know that from the beginning of Joe Biden's political career, family members have used his name to open doors.

Investing in Joe

In the summer of 2006, Joe's brother Jim partnered with Joe's son Hunter, and together they bought a hedge fund company, Paradigm Global Advisors. A Paradigm executive, who was there, later told Politico reporter Ben Schreckinger that on their first day of work, Jim and Hunter and Hunter's brother Beau arrived at Paradigm's midtown Manhattan offices with "two large men." They ordered Paradigm's chief of compliance to fire the president of the firm and had the two large men escort the man out of the building.

Then, according to the executive, Jim Biden addressed the remaining officials and staff of Paradigm, saying, "Don't worry about investors. We've got people all around the world who want to invest in Joe Biden."[82]

This took place mere months before Joe Biden would launch his second run for the White House. According to Schreckinger's source, Jim Biden stated unequivocally that he viewed Paradigm Global Advisors as a means of attracting foreign money that could not be legally donated to Joe Biden or his campaign. Jim allegedly said that foreign investors were "in a line of 747s filled with cash ready to invest in this company."

Hunter's brother Beau was running for attorney general of Delaware at the time. When he heard those words from Uncle Jim, he was shocked. "This can never leave this room," Beau allegedly told Jim, "and if you ever say it again, I will have nothing to do with this."

Both Jim and Hunter have denied, through a spokesperson, that these words were ever exchanged. But as Ben Schreckinger concludes, "the recollection of an effort to cash in on Joe's political ties is consistent with other accounts provided by other former executives" of Paradigm.[83]

Schreckinger says that there's no evidence that Joe Biden used his office to benefit his relatives; yet interviews, court documents, and news reports show that the Biden family "consistently mixed business and politics over nearly half a century, moving from one business to the next as Joe's stature in Washington grew."[84]

After Hunter Biden graduated from law school in 1996, he accepted a well-paying position at MBNA Bank, the largest private-sector employer in Delaware. Within two years, Hunter was promoted to executive vice president. Hunter left MBNA in 2001; yet the bank continued paying him consulting fees.

Meanwhile, Senator Joe Biden was working to pass a bankruptcy bill that would benefit MBNA by making it harder for borrowers to discharge credit-card debt. When the bill passed in 2005, Hunter's MBNA consulting fees ended.[85] Coincidence?

Conflict-of-Interest Questions

The media took little notice when Vice President Joe Biden took his son Hunter to China in December 2013. Yet a former White House aide told reporter Adam Entous of *The New Yorker* that the Obama administration worried about the "optics" of the vice president's son leveraging his political connections.

Entous interviewed members of Biden's vice-presidential staff and asked if anyone raised any conflict-of-interest questions. Several said that they didn't dare. "Everyone who works for him has been screamed at," said one former Biden advisor.[86]

Vice President Biden was assigned responsibility for U.S. policy toward Ukraine and China. Hunter Biden's business dealings just happened to be with Ukraine and China. Again, coincidence?

In May 2014, news broke of Hunter Biden's position on the Burisma board in Ukraine. Jen Psaki, then a spokesperson for the State Department, told reporters that the State Department saw no conflict-of-interest concerns. Why? Because Hunter was a "private citizen." Behind the scenes, however, there was a feeling that (as one White House aide put it) "Hunter was on the loose, potentially undermining his father's message."[87]

Nearly seven years later, Jen Psaki as White House press secretary *again* found herself explaining why Hunter Biden's business dealings were not an ethical problem for now-President Biden. At a White House daily briefing on February 5, 2021, a reporter asked Psaki about reports that Hunter "still owns a 10 percent stake in the Chinese investment firm formed with [Communist] state-owned entities. Do you have an update on the divestment from that investment?" Psaki replied that Hunter was "working to unwind his investment. . . . He's a private citizen."[88]

For a second time in almost seven years, Psaki relied on the flimsy private-citizen dodge to explain away the conflict of interest. Yes, Hunter is a private citizen, but he's the son of the president of the United States, and the president is anything *but* a private citizen. It is Joe Biden who has the conflict of interest, not Hunter. And it is Joe Biden who, in December 2020, told CNN, "My son, my family will not be involved in any business, any enterprise that is in conflict with or appears to be in conflict with where there's appropriate distance from the presidency and government."[89]

The "Smoking Gun" Laptop

On October 14, 2020, near the end of the 2020 presidential campaign, the *New York Post* published a front-page story about a series of "smoking gun" emails recovered from a water-damaged laptop. The computer was left by Hunter Biden at a repair shop in Wilmington, Delaware, in April 2019. In December 2019, after Hunter failed to pick up the repaired computer, the shop owner took possession under the terms of the service contract. On the hard drive he discovered a trove of emails and texts about Hunter's business dealings.

There were texts between two Hunter Biden associates, James Gilliar and Tony Bobulinski, on May 11, 2017. (Bobulinski was a venture capitalist hired by Jim and Hunter Biden as chief executive of Sinohawk Holdings, a partnership between the Biden family and Chinese energy mogul Ye Jianming.) One of the Gilliar's texts to Bobulinski read, "Let's get the company set up, then tell H and family the high stakes and get Joe involved." H, of course, is Hunter—and we all know who Joe is.

A May 13, 2017, email from Gilliar to Hunter outlined remuneration packages for six people involved in an unnamed business venture. The email listed equity shares for Biden family members, including 10 percent to be held by Hunter "for the big guy." After the *New York Post* broke the story, Bobulinski positively identified the big guy as Joe Biden.

Joe Biden's direct involvement worried Bobulinski. He later told Michael Goodwin of the *New York Post* that he asked Jim Biden, "How are you guys getting away with this? Aren't you concerned?" Jim Biden laughed and said, "Plausible deniability."

On May 20, 2017, Gilliar sent Bobulinksi an encrypted WhatsApp message that read, "Don't mention Joe being involved, it's only when u are face to face, I know u know that but they are paranoid." Bobulinksi replied, "OK they should be paranoid about things." Aware that Joe Biden was considering a presidential campaign in 2020, Bobulinski added, "You need to stress to H, does he want to be the reason or factor that blows up his dad's campaign."

Tony Bobulinski has verified the emails as authentic. He has given his records to the Senate Homeland Security Committee. In a press release, Bobulinski said:

> Hunter Biden called his dad "the Big Guy" or "my Chairman,"
> and frequently referenced asking him for his sign-off or
> advice on various potential deals that we were discussing. I've
> seen Vice President Biden saying he never talked to Hunter
> about his business. I've seen firsthand that that's not true,
> because it wasn't just Hunter's business, they said they were
> putting the Biden family name and its legacy on the line.[90]

The emails on Hunter Biden's laptop were like a smoking gun—persuasive evidence of a pattern of corruption by Biden, Inc. But would the media examine that evidence—or suppress it?

The Ukraine Cover-Up

On June 18, 2017, Hunter urgently requested $10 million from Ye Jianming as seed money for Sinohawk Holdings, adding that he extended "best wishes from the entire Biden family." That summer, Ye met with Hunter in Miami, where they discussed ways that Ye's company, CEFC China Energy, might invest in American companies. Later, Ye sent Hunter a thank-you gift—a 2.8-carat diamond.[91]

In early 2018, Ye was detained on suspicion of economic crimes. The arrest order came directly from Communist China's leader Xi Jinping. It was an astonishing fall for Ye, who had been listed by *Forbes* in 2016 as one of the 40 most powerful young people in the world.[92]

In January 2018, Joe Biden spoke at a Council on Foreign Relations event and told this story about an incident in Kiev after he was assigned responsibility for Ukraine:

> I was supposed to announce that there was another billion-dollar loan guarantee. And I had gotten a commitment from Poroshenko and from Yatsenyuk that they would take action against the state prosecutor. And they didn't. So they were walking out of the press conference. I said, "Nah, I'm not going to—we're not going to give you the billion dollars." They said, "You have no authority. You're not the president. The president said—." I said, "Call him." I said, "I'm telling

you, you're not getting the billion dollars." I said, "You're not getting the billion. I'm going to be leaving here in—." I think it was about six hours. I looked at them and said, "We're leaving in six hours. If the prosecutor is not fired, you're not getting the money." Well, son of a bitch, he got fired.[93]

Why did Vice President Biden threaten to withhold American taxpayer dollars from Ukraine? Was it because the Ukrainian prosecutor, Viktor Shokin, was investigating corrupt dealings by Burisma Holdings and Hunter Biden? Was Biden using his office to shield Hunter and Burisma from Shokin's investigation?

The media scorned this explanation. A *USA Today* story on October 3, 2019, was headlined, "Explainer: Biden, Allies Pushed Out Ukrainian Prosecutor Because He Didn't Pursue Corruption Cases." (In other words, Shokin was supposedly too soft on corruption.) On October 15, 2020, after President Trump accused Biden of trying to cover up Hunter's dealings, FactCheck.org ran a story headlined, "Trump Revives False Narrative on Biden and Ukraine." Around the same time, Snopes.com rated the claim that Biden wanted Shokin fired to protect Hunter "FALSE."[94]

But a joint majority report issued by two U.S. Senate committees, Homeland Security and Governmental Affairs and the Committee on Finance, tells a different story. Here's an excerpt:

On April 16, 2014, Vice President Biden met with his son's business partner, Devon Archer, at the White House. Five days later, Vice President Biden visited Ukraine, and he soon after was described in the press as the "public face of the administration's handling of Ukraine." The day after his visit, on April 22, Archer joined the board of Burisma. Six days later, on April 28, British officials seized $23 million from the London bank accounts of Burisma's owner Mykola Zlochevsky. Fourteen days later, on May 12, Hunter Biden joined the board of Burisma, and over the course of the next several years, Hunter Biden and Devon Archer were paid millions of dollars from a corrupt Ukrainian oligarch for their participation on the board.

In 2016, Ukraine's top prosecutor, Viktor Shokin, had an active and ongoing investigation into Burisma and its owner, Mykola Zlochevsky. At the time, Archer and Hunter Biden continued to serve on Burisma's board of directors. According to news reports, then-Vice President Biden "threatened to withhold $1 billion in United States loan guarantees if Ukraine's leaders did not dismiss [Shokin]." After that threat, Ukraine's Parliament fired Shokin.[95]

In 2018, the Department of Justice began investigating Hunter Biden's tax liability stemming from his dealings in China and Ukraine. In all, Hunter was involved in more than two dozen business ventures. One 2017 email revealed that Hunter had failed to report $400,000 in income from Burisma Holdings.[96]

The Media Cover-Up

The *New York Post* broke the story of Hunter's laptop two-and-a-half weeks before Election Day 2020. The mainstream media unanimously dropped a shroud of silence over the story. If you only got your news from the mainstream media, you didn't hear a whisper about the story. Twitter blocked any tweets containing a link to the *Post* story and even locked the *New York Post* out of its own Twitter account.

Matt Taibbi is a liberal journalist who has been covering politics for *Rolling Stone* since 2004 and who publishes "TK News by Matt Taibbi" on Substack.com. Though Taibbi and I would probably not agree on politics, I admire his dedication to covering this story. On October 24, 2020, frustrated by media suppression of the Hunter Biden story, Taibbi wrote:

> The flow of information in the United States has become so politicized—bottlenecked by an increasingly brazen union of corporate press and tech platforms—that it's become impossible for American audiences to see news about certain topics absent thickets of propagandistic contextualizing. Try to look up anything about Burisma, Joe Biden, or Hunter Biden . . . and you're likely to be shown a pile of "fact-checks" and explainers ahead of the raw information. . . . Other true information has been scrubbed or de-ranked, either by platforms or by a confederation of press outlets whose loyalty to the Democratic Party far now overshadows its obligations to inform.[97]

On April 8, 2021, MSNBC host Chris Hayes (@chrislhayes) tweeted, "So, like, did we ever find out the actual deal with the Hunter laptop? I mean, maybe the wildly improbably [sic] story about it was . . . true? or maybe it was a cover story for a hack, but do we know?"

I rolled my eyes when I read Hayes's tweet—then I quoted-tweeted it with my reply: "So, like, um, you know you, your network and your leftist media buddies all ignored and shunned this story when it came out."

The story of Biden, Inc., is the story of a decades-long pattern of corruption involving the Biden family. It involves compromising business deals in Ukraine and China worth millions or billions of dollars—with percentages allegedly allocated for "the big guy," Joe Biden himself.

That's obviously a huge scandal.

But as Matt Taibbi points out—and as we will explore more deeply in Chapters 17 and 18—suppression of the truth by the mainstream press and social media is a far bigger scandal.

And this is an ominous portent for our future.

8

The Threat to
Global Security

A T A MAY 2019 campaign rally in Iowa City, Joe Biden dismissed concerns that China is surpassing the United States
as a world superpower. "China is going to eat our lunch?" he said.
"Come on, man! I mean, you know, they're not bad folks, folks.
But guess what? They're not competition for us."

I agree that the Chinese people are not bad folks. They're a
wonderful people with an amazing cultural heritage. But China's
communist leaders—with their militarism, slave labor camps,
oppression of Hong Kong, and cover-up of the spread of COVID-
19—are very bad, folks. It's incredibly dangerous for an American
president to be so naive about the intentions of Communist China.

On February 10, 2021, three weeks into his presidency, Biden
spoke by phone with his counterpart in Communist China, Xi

Jinping, general secretary of the Chinese Communist Party (CCP) and president of the People's Republic of China (PRC). The conversation lasted two hours. The next day, in a meeting with senators about environmental and public works issues, Biden said of China, "If we don't get moving, they're going to eat our lunch!"[98]

First he says China's *not* eating our lunch, and now he says China *is* eating our lunch. Maybe President Biden is finally waking up to China's competitive threat to the United States. But is he focused on the *real* threat of Communist China?

The Real Threat

In his remarks to the senate delegation, Biden said nothing of China's increasingly belligerent militarism and threats to global stability. He didn't mention Communist China's role in unleashing a deadly pandemic on the world. Instead, he cited Chinese advancements in infrastructure, environmental technology, electric vehicle technology, and railway technology.

> They're investing a lot of money; they're investing billions of dollars and dealing with a whole range of issues that relate to transportation, the environment and a whole range of other things. They have a major, major new initiative on rail, and they already have rail that goes 225 miles an hour with ease. . . . So we just have to step up.[99]

In other words, what Joe Biden took away from his conversation with Chairman Xi is that Communist China has really fast choo-choo trains—and our trains need to keep up with China's trains. But trains are nineteenth-century technology. Someone should tell our president about Elon Musk's Hyperloop, a zero-emission, electromagnetic levitation, supersonic ground transport system. The first human passenger test of Hyperloop technology was conducted successfully by Virgin Hyperloop in November 2020.[100] The Hyperloop can take passengers from Washington, DC, to New York in just 30 minutes[101] (the same trip takes three hours by Amtrak).

Yes, there's a real threat that Communist China is going to eat our lunch, but it's not going to be in transportation technology. President Biden only seems concerned about Chinese competition when he can use it to promote increased spending on infrastructure projects that benefit his political ally, Big Labor.

In his two-hour phone call with Chairman Xi, President Biden talked about human rights abuses against the Uighur population and the people of Hong Kong, and he raised concerns about China's "coercive and unfair" trade practices—and I salute him for that. But I've seen no evidence in President Biden's policies or public statements that he has any true understanding of the *real* threat Communist China poses to the United States and the rest of the world.

And that should worry us all.

Biden's WHO Blunder

In one of his first official acts as president on January 20, 2021, Joe Biden signed the "Letter to His Excellency António Guterres," nullifying President Trump's letter of July 6, 2020, and informing the secretary-general of the United Nations that "[t]he United States intends to remain a member of the World Health Organization."[102] President Trump pulled the United States out of the World Health Organization (WHO), so President Biden reflexively dragged us back into the WHO. Now the United States taxpayer is again being gouged to pay for a "health organization" that has degenerated into a Beijing-run propaganda office. Once again, the United States will be the largest financial contributor to the WHO, while Communist China calls the shots.

The consequences of President Biden's ill-considered move became clear on February 9, the day before Biden's phone call with Chairman Xi, when a team of WHO "investigators" held a press conference in Wuhan. They announced their conclusion that the COVID-19 virus originated in nature and was transmitted to humans by some as-yet-unknown means. The WHO team's "conclusions" parroted Communist China's propaganda.

While delivering their conclusions under the watchful eye of their Communist overlords in Wuhan, the WHO team attempted to validate various far-fetched theories floated by the Communist Chinese government. The WHO team gave credence to the impossible notion that the virus came from imported frozen food. The WHO team praised the "high biosafety protocols" at the Wuhan Institute of Virology that made it "very unlikely that anything could escape from such a place."[103] In short, Communist China is completely innocent, nothing to see here, move along, move along.

On January 29, 2021, husband-and-wife biologists Heather Heying and Bret Weinstein were interviewed on the HBO show *Real Time with Bill Maher*. Host Bill Maher asked his guests about the Wuhan Institute of Virology. Maher said:

There is this lab, I think it's the only one in the world quite like it, in Wuhan, where it started. It would almost be a conspiracy theory to think it *didn't* start in the lab. And that theory was demonized at first: "Come on, that's conspiracy thinking, that it started in the lab." But it certainly is a fifty-fifty [chance], would you say that?

Bret Weinstein replied:

Oh, it's far more likely than that. As a matter of fact, I said (I think in June) that the chances that it came from the lab looked to me to be about 90 percent. So this was never a conspiracy theory. In fact, that term [conspiracy theory] is simply used to make it go away. It's an obvious hypothesis that is in need of testing, and we are only now, a year in, getting to the point where we can discuss it out loud without being stigmatized.

Heather Heying added:

A big part of the problem, of course, is that we are so politi-cized, we are so polarized and partisan now as a country that if the wrong guy proposed this to begin with—and for half the country, it was the wrong guy [referring to President Trump]—then the rest of the country says, no way, no how! We're going to call that a conspiracy theory, and we're never going to revisit it. The fact is, that's not how science works. . . . A leak from the lab? That was clearly a possibility from the beginning.[104]

The next day, the *Daily Beast* pounced on Bill Maher and his guests with a bizarre review headlined, "Bill Maher Pushes Steve Bannon Wuhan Lab COVID Conspiracy," claiming that "Maher welcomed a pair of podcast hosts, the husband-and-wife duo of

Bret Weinstein and Heather Heying."[105] These so-called podcast hosts are highly respected biologists and researchers. What's more, Maher, Weinstein, and Heying are all considerably left of center in their own politics, and the suggestion that they are Steve Bannon fans is just bizarre.

The 2018 Wuhan Warning

The Wuhan Institute of Virology was working with very dangerous microbes—and the undeniable truth is that one of them could have got loose and triggered a global pandemic. In fact, the U.S. State Department has been worried about the Wuhan Institute for several years.

From January through March 2018, the American Embassy in Beijing sent scientists to visit the Wuhan Institute. The laboratory not only let the American scientists tour the lab but bragged about those visits on its website. After the COVID-19 outbreak, the Wuhan Institute scrubbed the news release about the American visits from its website.

Privately, the American scientists were so alarmed by what they saw at the Wuhan laboratory that they cabled Washington, warning of frightening safety issues there. They *specifically* spoke of the laboratory's work on coronaviruses from bats and their potential for transmission to humans—and they warned of a possible coronavirus pandemic. Less than two years later, the plague U.S. officials warned of spread around the world.[106]

Yet the WHO "investigators" assure us that COVID-19 couldn't have come from the lab. In fact, the WHO team claimed—incredibly—the lab wasn't even working on a virus similar to COVID-19.

The WHO hindered the world's response to the pandemic. In mid-January 2020, as the virus spread from China to other nations, the WHO denied there was evidence of human-to-human transmission, endorsing Beijing's claims. When some WHO officials urged a global emergency declaration, others objected that a declaration would upset China. The WHO's failure to tell the truth deprived the world of precious time to prepare for the pandemic.

Taro Aso, deputy prime minister of Japan, has said that many in his country refer to the WHO as the "Chinese Health Organization" because of the WHO's ties to the Communist Chinese government.[107] The *New York Times* reports that Beijing is tightening its grip on the WHO:

> China's leader, Xi Jinping, has made it a priority to strengthen Beijing's clout at international institutions, including the WHO, seeing the American-dominated global order as an impediment to his country's rise as a superpower.

China contributes only a small fraction of the WHO's $6 billion budget, whereas the United States is one of its main benefactors. In recent years, though, Beijing has worked in other ways to expand its influence at the organization.[108]

China has lobbied the WHO to promote traditional Chinese medicine, an unscientific practice that kills endangered species (including tigers, rhinos, black bear, and musk deer) for its various powders and potions. Pressured by China, the WHO scrubbed from its website a warning against treating COVID-19 with traditional Chinese medicine.

The WHO is a corrupt UN bureaucracy that does the bidding of Communist China while America pays the bills. President Biden, in his reckless haste to undo the Trump legacy, committed a huge blunder, dragging the United States back into an unholy alliance with the WHO.

In *Duty: Memoirs of a Secretary at War*, intelligence analyst and former Secretary of Defense Robert Gates said of Joe Biden, "I think he has been wrong on nearly every major foreign policy and national security issue over the past four decades."[109] Unfortunately, Joe Biden continues to be dangerously wrong in his approach to Communist China.

Slavery and Genocide

On January 20, 2021, at the very moment President Biden delivered his inaugural address, the People's Republic of China announced sanctions against 28 officials of the departing Trump administration, including former Secretary of State Mike Pompeo, former UN Ambassador Kelly Kraft, former Health and Human Services Secretary Alex Azar, and others. This action by the Communist Chinese government was a threat to the Biden-Harris administration: Don't say bad things about Communist China. Don't make us mad, or we'll take action against you *personally*.

One of Mike Pompeo's final acts as secretary of state was to declare:

> The People's Republic of China (PRC), under the direction and control of the Chinese Communist Party (CCP), has committed crimes against humanity against the predominantly Muslim Uyghurs [sic] and other members of ethnic and religious minority groups in Xinjiang. . . . I believe this genocide is ongoing, and that we are witnessing the systematic attempt to destroy Uyghurs by the Chinese party-state.[110]

Pompeo mentioned other persecuted ethnic and religious groups in China. According to Open Doors USA, there are more than 97 million Protestant and Catholic Christians facing state-sponsored violence and persecution in China. The Communist Chinese government is trying to conform the church to communist ideology through bullying, beatings, imprisonment, and the shutdown of churches.[111] The atheist communist regime has retranslated the Bible and requires Chinese Christians to adopt this "correct understanding" of their Scriptures. Chinese Christians say that under Xi Jinping's rule, they are enduring the harshest persecution since the Cultural Revolution of Mao Zedong.[112]

Pompeo's successor, Tony Blinken, testified before the Senate Foreign Relations Committee hours after Pompeo released his statement. To his credit, Blinken seconded Pompeo's assessment. Asked about Pompeo's claim that China was committing crimes against humanity, Blinken responded, "That would be my judgment as well." He added, "President Trump was right in taking a tougher approach to China. I disagree very much with the way he went about it in a number of areas, but the basic principle was the right one."[113]

Some people on the left blame Trump administration policies for ratcheting up tensions between the United States and Communist China. That view is based on a misreading of the history of U.S.-China relations from the Nixon era to the present day. For decades, America's China policy has been shaped by an unfounded (even wishful) belief: If we would encourage China's economic growth and democratization through trade and economic exchanges, China would liberalize and become an ally and partner of America and the West. Chinese leaders from Mao to

Xi Jinping have encouraged this myth, and every president from Nixon through Obama has viewed Communist China through this distortion lens.

A Gold Medal for an Insult

The PRC has always been a repressive and rigidly Marxist-Stalinist-Leninist-Maoist regime. Communist China has been continuously obsessed with regional and even global hegemony. (*Hegemony* may be defined as "a high level of military, economic, and cultural ascendancy, enabling a nation to impose its will on other nations.")

Mandarin-speaking China expert Michael Pillsbury, author of *The Hundred-Year Marathon*, has chronicled China's patient, persistent quest for a China-centric new world order. This quest began in 1972, when Richard Nixon and Henry Kissinger opened up China to the West—or so they thought. In reality, Pillsbury asserts, Mao Zedong set a trap for the United States, and Richard Nixon took the bait. "In many ways," Pillsbury wrote, "it was not Nixon who went to China, but China that went to Nixon."[114]

Pillsbury brings deep first-hand knowledge to the subject. In 1973, when he was a young RAND Corporation China analyst, he had top-secret cleared access to Secretary of State Henry Kissinger's conversations with Communist Chinese leaders. He had roles in the Carter and Reagan administrations, helping to shape military and intelligence cooperation with Communist China—cooperation he now views as a huge foreign policy blunder. Pillsbury identifies July 1978 as the moment the United States, under President Jimmy Carter, began transferring scientific and technological knowledge to China. China also began sending thousands of students to American universities to study—and to spy. China has been taking American technology and using it against us ever since.

During the Clinton years, the Chinese Communists pulled off what they called "the Clinton coup" by identifying China-friendly members of the Clinton administration and cultivating ties with them. These allies, Pillsbury wrote, "persuaded the president to relax his anti-China stance. . . . Sanctions were eased, then lifted."[115]

On November 30, 2012, Chinese artist Cai Guo Qiang, who was being honored by the Smithsonian Institution, set up a Christmas tree on the National Mall. Then he exploded the tree with hundreds of Chinese-made fireworks. The audience, which included Democratic Congresswoman Nancy Pelosi and other luminaries of the left, applauded as the Christmas tree went up in smoke. Cinders, pine needles, and wood fragments formed a debris field that would take weeks to clean up. Hillary Clinton presented Cai Guo Qiang with a gold medal—the first U.S. State Department Medal of Arts, along with $250,000 from American taxpayers. The medal recognized his "contributions to the advancement of understanding and diplomacy."

Michael Pillsbury witnessed the exploding tree and applauded along with the audience—but he was troubled by what he saw. The next day, Pillsbury had a secret meeting with a "senior Chinese government defector." The defector couldn't believe that the United States had allowed Cai to stage the event and had given him the award. Didn't the Americans understand the themes of Cai's work—themes of "the decline of the United States and the rise of a strong China"? Didn't the Americans grasp the symbolism of the exploding tree? There, at the seat of American government, Cai had destroyed a Christmas tree, a symbol of the Christian

faith. Cai, a communist and a nationalist, had insulted America—
and the Americans had cheered and given him a medal.

Pillsbury concludes that the exploding tree symbolizes our mis-
understanding of Communist China's view of the West. He writes,
"Chinese leaders have persuaded many in the West to believe that
China's rise will be peaceful and will not come at others' expense."[116]

But China's rise has come at a huge price for the world.

The Thucydides Trap

When Xi Jinping came to power in 2012, many Western observers
saw him as a benign leader and even a reformer. But China's lies
about COVID-19 have cost the world millions of lives and trillions of dollars. China under Xi has corrupted the WHO, crushed
opposition in Hong Kong, enslaved more than a million people
in Xinjiang, threatened Taiwan and Tibet, clashed with India and
Japan, and sought sole dominion over the South China Sea.

Some analysts have warned the United States not to fall into
the *Thucydides trap*—a term coined by political scientist Graham
Allison. Named after Athenian general Thucydides, a Thucydides
trap is the competition for dominance between an emerging power
and an established power, leading to war.

H. R. McMaster, national security advisor from 2017 to 2018,
wrote an op-ed in the *Washington Post* urging the new administration not to misunderstand the Thucydides trap theory. McMaster
warned that it would be a tragic mistake to conclude that "U.S.
competition with China is dangerous or even irresponsible because
of 'Thucydides's Trap,'" Instead, the Biden-Harris administration
"should be confident in the free world's ability to compete effectively" with China. "The United States has been sorely tested by
pandemic, recession, social division and political strife, but our

republic has proved resilient. It is up to the task of working with partners to defend the free world from Chinese Communist Party aggression."[117]

The Biden-Harris administration faces immense challenges around the world. Our national defense assets, civilian infrastructure, and electric grid are under continuous cyber-assault from Russia, China, and other unfriendly nations. Iran will continue its dangerous provocations in the Persian Gulf. North Korea will rattle its missiles and nukes. These are crisis-level challenges that won't go away.

But most important of all, the fate of the world hinges on whether the Biden-Harris administration gets it right on Communist China.

9

The Biden Postpandemic Economy

I N HIS INAUGURAL ADDRESS on January 20, 2021, President Joe Biden delivered these noble-sounding sentiments: "Politics need not be a raging fire, destroying everything in its path. . . . We must reject a culture in which facts themselves are manipulated and even manufactured."[118]

At his first official press conference on March 25, 64 days after making those remarks, President Biden took a question from Nancy Cordes of CBS News. She asked his thoughts on Republicans trying to "restrict voting."

Biden replied, "What I'm worried about is how un-American this whole initiative is. It's sick. It's sick. . . . This makes Jim Crow look like Jim Eagle."

That wacky line sent millions of Americans scurrying to Google, asking, "Who is Jim Eagle?" The fact is that this was Joe Biden's attempt at a joke. Jim Crow? Jim Eagle? Get it? Yeah, ornithological puns. Hilarious.

Underneath President Biden's failed joke, however, lies an explosive claim. He was saying that Republican-sponsored election reforms in many states were *far worse* than the 4,000 lynchings of black Americans during Jim Crow, far worse than the 1873 Colfax massacre in Louisiana when the "White League" slaughtered more than 100 black Americans, and far worse than the 1921 massacre of as many as 300 black Americans in the destruction of the Greenwood freedom colony in Tulsa, Oklahoma.

What an outrageous claim! Surely that wasn't what President Biden really meant, was it? Yes, that's exactly what he meant.

Four Pinocchios

The next day, March 26, Biden doubled down on that claim, singling out the Georgia Election Integrity Act. He said:

> Among the outrageous parts of this new state law, it ends voting hours early so working people can't cast their vote after their shift is over. It adds rigid restrictions on casting absentee ballots that will effectively deny the right to vote to countless voters. And it makes it a crime to provide water to voters while they wait in line. . . . This is Jim Crow in the twenty-first century. It must end.[119]

On March 30, the *Washington Post* published an article headlined, "Biden Falsely Claims the New Georgia Law 'Ends Voting Hours Early.'" The *Post*'s left-wing so-called fact checker, Glenn

Kessler, called out President Biden for repeatedly claiming that the Georgia law would "end voting at 5:00 o'clock when working people are just getting off work." The truth, Kessler said, is that Georgia's polling places "are open from 7 a.m. to 7 p.m., and if you are in line by 7 p.m., you are allowed to cast your ballot."

In fact, Georgia's new early voting laws didn't restrict voting, as Biden claimed, but actually *expanded* voting opportunities. Kessler compared Georgia with Biden's home state, Delaware, and found very little difference between the two states' laws. Kessler concluded, "The president earns Four Pinocchios."[120] That's the equivalent of "Liar, liar, pants on fire!"

Biden's $100 Million Lie

On March 31, the *next day* after receiving four Pinocchios from the *Washington Post*, President Biden spoke with ESPN's Sage Steele. She told Biden that the Major League Baseball Players Association was urging the league to move its All-Star Game out of Atlanta. Biden responded, "I strongly support them doing that [moving the All-Star Game]. . . . It's just not right. This is Jim Crow on steroids, what they're doing in Georgia and 40 other states."[121]

There it was again—"Jim Crow on steroids." Even after being exposed by the *Washington Post*, Biden continues spouting the lie. And this time he added a new outrage, calling for the All-Star Game to be moved out of Atlanta. He had gone far beyond scoring political points against Republicans. His reckless lie was about to harm thousands of people, most of them African Americans.

Major League Baseball Commissioner Rob Manfred heard Biden's lie—and he abruptly announced that the All-Star Game was being moved from Atlanta to Denver, Colorado—a state that had virtually the same voting laws as Georgia.

In a *Wall Street Journal* op-ed titled, "Rob Manfred's All-Star Error," Fay Vincent, commissioner of baseball from 1989 to 1992, criticized Manfred for politicizing baseball "over a law he likely hadn't examined." Vincent explained:

> The players will get paid no matter where the game takes place. MLB will get the same television revenue. The only people hurt by Mr. Manfred's decision will be Atlanta's stadium workers and local vendors. . . .
>
> If Georgia is racist, how can baseball talk of doing business with China? Mr. Manfred failed to spell out specific criticisms of Georgia's voting law. Now he's put himself in the awkward position of having to defend Colorado's voting laws.[122]

It's true. Manfred's decision hurt stadium workers and local vendors, as well as business owners and workers not only around Atlanta's Truist Park but also throughout the greater Atlanta region. And in terms of demographics, Atlanta is 51.4 percent black, while Denver is lily-white.

Jobs Creator Network CEO Alfredo Ortiz responded:

> Small business owners in Georgia are barely making it out of the pandemic, and now they're faced with potentially higher taxes out of the Biden administration, a higher minimum wage, more red tape and regulation, and now this. . . . [Moving the All-Star Game out of Atlanta] is going to cost upwards of $100 million in economic damage and impact to the state . . . [including] minority-owned businesses that desperately needed this kind of revenue.[123]

This is Joe Biden's hundred million–dollar lie. With his reckless and dishonest attacks on Georgia's new voting law, the president has done enormous economic harm to the very people he *claims* he wants to help.

Joe Biden's incendiary Jim Crow remarks are totally in character. Remember his 2012 speech in Danville, Virginia, to a crowd of predominantly black voters? He said of Republicans (in an offensive parody of black vernacular), "They're going to put y'all back in chains."[124]

The "Jim Crow on steroids" lie was calculated and deliberate, intended to inflame racial hatred. President Biden—who said, "Politics need not be a raging fire, destroying everything in its path"—knowingly risks provoking a race war with this lie.

Why is he doing it? Because the Democrats plan to pass legislation that will erase the election laws of all 50 states and turn the Federal Election Commission into a wholly owned subsidiary of the Democratic Party. To do so, Joe Biden must demonize Georgia's new voting law. So he lied with complete disregard for the economic destruction he inflicted on the people of Georgia— including black Americans.

Selling the Sizzle and Hiding the Pork

In 2020 and 2021, Congress passed three COVID-19-related stimulus bills that included direct payments to individuals and families. The first was the $2.2 trillion Coronavirus Aid, Relief, and Economic Security Act (CARES Act) of March 2020, which included $1,200 stimulus checks. The second was the Consolidated Appropriations Act of December 2020, which included $600 stimulus checks. The $2.3 trillion spending bill combined $900 billion of stimulus relief with a $1.4 trillion omnibus spending bill for the 2021 fiscal year. Both bills passed with strong bipartisan support in Congress.

The third COVID-19-related stimulus bill was the $1.9 trillion American Rescue Plan Act passed in March 2021, which included $1,400 stimulus checks. Unlike the previous two stimulus bills, the American Rescue Plan passed on a straight party-line vote, with all Democrats in favor and all Republicans opposed (Kamala Harris cast her first tie-breaking vote as vice president).

Why did this third stimulus bill fail to attract any Republican votes? Why did bipartisanship collapse after Joe Biden became president? Answer: Because Democrats didn't need Republicans anymore. They could pass anything they wanted to on a straight party-line vote.

So instead of writing a bill designed to protect the American people and the economy from the impact of COVID-19, Democrats wrote a massive wish list of Progressive spending projects. President Biden and the Democrats *promoted* the bill as a COVID-19 relief package, but it was actually a massive overhaul of American society.

There's an old saying, coined by legendary salesman Elmer Wheeler: "Sell the sizzle, not the steak." In other words, when you're selling a product, sell the benefits, not the product itself. The sizzle of the American Rescue Plan Act was COVID-19 relief. The steak—or, rather, the pork—was the massive non-COVID-19-related list of Progressive goodies.

On February 19, 2021, President Biden visited the Pfizer manufacturing site in Kalamazoo, Michigan, and talked about how we need the American Rescue Plan to feed people who had lost their jobs, help people who were behind on their mortgage or rent, and get people vaccinated. He said, "The American Rescue Plan puts $160 billion into more testing and tracing, manufacturing and distribution, and setting up vaccination sites—everything that's needed to get vaccines into people's arms."[125]

President Biden was selling the sizzle and hiding the pork. The $160 billion of COVID-19-related spending he touted is 8.4 percent of the $1.9 trillion American Rescue Plan. Republican leaders did the math and began saying that less than 9 percent of the bill was related to COVID-19. Predictably, the mainstream media fact-checked that claim and declared it *false*.

For example, *Newsweek*'s fact checker pointed out that the Democrats considered funds for emergency paid leave and for safely reopening schools (even though private and parochial schools had remained open without billions of federal dollars). *Newsweek* quoted the Biden-Harris administration as saying, "Altogether, this would put over $400 billion toward these critical measures for addressing COVID-19." According to *Newsweek*, the Republican claim that only 9 percent of the bill went to COVID-19 relief was false because "more than 20 percent" of the American Rescue Plan was COVID-19 related.[126] Okay. Let's be generous and say that roughly 20 percent of the bill is COVID-19 related. This still means that 80 percent of the bill—$1.4 trillion worth— is pure unadulterated pork.

Addicted to Government Checks

The pork in the bill includes $350 billion in bailouts for state and local governments, including governments bankrupted by reckless Democratic spending. It contains $130 billion for schools, which will be spent *not* to improve education but to pay off the teachers' unions. Even worse, the schools get the money even if they refuse to reopen.

The American Rescue Plan creates a universal income guarantee for families by creating a child tax credit of up to $3,600 per child. For a household with three children, that's a $10,800 benefit, which the IRS would dole out in monthly cash payments.[127]

One of the social justice provisions of the bill is a $5 billion program that provides loan forgiveness for farmers and ranchers who belong to "socially disadvantaged" groups, as defined by the Food, Agriculture, Conservation, and Trade Act of 1990. The program pays 120 percent of the debtor's outstanding debt (the additional 20 percent is intended to cover taxes).[128] Another social justice program is a $50 million funding provision for EPA "environmental justice grants," whatever that means.

Calling this $1.9 trillion monstrosity a COVID-19 relief bill is a little like buying a $300,000 Lamborghini and calling it a portable cell phone charger. Yes, a Lamborghini has a phone-charging port, and you can try to convince your significant other, "I really needed a portable cell phone charger." But it's obvious what that purchase was really all about, just as it's obvious that the American Rescue Plan was never really about COVID-19 relief. It was about the Democrats being able to spend as much as they want on whatever they want, and no one can stop them.

The so-called American Rescue Plan doesn't rescue people. It traps them into dependence on government handouts. It creates incentives for people to stay home instead of going back to work. University of Chicago economist Casey B. Mulligan and Club for Growth cofounder Stephen Moore analyzed the American Rescue Plan for the *Wall Street Journal*. They concluded that the bill created "one of the largest expansions in government welfare benefits since the birth of the modern welfare state." They wrote:

> Many Americans will always choose the dignity of work over government handouts. But the Biden benefit package makes going back to work a money-losing proposition. If Mr. Biden and the Democrats want to encourage employment, they should suspend payroll taxes for jobs that pay $100,000 a year or less. This would provide all workers an immediate 7.5% raise and would cut the cost to employers of hiring unemployed workers back by the same percentage. . . .
>
> President Biden's bill will make millions more Americans dependent on checks from the government, not an employer. Could that be the point?[129]

I believe that that's *exactly* the point. If the Democrats can get middle-class Americans addicted to government checks, the Democrats will own the middle-class vote—and they can transform America into their idea of a socialist utopia.

A $1.9 Trillion "Free Lunch"

As this so-called COVID-19 relief bill was being debated, the COVID vaccine was being distributed and COVID-19-related deaths were declining. The Democrats realized that they had to get the bill passed while the public still felt a sense of urgency about the coronavirus. So the Democrats crammed the bill through Congress like meat through a sausage grinder. The American Rescue Plan was introduced in the House on February 24, passed three days later, reconciled with a Senate version on March 10, and signed into law on March 11.

In the midst of the process, long-time *Washington Post* columnist Steven Pearlstein wrote his final column, retiring after 33
years with the newspaper. A professor of public affairs at George
Mason University, Pearlstein had often written about economic
issues. Here are some choice observations from his last column:

> Welcome, fellow Americans, to the era of the free lunch.
>
> To hear it from liberal economists, progressive activists
> and Democratic politicians, there is no longer any limit to
> how much money government can borrow and spend and
> print. . . .
>
> Worries about debt and inflation are just so twentieth
> century, the figments of a now-discredited neoliberal imag-
> ination. We have entered a magical world where borrowing
> is costless, spending pays for itself, stocks only rise and the
> dollar never falls.[130]

Pearlstein reminded his readers that Joe Biden had promised to be a "moderate, deal-making president." But instead of
"bringing a polarized country together after a narrow election
victory, Democrats seem determined to spike the football in the
end zone."[131]

Steven Pearlstein summed it up well: President Biden's American
Rescue Plan is a $1.9 trillion "free lunch," a costly and dangerous
exercise in magical thinking. As long as the government printing
presses don't run out of ink, we can spend our way to prosperity,
right?

We'll see how long it lasts.

Redefining Infrastructure

One of Joe Biden's nicknames is "Amtrak Joe." He once calculated that he had ridden more than 2.1 million miles of track during his commutes between Delaware and Washington, DC. Peter Schweizer, author of *Profiles in Corruption*, was a guest on *Spicer & Co.* and told me a story about Joe Biden's Amtrak years. He said that if Senator Biden was running late to the train station, he would call Amtrak and tell them to hold his train until he got there. All the other commuters on the train had to wait for Amtrak Joe.

As a senator, Joe Biden didn't hesitate to use infrastructure—the Amtrak train system—for his own personal convenience. Now, as president, Joe Biden doesn't hesitate to use infrastructure to increase his political power.

On March 31, 2021, President Biden proposed a massive piece of legislation he called the "American Jobs Plan," with a price tag of $2.3 trillion. It is better known as the "infrastructure bill." After Senate Minority Leader Mitch McConnell studied the bill, he concluded, "This plan is not about rebuilding America's backbone. Less than 6 percent of this massive proposal goes to roads and bridges. It would spend more money just on electric cars than on America's roads, bridges, ports, airports, and waterways combined."[132]

On April 2, President Biden said, "Independent analysis shows that if we pass this [infrastructure] plan, the economy will create 19 million jobs—good jobs, blue-collar jobs, jobs that pay well." The president's surrogates went on the Sunday talk shows, touting the 19 million jobs figure. For example, Transportation Secretary Pete Buttigieg told NBC's *Meet the Press* that the infrastructure plan "is about a generational investment. It's going to create 19 million jobs."

Glenn Kessler of the *Washington Post* contacted Moody's Analytics and asked if the White House claims were true. The answer: No. According to Moody's analysis, *the economy would produce 15.65 million jobs in 10 years if no stimulus legislation were passed.* Moody's estimated that the infrastructure bill would only add 2.7 million jobs over 10 years. Divide $2.3 trillion by 2.7 million jobs, and you get a cost of about $852,000 per job. Would you call that a bargain?[133]

Though you and I have a pretty good idea about what counts as infrastructure, the definition of that term is very squishy among Progressives. Democratic Senator Kirsten Gillibrand of New York took to Twitter to make the case for the $2.3 trillion tax-and-spend infrastructure scheme. On April 7, 2021, she tweeted, "Paid leave is infrastructure. Child care is infrastructure. Caregiving is infrastructure."

Conservative commentator Ben Shapiro tweeted back, "Unicorns are infrastructure. Love is infrastructure. Herpes is infrastructure. Everything is infrastructure."[134]

Later that day, President Biden waded into the discussion, arguing that the definition of *infrastructure* has "always evolved to meet the aspirations of the American people and their needs. And it is evolving again today."[135] In other words, infrastructure is whatever we say it is.

The New Democratic Dictionary

You may recall a scene in George Orwell's *Nineteen Eighty-Four*. The protagonist, Winston Smith, stands before the Ministry of Truth building and reads the words written on the façade: "War

Is Peace, Freedom Is Slavery, Ignorance Is Strength."[136] When language has become so elastic that words can mean anything or nothing at all, we have entered Orwell territory.

Conservatives believe that *words mean things*, but Democrats treat language as Silly Putty. In the late 1990s, part of President Clinton's defense in his impeachment trial was, "It depends upon what the meaning of the word 'is' is."[137]

Democrats believe that a COVID-19 relief bill can contain 9 percent COVID-19 relief and 91 percent pork. They believe an infrastructure bill can contain 6 percent infrastructure funding and 94 percent pork. If truth-in-advertising laws applied to legislation, these bills would have to be labeled the "American Pork Bill I" and the "American Pork Bill II." And by the way, the word *taxes* must never be used in connection with these bills—always call taxes *investments*.

In 2021, Democrats redefined the word *bipartisan*. Now, even when passing a massive spending bill by a straight party-line vote, they still claim the bill is bipartisan because polls show that it is supported by some Republicans and independents. Joe Biden explained his version of bare-knuckle bipartisanship this way: "If you looked up 'bipartisan' in the dictionary, I think it would say support from Republicans and Democrats. It doesn't say the Republicans have to be in Congress."[138]

During the 2020 presidential campaign, candidate Joe Biden repeatedly ducked the question, "Are you going to pack the court?" Then, when President Trump nominated Judge Amy Coney Barrett to the Supreme Court, Biden redefined *court packing* and turned the accusation against Trump, saying, "The only court packing going on right now is going on with Republicans. It's not constitutional what they're doing."[139] It was a devilishly brilliant tactic to deceive voters about the meaning of the term *court packing.*

In April 2021, House Democrats unveiled their court-packing bill, the Judiciary Act of 2021. The lead sponsor of the bill, Jerry Nadler of New York, was in fine Orwellian form, claiming that the Democrat plan to expand the court with Democratic nominees was not an attempt to pack the court but to "unpack" it.[140]

In the Lexicon of the Left, *illegal aliens* have become "undocumented immigrants"—or, more simply, "immigrants," blurring the distinction between legal and illegal immigrants. It won't be long before Democrats begin calling them "unregistered Democrats." The emergency at the southern border is not a *crisis;* it's a "challenge." The rooms used to house unaccompanied minors are called *cages* under President Trump but *reception centers* under President Biden.

Another newly coined term is *mixed economy.* Democrats use this term to hide the fact that they are mixing socialist ideas (like "Medicare for all") into the capitalist economy. Whenever you see the Democrats using terminology that you don't understand, they're probably hiding terrible ideas behind verbal sleight of hand.

George Orwell put it this way: "Political language . . . is designed to make lies sound truthful and murder respectable, and to give an appearance of solidity to pure wind."[141]

Money like Confetti

My father, Mike Spicer, loved sailing so much that he founded a yacht brokerage business in Newport, Rhode Island. Running a yacht brokerage may sound like an upscale and elegant way to make a living, but our family income could vary widely from year to year, based on the swings of the economy.

In 1991, when I was 17, Senate Majority Leader George Mitchell of Maine persuaded George H. W. Bush to sign a budget deal that included a 10 percent tax on luxury items costing $100,000 or more. This tax became known as the "yacht tax." There's a wise old saying that Democrats repeatedly ignore: "You get less of what you tax and more of what you don't."

In the years before the tax was enacted, American boat builders were annually producing up to 16,000 yachts costing $100,000 or more. One year after the yacht tax was passed, that number sank to 4,250. My home state of Rhode Island lost 12,000 jobs that were directly or indirectly tied to yacht sales. My father's yacht brokerage business was devastated—and so was I, because I worked in a boatyard during the summer, cleaning and maintaining boats. The tax took a heavy toll on my income.

The yacht tax was supposed to soak the rich. But the rich didn't get soaked—they just stopped buying yachts. Who got hurt? Working people—people like me.

From that experience, I learned the direct impact of federal tax policy on ordinary working people. That lesson cemented my conservative values at an early age. It's one of the reasons why, when I hear Democratic proposals to tax and spend, alarms go off in my mind.

Joe Biden's tax-and-spend economic agenda is the most radical plan ever proposed by a Democratic president. It is much bigger, costlier, and riskier than any economic plan proposed by Franklin Roosevelt, Jimmy Carter, Barack Obama, or Hillary Clinton. Biden began by shoving a gigantic $1.9 trillion stimulus package through Congress and then immediately followed up with an even bigger "infrastructure" package, accompanied by steep tax hikes on individuals and businesses.

President Biden is misreading economic history. Wasn't he paying attention when President Trump cut taxes, slashed regulations, and unleashed the American economy? Joe Biden is stubbornly committed to the failed Keynesian notion that if you just print up a bunch of money and spread it around like confetti, good things magically happen. That notion fails every time it's tried.

In all of history, no one has ever made a multitrillion-dollar wager before. The Biden-Harris administration has bet the entire U.S. economy, and perhaps the world economy, on the proposition that we can keep printing fiat money and piling up trillions of dollars of debt—and the future's going to be rosy.

The administration had better keep those printing presses running night and day. In the Biden-Harris postpandemic economy, it may soon take a wheelbarrow full of dollars to buy a loaf of bread.

10

The Assault on Religious Liberty

IN JANUARY 2018, A person named Jessie came to Hope Center, a faith-based homeless shelter in Anchorage, Alaska. Jessie—a biological male who identified as a woman—wanted a place to sleep after being turned away at another shelter for fighting.

Hope Center only housed women at night. Having a biological male sleeping in a bed three feet away from a woman who was traumatized by domestic violence made no sense. There were other facilities nearby that sheltered biologically male clients.

Inebriated and bleeding from a forehead wound, Jessie needed medical attention. So the shelter paid for a taxi to transport Jessie to a hospital.

The next day, Jessie returned to Hope Center and was again turned away.

A few weeks later, Jessie filed a complaint with the Anchorage Equal Rights Commission claiming the shelter had violated the city's anti-discrimination ordinance. The commission pressured Hope Center to accept transgender clients, but the shelter refused.

Finally, in August 2018, Hope Center filed a lawsuit against the city, claiming that the city had violated the shelter's religious liberty under the First Amendment. The complaint stated, "Hope Center believes that a person's sex (whether male or female) is an immutable God-given gift and that it is wrong for a person to deny his or her God-given sex." It would violate the shelter's religious convictions to house someone the center views as a man alongside women, especially female victims of violence.

In September 2019, a judge issued an injunction in favor of Hope Center. The judge didn't rule on the religious liberty claims. The narrow ruling simply noted that the Anchorage anti-discrimination code contained exceptions for hospitals, long-term care facilities, convents, monasteries, and, yes, shelters.[142]

So Hope Center prevailed—for now.

To most Christians, gender is a big deal. Genesis 1 states that when God created human beings as male and female, He looked on what He had made and it was very good. Jesus affirms the Genesis account in Matthew 19:4. So devout Christians believe it is wrong to erase those biological distinctions.

In June 2019, the Vatican released "Male and Female He Created Them," a document calling on Catholics to demonstrate love and respect for transgender people while standing firmly on the biblical doctrine and biological fact that one's gender is a feature of one's biological sex. The concept of transgender identity, the Vatican adds, seeks to "annihilate the concept of nature."[143] So, for most Catholic and Protestant Christians, there can only be two sexes, male and female, and two genders, men and women.

The Biden-Harris administration is already launching an all-out assault on faith-based institutions all across the country. It's only a matter of time before people of faith in America begin losing the right to act in accordance with their religious conscience in the public square. The assault on our religious liberty is well underway. It will impact all of us. We must be ready to take a firm but respectful stand for our faith and our convictions.

A License to Discriminate?

The First Amendment has been under increasing assault in recent years. The Trump administration fought hard against legal and regulatory threats to religious liberty. For example, in the 2017 Supreme Court case involving Masterpiece Cakeshop baker Jack Phillips (who conscientiously declined as a Christian to bake a cake for a same-sex wedding), the Department of Justice filed a brief in support of Phillips's First Amendment rights.[144]

On October 6, 2017, the Department of Justice issued a 25-page memo, signed by Attorney General Jeff Sessions, offering guidance to federal agencies on protecting religious liberty. The memo contains powerful insights into how to protect First Amendment religious freedom while also protecting the legal rights of same-sex couples and transgender individuals. The memo opens with a compelling statement by the man known as the "Father of the Constitution":

As James Madison explained in his *Memorial and Remonstrance Against Religious Assessments,* the free exercise of religion "is in its nature an unalienable right" because the duty owed to one's Creator "is precedent, both in order of time and in degree of obligation, to the claims of Civil Society." Religious liberty is not merely a right to personal religious beliefs or even to worship in a sacred place. It also encompasses religious observance and practice. Except in the narrowest circumstances, no one should be forced to choose between living out his or her faith and complying with the law.[145]

The memo sets forth a set of principles to guide federal agencies and departments in how to carry out their duties while protecting First Amendment religious liberty, including:

The freedom of religion is a fundamental right of paramount importance, expressly protected by federal law.

The freedom of religion extends to persons and organizations.

Americans do not give up their freedom of religion by participating in the marketplace, partaking of the public square, or interacting with government.

Government may not officially favor or disfavor particular religious groups.

Government may not interfere with the autonomy of a religious organization.

Religious employers are entitled to employ only persons whose beliefs and conduct are consistent with the employers' religious precepts.[146]

In an interview with the *Philadelphia Gay News*, Joe Biden promised to do away with all the First Amendment protections outlined in the DOJ memo and other Trump-era policies. Biden said:

> Religion should not be used as a license to discriminate, and as president, I will oppose legislation to deny LGBTQ+ equal treatment in public places. I will immediately reverse discriminatory practices that Trump put in place and work to advance the rights of LGBTQ+ people widely.[147]

Is the DOJ memo on religious liberty a "license to discriminate," as Joe Biden claims? Of course not. The memo merely places our human rights and civil duties in their rightful priority. As Madison observed, the Constitution acknowledges that our first duty is to our Creator, and our duties to civil law come second. No American should ever be forced to choose between obeying God and obeying the government.

The Biden-Harris administration and Democratic leaders in the House and Senate are working tirelessly to abolish these protections of religious liberty. They believe that our duty to government supersedes our duty to God and conscience. They believe that the political agenda of far-left pressure groups carries more weight than the First Amendment. They believe that religious organizations and religious business owners should be forced to violate their conscience in order to accommodate the radical-left political agenda.

The So-Called Equality Act

One of the Democrats' first assaults on religious liberty is the so-called Equality Act. While campaigning, Joe Biden vowed to sign the Equality Act during his first 100 days. The act establishes new federally protected categories of gender identity and sexual orientation and inflicts chaotic change across every segment of American society:

- Biological males who identify themselves as women would have to be admitted to women's private spaces, including women's sports leagues, shelters, locker rooms, and restrooms.
- Employers would be forced to offer costly healthcare coverage for sex reassignment surgery or hormone therapy for people with gender dysphoria.
- Parents would be barred from seeking counseling for children who struggle with gender identity confusion.
- Anyone who opposes the LGBTQ agenda would be in violation of federal law.

Doreen Denny of Concerned Women for America underscored the threat posed by the Equality Act:

Governments that impose ideological viewpoints in law that deny God's creation, like the Equality Act, threaten our fundamental rights of conscience and religious belief. . . . This is an assault on the dignity of women and directly threatens our safety and status under the law.[148]

In February 2021, Emilie Kao appeared on *Spicer & Co.* to talk about the Equality Act. Emilie is the director of the Richard and Helen DeVos Center for Religion and Civil Society at the Heritage Foundation. I said:

Emilie, they do this in Washington all the time. They call it the "Equality Act" with the idea that people will say, "Equality! Who would be against equality?" But what does the Equality Act mean in terms of its impact on our lives?

She said:

It's very important that Americans understand that the Equality Act creates *inequality* by imposing a secular sexual orthodoxy on the entire nation. It would affect not only businesses but religious employers. It would also affect children and their parents. It would impose a destructive gender ideology on children in education and in medicine. It's clearly going to erase protection under the law for women and girls. By saying, "I identify as a woman," a man can enter into any women's space, any women's athletic competition.

Emilie was quick to acknowledge the need for compassion and equality for all people, adding, "We want equality for everybody, but the Equality Act imposes inequality and treats women as second-class citizens."

The First of All Freedoms

On January 16, 1993, President George H. W. Bush proclaimed the first Religious Freedom Day, commemorating the anniversary of the 1786 passage of the Virginia Statute for Religious Freedom. That statute was authored by Thomas Jefferson, and it served as a model for the opening lines of the First Amendment. President Bush noted in his Religious Freedom Day Proclamation that freedom of religion is the "first of all freedoms enumerated in our Bill of Rights."

Every president since Bush has issued a Religious Freedom Day Proclamation on January 16. In 1999, President Bill Clinton called religious freedom a "fundamental human right . . . without which a democracy cannot survive." In 2009, President George W. Bush proclaimed religious freedom "one of this land's greatest blessings."

In 2013, President Barack Obama opened his proclamation with the statement, "Foremost among the rights Americans hold sacred is the freedom to worship as we choose."[149] Since then, many Democrats and Progressives have adopted the phrase "freedom of worship" while avoiding the phrase "free exercise of religion." The "free exercise" wording comes from the opening line of the First Amendment: "Congress shall make no law respecting an establishment of religion, or prohibiting the free exercise thereof."

It may seem trivial, but there's a big difference between freedom of worship and the free exercise of religion. Those on the left understand the difference, and that's why they speak of freedom of worship and avoid the words of the First Amendment.

Words matter. When politicians speak of freedom of worship, they are saying that you are free to worship any way you choose in your home or in your house of worship. But they don't want your religion to affect the way you live your life in public or the way you conduct your business. Democrats and Progressives say that you are perfectly free to pray and worship in any way you choose—as long as you do so behind closed doors.

But if you are a Christian businessperson, you must set aside your convictions and pay for your employees' abortions. If you are a Christian baker, you must set aside your conscience and create a cake that celebrates a same-sex wedding. You may practice your faith in your house of worship one day a week. The rest of the week, your conscience belongs to the State, not your Creator.

But the First Amendment guarantees much more than freedom of worship. It guarantees the *free exercise* of religion. This means that you are free to practice your religion wherever you are, 24 hours a day, 7 days a week, in every aspect of your life.

The Biden-Harris administration wants to deprive you of the right to live out your conscience and obey your God.

Kamala Harris, Hobby Lobby, and "Do No Harm"

In 2012, Hobby Lobby Stores, Inc., a chain of arts and crafts stores owned by the David Green family, filed a lawsuit against the U.S. government over a mandate in the Patient Protection and Affordable Care Act ("Obamacare" law) requiring companies to provide abortifacients. Hobby Lobby argued that the mandate was a violation of the Christian owners' First Amendment right to free exercise of religion.

Kamala Harris, in her role as attorney general of California, joined an amicus brief (a "friend of the court" brief) from the attorney general of Massachusetts arguing that Hobby Lobby should be required to provide abortifacient coverage for its employees. Harris reasoned that for-profit corporations are not permitted to hold "personal" religious beliefs, even when those corporations are wholly owned by a Christian individual or family. She wrote:

> Certain rights by their nature are "'purely personal' guarantees" that cannot be held by a business corporation (or, in some cases, by any corporation or collective entity). . . . Rights

to the free exercise of religious beliefs, whether created by statute or by the Constitution, likewise protect the development and expression of an "inner sanctum" of personal religious faith. Free-exercise rights have thus also been understood as personal, relating only to individual believers and to a limited class of associations comprising or representing them. . . . Unsurprisingly, there is no tradition of recognizing or accommodating the exercise of such inherently personal rights by ordinary, for-profit business corporations.[150]

According to Kamala Harris, if you run a for-profit business, whether it's a little Colorado bakeshop or a multibillion-dollar chain of hobby stores, the First Amendment doesn't apply to you. You are free to practice your religious faith in any way you choose, as long as you keep it within your private "inner sanctum." You are not allowed to apply the precepts of your faith to the way you conduct your business. In the public square, you must obey the almighty State, not almighty God.

With the center-left Justice Anthony Kennedy as the swing vote, the U.S. Supreme Court ruled five to four in favor of Hobby Lobby.

But Kamala Harris wasn't finished. Elected to the U.S. Senate in 2017, she introduced the Do No Harm Act. It would amend the Religious Freedom Restoration Act of 1993, stripping religious business owners of their First Amendment rights and forcing them to obey government healthcare edicts that violate their religious convictions and moral conscience.

In a press conference promoting the Do No Harm Act, Harris said, "The freedom to worship is one of our nation's most fundamental rights."[151] She didn't dare quote the actual wording of the First Amendment, which guarantees not merely freedom to worship but the *free exercise of religion* in every aspect of our lives.

"You Have to Take a Stand"

Attorney David A. Cortman is senior counsel and vice president of U.S. litigation with the Alliance Defending Freedom (ADF). He has argued several First Amendment cases before the Supreme Court. Appearing on *Spicer & Co.* in February 2021, he told me about a case he was litigating, *Washington v. Arlene's Flowers, Inc.*

The owner of Arlene's Flowers, Barronelle Stutzman, had two gay friends, Robert Ingersoll and Curt Freed, who had been loyal customers and friends of hers for nine years. Ms. Stutzman had an excellent relationship with these two men. But when Ingersoll and Freed told her they were getting married and they wanted her to provide the flowers for the wedding, she replied that, as a Christian, she couldn't do so.

With representation by the American Civil Liberties Union (ACLU), Ingersoll and Freed sued Barronelle Stutzman under the anti-discrimination laws of Washington state. ACLU attorneys offered to settle the suit in exchange for a public apology, a $5,000 donation to a local LGBT youth center, and a promise not to discriminate based on sexual orientation. A second lawsuit, filed by the state attorney general under Washington's consumer protection statutes, was combined with the Ingersoll-Freed lawsuit.

David Cortman and the Alliance Defending Freedom represented Ms. Stutzman in court, arguing that she should not be forced to violate her religious beliefs. When the Benton County Superior Court ruled against her, Cortman took the case to the Washington Supreme Court, which ruled against her. The court stated that a floral arrangement is not protected free speech and that providing flowers doesn't constitute endorsement of same-sex marriage.

Ms. Stutzman appealed to the U.S. Supreme Court, making the same argument that had succeeded in the Supreme Court case involving the Colorado baker. On June 25, 2018, the Supreme Court vacated the Washington Supreme Court judgment and remanded the case to that court for further consideration. One year later, the Washington Supreme Court unanimously ruled against Stutzman. As I write these words, David Cortman and the Alliance Defending Freedom are taking Ms. Stutzman's case back to the U.S. Supreme Court.

David told me on the show:

Every person should be treated with dignity and respect, regardless of sexual orientation. At the same time, we have to make sure that everyone's constitutional rights are watched over and cared for, no matter what your beliefs are. Barronelle Stutzman served everyone in her flower business. In fact, the person who sued her was a best friend. But people shouldn't be forced to violate their religious beliefs. . . . You have to take a stand. First, you work through the legislature. If that doesn't work, you go through the courts. Our constitutional rights are too valuable to surrender them.

In the New Testament book of Acts (chapter 5), there is a scene where Peter and the apostles stand before the ruling council, the Sanhedrin. The leaders tell the apostles to stop preaching and practicing the Christian faith. But Peter boldly replies, "We must obey God rather than men."

The Biden-Harris administration and the Democratic Party are determined to force Americans to compromise their faith and surrender to the secular Progressive agenda. I urge you to take a stand for religious liberty. Be as bold and uncompromising as Peter. If they come for your religious freedom, tell them, "We must obey God rather than men."

11

The Assault on
Human Life

F OUNDED IN FRANCE IN 1839, the Little Sisters of the Poor is a
Catholic order of nuns who operate 29 care homes across the
United States. The nuns take vows of chastity, poverty, obedience,
and hospitality, and they serve Christ by serving the elderly poor.

When the Patient Protection and Affordable Care Act (ACA or
"Obamacare") was enacted in March 2010, it required employers
to offer health insurance plans that included contraceptives, abortifacients, and sterilizations—all of which violate the precepts of
the Catholic Church. Though the ACA exempted churches, it did
not exempt faith-based ministries such as the Little Sisters of the
Poor. These ministries were subject to fines if they did not comply—and the Little Sisters refused to comply.

St. Paul once wrote that all who will live godly in Christ Jesus will suffer persecution. The Obama administration was determined to make good on that biblical promise and proceeded to persecute the Little Sisters all the way to the U.S. Supreme Court. In 2016, the Supreme Court directed the Obama administration to compromise with the Little Sisters and "arrive at an approach going forward" to end the standoff. The Obama administration failed to achieve that goal before leaving office.

In 2017, the Trump administration took over and structured an accommodation that resolved the Little Sisters' problems with the ACA mandate. In October of that year, Health and Human Services issued an updated religious exemption rule that protected religious nonprofit organizations such as the Little Sisters of the Poor.

Case closed, right? Wrong.

The next month, November 2017, attorneys general from several states, including Pennsylvania and California, ramped up the persecution of the Little Sisters. They went to court and obtained a *nationwide injunction* against the new HHS rule. Pennsylvania and California sued the federal government, asking the judges to force the Little Sisters to comply with the Obamacare mandate or face millions of dollars in penalties.[152]

In July 2019, the Third Circuit Court of Appeals ruled against the Little Sisters in the Pennsylvania case. In October 2019, the Ninth Circuit Court of Appeals ruled against the Little Sisters in the California case. At that point, the Little Sisters asked the U.S. Supreme Court for a definitive ruling.

On July 8, 2020, the Supreme Court delivered a decisive seven to two ruling in favor of the Little Sisters of the Poor. The court affirmed the religious liberty exemptions for faith-based organizations. The Little Sisters of the Poor would *not* have to pay for abortions under the Obamacare mandates. After spending over a decade fighting federal and state governments in the courts, the Little Sisters could finally get back to serving the poor in peace.

The Little Sisters set an example for us all, refusing to back down in the face of government pressure. They were determined to serve the elderly poor without lending support or endorsement to abortion. They correctly understood that the assault on their freedom was an assault on the sanctity of human life.

"I Never Sued the Nuns!"

Is this really why government exists? To harass and intimidate nuns who are simply living out their faith and serving the poor? It's hard to believe, but there are people in government who get up in the morning and say, "I'm going to punish a Catholic ministry today! I'm going to scare nuns and force them to pay for abortions!" I mean, such a person would have to be a mustache-twirling villain of the Snidely Whiplash variety, right?

Well, meet one of the persecutors of the Little Sisters of the Poor—President Biden's secretary of health and human services, Xavier Becerra. In November 2017, after the Little Sisters had already prevailed once in the Supreme Court, it was Xavier Becerra who made the decision for California to sue *again* in federal court to take away the nuns' religious exemption. He lost that case in 2020—but the following year, President Biden tapped Becerra to lead HHS, the very agency he had unsuccessfully sued in 2017.

In February 2021, Becerra was in a Senate confirmation hearing for the Biden cabinet post, trying to explain away his relentless pursuit of the Little Sisters of the Poor. Senator John Thune of South Dakota said to him, "It does seem like, as attorney general, you spent an inordinate amount of time and effort suing pro-life organizations, like Little Sisters of the Poor, or trying to ease restrictions or expand abortion."

Apparently realizing how bad his pursuit of the Little Sisters looked, Becerra replied, "I have never sued the nuns, any nuns. I've never sued any affiliation of nuns, and my actions have always been directed at the federal agencies."[153]

It's a flimsy alibi. Becerra did, in fact, sue to force a religious order of nuns to pay for Obamacare's contraceptive and abortifacient mandate. Moreover, the case is named *State of California v. Little Sisters of the Poor*. It doesn't get any plainer than that. Had Becerra won his case, the Little Sisters would have lost millions of dollars, along with their First Amendment rights. Becerra pursued the nuns in court for three years.

Despite his evasive testimony, Becerra did sue nuns—an act of cold-hearted villainy that would have done Snidely Whiplash proud. As Senator Tom Cotton of Arkansas tweeted on February 24, 2021, "Xavier Becerra is now claiming he didn't sue nuns because he wants to get confirmed. But Becerra did sue nuns. He repeatedly harassed the Little Sisters of the Poor. That's why he should be rejected by the Senate."[154]

In selecting Xavier Becerra to head HHS, President Biden signaled his intention to move America to the extreme edge of pro-abortion policy. No American politician has ever demonstrated more enthusiasm for unrestricted abortion than Xavier Becerra.

Ground Zero for the Protection of Life

Another landmark Supreme Court case bears Becerra's name: *National Institute of Family and Life Advocates v. Becerra*. That case involves the 2015 California Reproductive Freedom,

Accountability, Comprehensive Care, and Transparency Act (FACT Act). The FACT Act persecuted Christian crisis pregnancy centers—ministries that offer counseling, adoption services, and other alternatives to abortion. It required the centers to post notices advertising state-sponsored abortion clinics.

Advertising abortion services, of course, violates the pro-life mission of a crisis pregnancy center. The FACT Act intruded on the First Amendment rights of these Christian ministries in two ways: (1) It infringed on the free exercise of religion of these ministries, requiring them to advertise a service that, according to their beliefs, is murder, and (2) it infringed on their First Amendment right of free speech. Freedom of speech is both the freedom to speak your mind *and* the freedom *not* to speak a message imposed on you by the government.

Becerra prosecuted the case vigorously, and the crisis pregnancy centers lost every round in the lower courts, including the frequently overturned far-left Ninth Circuit Court of Appeals. But in June 2018, the U.S. Supreme Court repudiated Becerra's attack on the First Amendment and on human life, ruling five to four that the FACT Act mandates were unconstitutional.

In addition to Xavier Becerra's persecution of nuns and crisis pregnancy centers, he has pushed for expanded access to morning-after abortion pills and has supported lawsuits against abortion restrictions in California and other states. He took over (from his predecessor, Kamala Harris) the prosecution of pro-life activist David Daleiden, whose undercover videos appeared to show that Planned Parenthood was illegally profiting by selling fetal tissue from abortions. So here's a troubling question: Did President Biden choose Becerra for HHS secretary solely because of his extreme-left record on abortion?

Hiding behind His Mother's Rosary

In Becerra's Senate confirmation hearings in February 2021, Senator Steve Daines of Montana expressed "serious concerns" about the nominee's "radical views" on abortion, asking the nominee to name "one abortion restriction that you might support."

Becerra responded with a nonanswer answer: "I have tried to make sure that I am abiding by the law, because whether it's a particular restriction, or whether it's the whole idea of abortion, whether we agree or not, we have to come to some conclusion."

When Senator Daines continued to press for an answer, Becerra hid behind his wife and mother, saying that his wife is an obstetrician-gynecologist who has provided medical care for babies "for decades" and that his mother prayed the Rosary for him and had "blessed" him the morning of the confirmation hearing. Not only is all this irrelevant to the question he was asked, but it's also highly offensive that he seeks to cloak these evil policies with the prayers of the holy Rosary.

So Senator Daines got down to specifics: Would Becerra support banning abortions of Down syndrome babies? Sex-selection abortions? What about partial-birth abortion, which was banned by federal law in 2003? (Becerra had voted against the ban as a congressman.) Again and again, Becerra declined to answer the question. He would only make the nonresponsive response, "I respect the different views that are out there, but what's important is to make sure that my view is in accordance with the law."[155]

In accordance with which laws? There are many laws that relate to abortion, and over his career he has invested his time and resources enforcing some laws while ignoring others. He has obsessively *attacked* the free exercise of religion rights of Christian organizations under the First Amendment, which is the most fundamental law we have. Becerra should not have gotten away with dodging these all-important questions.

Valerie Huber, former U.S. special representative for global women's health at HHS, said of Xavier Becerra, "Having someone who is such a radical pro-abortion advocate will move that agenda to its limits." Huber noted that the Biden-Harris administration had rescinded the Mexico City policy. That policy, first implemented by the Reagan administration, barred federal funding of foreign organizations that promote or provide abortions. This action, she said, gives Biden and Becerra "plenty of space for mischief-making that could result in abortion being deemed an international human right." Huber added that HHS is "ground zero for either the protection of life or the promotion of abortion."[156]

Why the Pro-Life Issue Matters

I'm writing from the perspective of a Catholic. And while I can't speak for evangelicals, charismatics, and other conservative Christians, I believe that they would broadly agree with what I'm about to say.

In Christianity in general and Catholicism in particular, there is a lot of room for different political viewpoints. Christians may legitimately differ over tax policy, economic policy, regulatory policy, foreign policy, the use of military force, and on and on. Within the Catholic Church, we hear many voices speaking from liberal convictions and from conservative convictions, and yet we are all One Church. Whatever our political disagreements, we accept one another as faithful Catholics who share the same sacraments and serve the same Lord.

But there are definite limits that a devout Catholic must not overstep. One of those limits is the issue of abortion. Church doctrine and the Bible impose a solemn obligation on every Catholic believer to seek justice for all human beings from the moment of conception until the moment of death. The fifth commandment applies to all human life, before and after birth: Thou shalt not kill.

You might ask, "Does a Catholic president have a right to impose his religious beliefs on American society?" But that's a prejudicial question. Presidents don't have kingly powers. They are leaders who use influence and persuasion to achieve goals. The real question is, "Does a Catholic president have a moral and spiritual duty to influence American society away from selfishness and death and toward compassion and life?" And the answer is, "Yes." And every president, Catholic or not, has a duty to uphold the principles of the Declaration of Independence, which states that we are endowed by God with *unalienable rights* to life, liberty, and the pursuit of happiness—and the right to life is listed first.

Abortion, in the view of the Catholic Church, is not merely a sin in the same category with adultery, fornication, envy, lying, or theft (as grievous as those sins are). Abortion has the added dimension of being a grave injustice—the murder of an innocent human being. A leader who actively promotes the mass killing of innocent human beings has multiplied this grave injustice many times over. This is why Pope Francis in 2019 said, "I take this opportunity to appeal to all politicians, regardless of their faith convictions, to treat the defense of the lives of those who are about to be born and enter into society as the cornerstone of the common good."[157]

A Matter of Justice

Joe Biden began his first term in the U.S. Senate in 1973, the same year the *Roe v. Wade* decision was handed down by the Supreme Court. Biden stated at the time that *Roe v. Wade* was wrongly decided, and the following year, he told *Washingtonian* magazine that the decision "went too far." In a letter to his constituents in 1994, he said that he had voted against federal funding for abortion "on no fewer than 50 occasions." He explained his reasoning: "Those of us who are opposed to abortions should not be compelled to pay for them." And in March 1986, Biden told a Catholic newspaper, "Abortion is wrong from the moment of conception."[158]

In his 2007 book *Promises to Keep*, Joe Biden recalls a conversation he had with Connecticut Senator Abe Ribicoff over an upcoming vote on abortion:

> "How are you going to vote on this, Joe?"
>
> "It's a difficult vote."
>
> "I know that," he said, "but how are you going to vote on it? What's your position?"
>
> "Well, my position is that I personally am opposed to abortion, but I don't think I have the right to impose my view—on something I accept as a matter of faith—on the rest of society. I've thought a lot about it, and my position probably doesn't please anyone. I think the government should stay out completely."
>
> "What's that supposed to mean?" he asked as we headed toward the Capitol corridors.

"Well, I will not vote to overturn the Court's decision. I will not vote to curtail a woman's right to choose abortion. But I will also not vote to use federal funds to fund abortion."

"That's a tough position, kid," he said on the escalator.

"Yeah, everybody will be upset with me," I told him, "except me. But I'm intellectually and morally comfortable with my position."[159]

This little anecdote suggests that Joe Biden has never really internalized the meaning of the Catholic Church's teachings on abortion. He seems to think that it's merely a Catholic doctrinal issue, such as the doctrine of transubstantiation. On matters of doctrine, Catholics can have strong convictions while not wishing to impose them on society. Abortion is a whole different category of Catholic teaching. It's a social justice issue. It's an issue of the killing of innocent human life.

If we follow the science regarding prenatal life, we cannot escape the fact that a fetus is not part of the mother's body but a genetically distinct human being capable of feeling pain at an early stage and capable of life outside the womb as early as 22 weeks. So if you are truly convinced that life begins at conception and that an unborn baby is a human being, then abortion is murder. If Joe Biden were a senator in the early nineteenth century, could he reasonably say, "I am personally opposed to human slavery, but I don't think I have the right to impose my view on the rest of society"? This is not a nuanced position. This is a morally confused position.

All Catholics have a moral and spiritual obligation to seek justice for all human beings, born and unborn, at home and abroad. For a Catholic senator, vice president, or president, that obligation is magnified, not diminished, because God has elevated him to that position to bless and influence society. He should not impose his beliefs, but he is obligated to exercise influence.

Living as "Salt and Light"

In the Sermon on the Mount, Jesus calls His followers to be "salt" and "light" in the world. What does this mean? Salt is a preservative—it guards against corruption and decay. And light gives illumination and chases away the darkness. Abortion—the mass slaughter of the innocent—is a corrosive and dark force in our society.

Jesus said, "So let your light shine before men, that they may see your good works, and glorify your Father who is in heaven" (Matthew 5:16, Douay-Rheims American Edition). As a self-described devout Catholic, President Biden has a duty to shine the light of God's truth into the darkness. Instead, he serves a dark, anti-life, anti-Christian, pro-abortion agenda. He has joined the radical-left assault on human life. It does the world no good for Joe Biden to speak against injustice even as his actions *compound* injustice.

Through his executive actions, his policies, and his cabinet selections, President Biden has signaled his intention to take America back to the days of persecuting faith-based ministries (here they come again, Little Sisters). He has already rescinded the Mexico City policy, and he seeks to overturn the Hyde Amendment and force American taxpayers to fund abortions at home and around the world. (Biden supported the Hyde Amendment and Mexico City policy until 2019, when he moved to the extreme left to compete in the Democratic primaries.)

President Biden plans to deprive us of our First Amendment right to a religious conscience by forcing us to pay for the unjust mass murder of unborn children.

So I hope you'll join me in praying that President Biden will come to realize that God did not give him a position of power and influence for nothing. Theodore Roosevelt called the presidency a "bully pulpit." It does the world no good for President Biden to be "personally opposed" to abortion if he will not use his bully pulpit to promote justice and change the world for the better.

And let's pray to be agents of influence and justice in our own neighborhoods and workplaces. The right to life is sacred, it's under assault, and we cannot be silent.

12

The Radical Education-Indoctrination Agenda

FOUR DAYS BEFORE HAYDEN Hunstable's thirteenth birthday, he was helping his father and grandfather, handing them tools as they worked on a plumbing problem in their house. When the job was finished, the grandfather left. Hayden's father, Brad Hunstable, thanked young Hayden for his help, hugged him, and gave him a kiss on the head.

A half-hour later, Hayden's eight-year-old sister ran from Hayden's bedroom, crying. She had just discovered that her brother had hanged himself.

Brad Hunstable ran upstairs, pulled Hayden down, and called 911 on his cell phone. As the dispatcher talked to him, Hunstable gave CPR to his son. "I couldn't save him," the grieving father later recalled. "He was gone. I saw something horrific that day, and I don't wish it upon anybody. I still get nightmares about it."

Hayden Hunstable died at his home in Aledo, Texas, on April 17, 2020. By that time, his school had been shut down for two months. Brad Hunstable had noticed a change in Hayden's moods, but the boy had never said a word about suicidal thoughts.

"We were seeing increased anxiety [in Hayden] from the pandemic," Brad Hunstable said. "He wanted to play football; he wanted to see his friends. You know, he couldn't have a birthday; it was four days away. He hated online schooling. . . . I think everything just got on top of him; he felt overwhelmed, and he made a tragic decision."

Brad Hunstable channeled his grief into action, founding Hayden's Corner, an organization to provide suicide-prevention support. He hopes to help pass legislation to teach resilience classes as core curriculum in elementary, junior high, and high schools across the nation.[160]

A Pandemic of Isolation, Depression, and Suicide

Hayden Hunstable was far from alone in suffering unbearable depression because of being isolated from his friends by the COVID-19 lockdowns. FAIR Health, an independent nonprofit organization that maintains a database of privately billed health insurance claims, analyzed more than 32 billion private health-care claim records from January to November 2020—the first 11 months of the pandemic—and compared those records with the same 11 months during prepandemic 2019. The results were shocking.

FAIR Health found that while medical claims declined by approximately half during the pandemic months, mental health claims for young people aged 13 to 18 years roughly doubled. Medical claims for the 13- to 18-year age group who inflicted physical harm on themselves also roughly doubled from 2019 to 2020. Medical claims for overdoses and substance use disorders sharply increased in 2020 versus 2019.

In a March 2021 white paper titled, "The Impact of COVID-19 on Pediatric Mental Health," FAIR Health researchers concluded:

> The COVID-19 pandemic has had a profound impact on mental health. Infection-related fears, bereavement, economic instability and social isolation have triggered and exacerbated mental health [problems]. . . . Young people have proven especially vulnerable to mental health issues related to the COVID-19 pandemic. School closures, having to learn remotely and isolating from friends due to social distancing have been sources of stress and loneliness.[161]

Across the nation, the devastating impact of school closures, isolation, and depression has triggered an epidemic of child suicides. For example, in the Clark County School District in Nevada, 18 children committed suicide in a 9-month period after schools closed in March 2020—exactly double the number of child suicides in the district the previous year. In January 2021, an alarmed and shaken Clark County School Board ordered a phased-in reopening of schools to rescue students from isolation as quickly as possible.

Jesus Jara, the Clark County superintendent of schools, said, "We have to find a way to put our hands on our kids, to see them, to look at them. They've got to start seeing some movement, some hope."[162]

In San Francisco, UCSF Benioff Children's Hospital reported a 66 percent increase in emergency room visits of suicidal children and a 75 percent increase in children and youths needing hospitalization for major mental health issues, including anxiety, depression, and eating disorders. Worried San Francisco parents reported disturbing changes in their children's emotions and behavior.

One mother looked in on her 15-year-old daughter, who was supposed to be doing distance learning, and found her "curled up in a fetal position, crying, next to her laptop." The mother said that her daughter often cried in the middle of the day because of the isolation and fear of the pandemic. The mother said that her daughter was losing faith not only in the school district but also in the world itself.[163]

Why Classrooms Are Dark and Empty

You'd think that the San Francisco School Board would be working feverishly to get schools reopened and rescue these kids from depression. But no; during January 2021, the San Francisco Unified School District Board devoted most of its time and energy to a plan to rename 44 schools that were supposedly named for white supremacists. Cancel culture enthusiasts on the school board wanted to remove the names of George Washington, Abraham Lincoln, and Dianne Feinstein. While board members focused on scrubbing names from the *outsides* of the schools, they had no plan for getting kids back *inside* those schools. Even the far-left mayor of San Francisco, London Breed, expressed frustration with the board's inaction.

In February, City Attorney Dennis Herrera went to San Francisco Superior Court and took the unprecedented step of filing a lawsuit against the city's own school district. The filing included heartbreaking testimony from doctors, parents, and hospitals about the suffering of the city's children. Herrera noted that while San Francisco's 52,000 public school students had been locked out of classes for nearly a year, the city's 114 private, parochial, and charter schools had been safely reopened to more than 15,800 students and 2,400 teachers and staff. Those schools reported *fewer than five cases* of suspected in-person COVID-19 transmission.[164]

San Francisco's public health officials had cleared the city's public schools to reopen in September 2020—but when Herrera filed suit against the school district in February 2021, the classrooms were still dark and empty. Why?

The teachers' unions.

Despite scientific data from the Centers for Disease Control and Prevention (CDC) showing that schools can open safely with simple precautions such as masks, distancing, and cleaning, the unions held out. Doctors and nurses were on the front lines of the COVID-19 pandemic, doing their jobs. Grocery store workers were doing their jobs. Airlines were safely flying passengers in packed airplanes.

But the teachers' unions wouldn't let teachers return to one of the safest work environments in the pandemic. Though the school shutdowns were ruining lives and killing children, the unions stubbornly refused to let teachers rescue kids from the cruelty of isolation and depression.

I have great respect and admiration for teachers. Most teachers chose this profession out of a love of children and a love of learning. Many would like to return to the classroom, but they don't dare take a public stand against the union leadership.

It's not teachers but *unions* that are hurting our children. Union leaders are using the pandemic as an excuse to stage an unofficial work stoppage to extort billions of dollars from the federal government. And they have powerful allies on their side—President Joe Biden and Vice President Kamala Harris.

A Seat at the Table

The day after President Biden's inauguration, First Lady Jill Biden welcomed the presidents of the nation's two largest teachers' unions to the White House. Mrs. Biden, a teacher herself, greeted Becky Pringle of the National Education Association and Randi Weingarten of the American Federation of Teachers. She said, "I'm ready to get to work with you and the unions that support you every day. I could not wait one more day to have this meeting, because I have never felt prouder of our profession. . . . On behalf of a grateful nation, thank you."

Mrs. Biden added that the teachers' unions would "always have a seat at the table" and that her husband, President Biden, "is going to be a champion for you because he knows that's the best way to serve our students."[165]

As we have seen during the pandemic, the unions are not serving students—they're serving themselves and harming the physical and mental health of schoolchildren. Tragically, children and parents don't have a seat at Joe Biden's table. There is no one representing their interests in the Biden-Harris administration.

In January 2021, Chicago public schools announced a strong set of classroom safety measures and set a February 1 deadline for reopening schools for in-person learning. The union balked, defiantly demanding widespread vaccinations and additional safety protocols before allowing teachers back in the classroom.

President Biden sided with the union, saying, "It's not so much about the idea of teachers aren't going to work. The teachers I know, they want to work. They just want to work in a safe environment."

The union tweeted its gratitude to President Biden for his support of its position: "Thank you, President Biden. Exactly what educators have been saying."

On the Senate floor, Minority Leader Mitch McConnell had a different take on President Biden's support for the union. "That's more goalpost moving," he said. "Congress has poured more than $110 billion into making education safe. As of last week, states and school districts had only spent about $4 billion of the roughly $68 billion we set aside for K–12 schools. That leaves $64 billion in the pipeline already."

In addition to the money for schools already in the pipeline, President Biden had asked for another $130 billion for reopening K–12 schools in his $1.9 trillion "COVID-19-related" stimulus package. The teachers' unions made political donations of $43.7 million in 2020, almost entirely to Democrats, according to the Center for Responsive Politics.[166] It looks like they got their money's worth from Joe Biden.

In January 2021, the CDC released guidelines for safely reopening schools with masks and social distancing. Around the same time, several CDC scientists co-authored an article in the *Journal of the American Medical Association (JAMA)*, citing evidence that school reopenings had almost no impact on the spread of COVID-19. A study of 90,000 students and staff found just 32 infections through school versus 773 infections of students and staff outside of school. No teachers or staff were infected by students. Clearly, one of the safest places to be during the pandemic was in a classroom.

On February 12, the CDC surprisingly issued new guidelines that were more strict and more complicated and involved a confusing color-coded chart that limited the options of schools wishing to reopen. In fact, according to a CNN analysis, 99 percent of American schoolchildren fell into the "red zones," the zones least likely to reopen. Almost 3 months later, we found out why the CDC had issued these oppressive new guidelines: The American Federation of Teachers (AFT) told the CDC what to do, and the CDC obeyed.

The watchdog group Americans for Public Trust filed a Freedom of Information Act request for emails between by the union, the CDC, and other White House officials. Americans for Public Trust provided those emails to the *New York Post*, which broke the story on May 1. Those emails showed that the CDC was taking direction from the teachers' union in the same way the World Health Organization took marching orders from China. Instead of following the science and issuing guidelines based on the health of the children, the CDC allowed itself to be bossed by the AFT.

The emails show that specific wording supplied by the union was cut and pasted almost verbatim into the CDC guidelines. Top Biden administration officials were also involved in the flurry of emails.[167] These emails are the "smoking gun" showing that the CDC needlessly slowed the reopening of schools to placate a powerful Biden political ally, the American Federation of Teachers. Is anyone looking out for your kids in the Biden administration, in the teachers' unions, or even in the CDC?

A Pandemic of Woke Indoctrination

In March 2021, United Teachers Los Angeles (UTLA) posted a video of the union president, Cecily Myart-Cruz. She complained that state officials and LA parents have been pressuring the union to reopen schools. California Governor Gavin Newsom and the state legislature had crafted a plan for reopening schools that had been locked down for a year, but Myart-Cruz dismissed the plan as "a recipe for propagating structural racism."

She added, "Some voices are being allowed to speak louder than others. We have to call out the privilege behind the largely white, wealthy parents driving the push for a rushed return. Their experience of this pandemic is not our students' families' experiences."[168]

Cecily Myart-Cruz has tipped her hand, showing us that woke critical race theory is one of the driving forces keeping our classrooms locked and empty. The notion that structural racism and white privilege are behind the effort to reopen schools is ludicrous. All kids, regardless of race or economic status, need to be in school. (We'll examine the origins of critical race theory in Chapter 16.)

Two weeks before Myart-Cruz complained about being pressured for a rushed return to the classroom, the CDC released guidelines for safely opening public schools. The five CDC strategies were mask wearing, social distancing, handwashing, cleaning/ventilation, and contact tracing/quarantine protocols.[169] But Myart-Cruz and her union shrugged off the CDC guidelines, blamed structural racism, and dug in their heels.

One of the greatest threats to our children and their education—next to the teachers' unions—is the woke critical race theory that many want to impose on our children. In fact, parents across the country are discovering that there is a pandemic of woke indoctrination sweeping through their schools. Here are some examples.

In Cupertino, California, a city with median home values of $2.3 million, a teacher at Meyerholz Elementary School led a class of third graders in an exercise based on critical race theory. The teacher told these children, ages eight and nine, to find their place on an identity map that listed such characteristics as race, gender, economic class, religion, and family structure. Then the teacher told them to deconstruct their identity and figure out where they ranked according to their power and privilege.

The teacher then told these children that they were part of a "dominant [system of] white, middle class, cisgender, educated, able-bodied, Christian, English speaker[s]," whose purpose was to "hold power and stay in power." The teacher then had the children read from *This Book Is Anti-Racist: 20 Lessons on How to Wake Up, Take Action, and Do the Work*, by Tiffany Jewell, a book for indoctrinating children in critical race theory. In that book, children learn that "a white, cisgender man, who is able-bodied, heterosexual, considered handsome and speaks English, has more privilege than a black transgender woman."

Parents were shocked and angered when they discovered the destructive ideas this teacher was inflicting on their children. Said one mother, an Asian American, "They were basically teaching racism to my eight-year-old." A group of parents met with the principal and demanded that this instruction be stopped. The principal consented—but this indoctrination was not the result of one radical teacher going rogue. It had been approved by the principal as part of a "process of daily learning facilitated by a certified teacher."[170]

The Privileged and the Targeted

In Minnesota, at Sunrise Park Middle School near St. Paul, sixth-grade students were introduced to critical race theory by their choir teacher. At the beginning of an exercise called a "social-emotional lesson," she gave students a handout that read, in part, "Today, we will look at different types of oppression, and whether each of us is in the privileged group or the targeted group." Then she separated the students according to whether they were privileged or targeted.

The children were shown a chart from which they learned the five types of oppression: racism, sexism, religious oppression, heterosexism, and xenophobia. The privileged students were those who were white, male, heterosexual, and Christian and were born in the United States. Anyone who was nonwhite, female, non-Christian, LGBTQ, or foreign born was undoubtedly shocked and troubled to discover, "Oh no, I'm targeted!"

No parent would imagine that this kind of neoracist indoctrination would be taking place in a sixth-grade choir class. Once again, this was not a case of one radical teacher going rogue. The lesson was endorsed by the school with a stated goal of helping students "understand that everyone is different and everyone experiences the world differently."[171]

In Illinois, at the Naperville 203 Community Unit School District, teachers arrived for work to discover that they would be undergoing anti-racism training. Training sessions to teach educators about their implicit bias and white privilege are now mandated in Illinois public schools. In the course of the training, white teachers were shamed for being white and told that the educational system is based on "a foundation of whiteness" and that American teachers are "spiritually murdering" their students.

Ten speakers took part in the training, and the keynote speech was delivered by a self-styled anti-racist coach, Dena Simmons. She is listed on the website of a National Speakers Bureau with a speaker's fee range of $10,000 to $20,000.[172] Did the Naperville School District pay these outrageous fees to have Ms. Simmons spout this destructive ideology?

In San Diego, California, teachers were subjected to white privilege training, berated and told they were racists, and required to commit to becoming anti-racists. They were also told that they must submit to a "new racial orthodoxy." The mandatory sessions were required by both the teachers' union and the San Diego Unified School District.

The training session began with a land acknowledgment ceremony in which teachers were told to acknowledge that the United States occupies stolen land. Curriculum for the training included video clips of *White Fragility* author Robin DiAngelo and Ibram X. Kendi, author of *How to Be an Antiracist*.[173] Similar training sessions are conducted in school districts across the country.

Toxic Food for Thought

At New York City's East Side Community School on the Lower East Side, a public school principal distributed materials to all the school's parents, asking them to reflect on their whiteness. The materials were said to be "meant for reflection" and "food for thought." Included in these toxic materials was a document that ranked "The 8 White Identities," ranging from white supremacist to white abolitionist. Parents were encouraged to study the materials and determine which white identity they represented.[174]

The woke radicals are coming for our children, for their minds and hearts and souls. They're coming for us as parents, demanding that we confess to thought crimes that we've never committed, confess that we are horrible people regardless of the content of our character, purely because of the color of our skin.

I know it's easy to become angry when you think of these people with their hateful neoracist ideas trying to impose these false ideologies on your precious children. But don't give in to hate. Instead, take deliberate, purposeful action.

Your children belong in school, not in front of a Zoom screen. But make sure that you know what your children are being taught in school. Make sure that you talk to them and ask them what they are learning. Make sure that you know the teachers and administrators at your school. Attend school board meetings. Join forces with other parents.

Above all, take a stand against the radical indoctrination of your children.

13

The Green Raw Deal

O<small>N</small> M<small>ONDAY</small>, F<small>EBRUARY</small> 15, 2021, eleven-year-old Cristian Pavon Pineda was excitedly playing in the snow outside his family's mobile home in Conroe, a suburb of Houston. The sixth grader had never seen snow before. The snowstorm was more severe than any living Texans had ever experienced. It caused massive power outages, food and water shortages, and deaths all across the state. Cristian's home had been without electricity and heat for two days.

That night, as the temperature outside dropped to 12 degrees, Cristian's mother bundled him up alongside his three-year-old brother under a pile of blankets. The next morning, she went in to check on Cristian and his brother—and found Cristian dead. The suspected cause: hypothermia.

The "Great Texas Blackout of 2021" took the lives of more than 80 people. Causes ranged from hypothermia to carbon monoxide poisoning to house fires to traffic accidents. Those deaths were caused by political decisions. A decade earlier, federal regulators had explicitly warned Texas that its electric grid would likely fail under extreme cold conditions. That warning went unheeded.

The storm froze wind turbines, solar panels, and natural gas pipeline equipment. Unlike other states, Texas has its own independent power grid, separate from the two major interstate power grids. Suddenly, the most energy-rich state in the Union could not generate its own power—and it could not import electricity from other states. Nearby states were just as cold but kept the power on. The tragedy of the Texas blackout was partially the result of the growth of the green energy industry.

Texas conducted an experiment with a limited version of the Green New Deal: 42 percent of the state's electricity came from wind energy. But when the storm froze half the state's wind turbines, that figure dropped to 8 percent. Texas lacked an adequate infrastructure of coal and nuclear power plants to make up for the sudden shortfall in renewable energy.

For decades, political leaders of both parties have enacted laws that create cash incentives to convert the power grid to renewable—and unreliable—energy sources. Across the nation, we are retiring coal and nuclear plants in favor of undependable green energy sources. As the *Wall Street Journal* noted, many states:

> have renewable mandates that will force more fossil-fuel gen-
> erators to shut down. New York has required that renewables
> account for 70 percent of state power by 2030. Then layer on

Democratic policies at the federal level that limit fossil-fuel production and distribution.[175]

When you look at the environmental and energy policies of the Biden-Harris administration, it's clear that Joe Biden refuses to learn the lessons of the Great Texas Blackout of 2021. President Biden and his Democratic allies are dragging the entire nation into a suicide pact with the radical environmental left. I call that suicide pact the "Green Raw Deal."

The Green New Deal: Biden's Crucial Framework

During the first Biden-Trump debate in Cleveland on September 29, 2020, moderator Chris Wallace asked Joe Biden whether America needed to balance environmental concerns with economic concerns. When Biden started to talk about rejoining the Paris Agreement and building a green infrastructure, Trump said, "He's talking about the Green New Deal." Over the next few minutes, Biden made a confusing and contradictory series of statements:

> "That is not my plan. The Green New Deal is not my plan."

> "The Green New Deal will pay for itself as we move forward."

> "No, I don't support the Green New Deal."

> "I support the Biden plan that I put forward. The Biden plan, which is different than what he [Trump] calls the radical Green New Deal."[176]

Moments later, Twitter went wild with tweets about this statement on Joe Biden's campaign website, which seemed to contradict the candidate's statements in the debate: "Biden believes the Green New Deal is a crucial framework for meeting the climate challenges we face." Also on that webpage: "As president, Biden will lead the world to address the climate emergency and lead through the power of example, by ensuring the U.S. achieves a 100 percent clean energy economy and net-zero emissions no later than 2050."[177]

Whether Joe Biden embraces the crucial framework of the Green New Deal or advances his own Joe Biden version, he intends to take America down a perilous road of complete reliance on unreliable energy sources. He intends to rerun the failed Texas blackout experiment all over again—but on a national scale and with the security and survival of the American people as the stakes.

The term *Green New Deal* was probably coined by columnist Tom Friedman in January 2007. In a column called "A Warning from the Garden," Friedman wrote:

> The right rallying call is for a "Green New Deal." If we are to turn the tide on climate change and end our oil addiction, we need more of everything: solar, wind, hydro, ethanol, biodiesel, clean coal and nuclear power—and conservation.
>
> It takes a Green New Deal because to nurture all of these technologies to a point that they really scale would be a huge industrial project.[178]

The radical-left Green Party was an early adopter of the Green New Deal notion. Jill Stein ran as the Green presidential candidate in 2012 and 2016. In 2019, Alexandria Ocasio-Cortez of New York sponsored Green New Deal legislation in the House, and Ed Markey of Massachusetts sponsored it in the Senate, where it failed to advance. Ocasio-Cortez posted the Green New Deal FAQ to her office website, where it attracted such scorn and laughter that she eventually took it down. Some of the agenda items of the Ocasio-Cortez Green New Deal include:

- Eliminate all production of affordable, reliable fossil fuels— oil, coal, and natural gas.
- Eliminate nuclear energy.
- Eliminate and replace all internal combustion engine vehicles.
- Completely upgrade or replace *every building* in America for state-of-the-art energy efficiency.
- Replace air travel with high-speed rail. That's right, no air travel.
- Provide government-guaranteed jobs "with a family sustaining wage, family and medical leave, vacations, and retirement security."
- Provide government-guaranteed "safe, affordable, adequate housing" for every American.
- Provide "economic security for all who are unable or unwilling to work." That's right, unable or *unwilling* to work!

You might think that I'm exaggerating or making this up, but it comes straight from the "Ocasio-Cortez Green New Deal FAQ" that was entered into the record of a House oversight subcommittee hearing in February 2019.[179] And yes, this is the agenda Joe Biden calls the "crucial framework" of his own Joe Biden plan. This is the plan that a number of Democratic presidential hopefuls fully endorsed during the 2020 primary race, including Kamala Harris, Elizabeth Warren, Cory Booker, Kirsten Gillibrand, Julián Castro, and Beto O'Rourke.

It's worth noting that in May 2019, Alexandria Ocasio-Cortez's chief of staff, Saikat Chakrabarti, admitted that the Green New Deal was not devised as a solution to climate change but as an agenda for a socialist takeover of the American economy. According to the *Washington Post*, Chakrabarti told Sam Ricketts, climate director for Washington Governor Jay Inslee, "The interesting thing about the Green New Deal is it wasn't originally a climate thing at all. Do you guys think of it as a climate thing? Because we really think of it as a how-do-you-change-the-entire-economy thing."[180]

Joe Biden doesn't support the wilder, more Marxist aspects of the Green New Deal—the job and food and housing guarantees, but he is taking ambitious steps to move America away from affordable, reliable energy and toward a goal of a "100 percent clean energy economy and net-zero emissions"—and toward a national-scale Texas blackout experiment.

Implementing Joe Biden's Green Raw Deal

As we saw in Chapter 3, President Biden began implementing his radical climate agenda on day one. He signed an order recommitting the United States to "every article and clause" of the Paris Climate Agreement. The Paris Agreement imposes huge costs on American businesses and families, including soaring energy and consumer goods costs, massive job losses, and huge income losses for families. Why should Americans be punished when the United States already leads the world in controlling greenhouse gas emissions? The Paris Agreement would impose such crippling burdens on our economy that it would impede our ability to reduce emissions.

In terms of total global carbon dioxide (CO_2) emissions, the top three polluting nations are Communist China (30 percent of global emissions), the United States (15 percent), and India

(7 percent). The 27 nations of the European Union plus former EU member Great Britain together contribute 9 percent.[181] While the United States has made great strides in reducing carbon emissions, China and India are scarcely held accountable for making any near-term progress in cleaning up their air. China plans to continue *increasing* CO_2 emissions in the near term and does not promise to begin reducing CO_2 emissions until around 2030. India says that it needs to receive about $2.5 trillion in aid from the United States and other countries in order to achieve its emissions reduction goals by 2030.

The Paris Agreement imposes crippling economic demands on the United States—while China, an enormously wealthy and technologically advanced nation, gets a free pass to spew increasing volumes of pollution for the next decade. This increases pressure on American companies to move manufacturing and supply chains to China to take advantage of China's cheap, planet-polluting energy. If climate change is as urgent a threat as environmentalists claim, shouldn't China do its fair share to save the planet?

The United States is dramatically reducing emissions, thanks to private-sector technological innovation. Meanwhile, the Paris Agreement permits big polluters like China and India to continue befouling the planet. In fact, we don't even know how much carbon those two countries are spewing into the atmosphere. A report by the BBC states that "levels of some emissions from India and China are so uncertain that experts say their records are plus or minus 100 percent."[182]

Just as China has repeatedly lied about the COVID-19 plague it unleashed on the world, it is lying about its carbon emissions. China's leaders have no regard for the truth—or for international agreements. China signed the Paris Agreement because it serves

China to do so. Our leaders signed it even though it harms our interests and aids our adversaries.

Each nation is on the honor system in reporting emissions and improvements under the Paris Agreement—these self-reports are called *stock takes*. There are no enforcement or verification measures for these stock takes. Communist China's reports are notoriously riddled with errors and lies.

Professor Glen Peters of Oslo's Centre for International Climate Research told the BBC:

> The core part of . . . [the Paris Agreement is] the global stock
> takes which are going to happen every five years, and after
> the stock takes, countries are meant to raise their ambition,
> but if you can't track progress sufficiently, which is the whole
> point of these stock takes, you basically can't do anything.
> So, without good data as a basis, Paris essentially collapses. It
> just becomes a talkfest without much progress.

This failed, corrupt "talkfest" is what President Trump rescued the United States from in 2017. And it's what President Biden returned us to with the stroke of a pen on his first day in office.

The Keystone Pipeline Cancellation

On his first day in office, President Biden signed Executive Order 13990: "Restoring Science to Tackle the Climate Crisis." The centerpiece of this order is Section 6: "Revoking the March 2019 Permit for the Keystone XL Pipeline." Biden's order makes no environmental or economic sense. It only makes *political* sense as a gesture to the radical environmentalist fringe.

The 1,200-mile Keystone XL Pipeline system was commissioned in 2010. It is jointly owned by Canada's TC Energy Corporation and the province of Alberta, Canada. The pipeline was intended to carry crude oil from the Western Canadian Sedimentary Basin in Alberta to refineries and distribution centers in Illinois, Oklahoma, and Texas.

The Obama State Department concluded that Keystone would have no adverse impact on greenhouse gas emissions because the Alberta crude oil would be extracted whether it passed through the pipeline or not. In fact, killing Keystone would force Alberta crude oil to be shipped by rail or truck, resulting in much higher carbon emissions plus a greater risk of leaks. Even though it made no environmental sense to kill the pipeline, President Obama was committed to the Paris Agreement, so he shut Keystone down in 2015.

President Trump greenlighted Keystone XL on January 24, 2017. In fact, I was present in the Roosevelt Room for President Trump's signing of the executive action reversing President Obama's veto of the Keystone and Dakota Access pipelines. A number of White House staffers were on hand as President Trump prepared to sign the document. With his pen poised over the paper, Mr. Trump looked up and said, "I assume these projects are all being built with American steel."

After an uncomfortable silence, someone said, "That wasn't part of the executive order, sir. In fact, much of the steel would probably come from foreign sources."

The president's brow furrowed, and he set the pen on the desk. "I can't sign this order," he said. "It needs to be revised. We need to do everything possible to utilize American steel. I'm not going to do this unless it benefits American workers to the greatest extent possible." That was Donald Trump's mindset: American workers came first. The document was revised to the president's satisfaction, and he signed it.

Unfortunately, environmental activists tied up President Trump's order in the courts for more than two years. Finally, in March 2019, President Trump was able to issue the Keystone permit. However, those two years of legal wrangling proved fatal to the project when President Trump was unable to win reelection.

TC Energy and the unions lobbied President-elect Biden, explaining the environmental and economic benefits of the Keystone project: the union construction jobs it would create, the steel pipe that would be made in America, the $10 million green job training program TC Energy would fund, the hundreds of millions of dollars the pipeline would pour into the U.S. economy, and the 100 percent clean and renewable energy used to operate the pipeline. These arguments fell on deaf ears.

Killing Jobs, Snubbing an Ally, Aiding Our Enemies

On his first day in office, President Joe Biden pulled Keystone's permit. He knew he was killing a minimum of 11,000 good-paying pipeline jobs (plus unknown thousands of ancillary jobs along the pipeline route). By hampering the ability of the United States and Canada to bring this oil to market, Biden gave a huge gift to our oil-producing adversaries, Russia and socialist Venezuela.

President Biden paid lip service to building America's infrastructure, claiming that his Build Back Better program would create good-paying jobs without increasing carbon emissions. Continuing the Keystone XL project would have been in line with that promise. Instead, Joe Biden killed good-paying jobs and forced oil producers to ship their product in carbon-spewing trains and trucks.

As the *Wall Street Journal* editorial board lamented on Inauguration Day, "President Biden issued a blizzard of executive orders on his first day in office, including a diktat to revoke the permit for the Keystone XL pipeline. This is a slap at Canada, and it sends a message to investors that playing by U.S. rules provides no immunity from arbitrary political whim."[183] In addition to killing the pipeline, President Biden's executive order paused oil and gas leasing in the Arctic National Wildlife Refuge.

President Biden's cancellation of Keystone XL is a gift to Russia, Venezuela, and environmental radicals—and a snub to Canada. But who else does this executive action benefit? It's too early to say, but one of the biggest winners might be Communist China. Canada's Trans Mountain Pipeline System currently moves 300,000 barrels of oil daily from Alberta, across British Columbia, to refineries and tankers on the Pacific Coast. Most of that oil currently remains in Canada and the United States.[184] But President Biden has just given Canada an incentive to sell a bigger share of Canadian oil to China.

Long after Joe Biden's inauguration, his son Hunter continued to hold a 10 percent stake in a China-based private-equity firm, Bohai Harvest RST (BHR Partners), a company invested primarily in mining, technology, and energy. Does President Biden's canceling of Keystone XL improve the value of Hunter's investments in Communist China? Time will tell.

President Biden and his fellow Democrats like to chant the mantra, "Follow the science!" Yet the science tells us that American prosperity is built on a foundation of affordable, reliable energy, including energy that can be safely, cleanly transported through the Keystone XL Pipeline. We can and should make a careful, gradual transition to more renewable forms of energy as we learn how to make green energy more reliable.

But Joe Biden's embrace of the Green Raw Deal endangers American prosperity and national security, aids our adversary Communist China, and violates both science and common sense.

14

The Biden Open Borders Agenda

O N MARCH 2, 2021, surveillance cameras recorded two SUVs driving through a breach in the fence at the California-Mexico border. A section of the fence located near the Gordon's Well Road exit off Interstate 8 had been torn down by smugglers. The two vehicles, a 1997 Ford Expedition and a Chevy Suburban, crossed into California just before 6:00 in the morning.

Both cars had the rear seats removed so that they could be packed tightly with passengers. Neither vehicle got far. The Suburban pulled onto Interstate 8 and traveled west for about 30 miles when the engine caught fire. The driver pulled off the road, and 19 people escaped from the burning car without injury. They were later picked up by Border Patrol agents.

The 22-year-old driver of the Ford Expedition took back roads, heading toward California Highway 115. He reached the intersection of Norrish Road and Highway 115, not far from the town of Holtville. The Expedition was rated to carry 2,000 pounds. The smugglers had stuffed 25 people inside, so it carried closer to 4,000 pounds. The extra weight would strain the SUV's ability to steer, accelerate, and brake. The young driver probably didn't realize how unresponsive the SUV had become.

It was a bright sunny morning. The flat farmland offered an unobstructed view. Yet, for some unknown reason, the driver pulled out onto Highway 115 directly in front of a truck hauling two trailers filled with gravel. The truck driver braked hard, jack-knifing his trailers, but he couldn't stop in time.

The truck slammed into the Expedition, shoving the SUV off the pavement, sending people and belongings flying. When police and ambulances arrived, they found an unbelievably gruesome scene. Dazed survivors walked in the field or knelt beside the dead. Some were still crawling out of the wreckage. In all, 13 people died, and the rest suffered major injuries.

One of the dead was 23-year-old Yesenia Cardona, who had been a law student at Guatemala's University of San Carlos. She and her mother, 46-year-old Verlyn Cardona, left Guatemala a month after Joe Biden's inauguration. They were two of eight people who remained in the Expedition after the crash. The other 17 passengers were ejected. Verlyn survived the crash, regaining consciousness to find her daughter lying across her legs, dead.

Guatemala's consul general in Los Angeles, Tekandi Paniagua, told the *L.A. Times* that smugglers are telling Guatemalans that the Biden-Harris administration is loosening restrictions on immigration—so now is the time to move north.[185] President Biden has encouraged these beliefs through his policy pronouncements and executive actions on the border wall and border security.

The Biden-Harris administration broke the border. The result is a humanitarian nightmare.

False Progressive Compassion

As we saw in Chapter 3, one of President Biden's first acts on day one of his administration was to terminate construction of the wall on the southern border. This action had both practical and symbolic consequences. As a practical matter, halting construction of the wall leaves much of our southern border open and undefended. But the symbolic consequences of this action are even worse. With the stroke of a pen, President Biden announced to the world an abrupt and disastrous change in our immigration policy. Both the desperate poor and the criminal cartels of Mexico and Central America were listening.

Walls are important to all of us, practically and psychologically. We live in houses because the walls of a house are protective barriers. Walls keep us safe. Walls help us to feel psychologically secure and protected from the outside world.

A few weeks after the inauguration of President Biden, I visited Capitol Hill. There's a wall around the Capitol, placed there by order of Speaker of the House Nancy Pelosi. I had to be screened by armed guards at a security checkpoint to pass through the gate. Since January 6, 2021, Nancy Pelosi has been afraid of an incursion at the Capitol—and she knows that walls work.

But neither Nancy Pelosi nor President Biden has any enthusiasm for protecting America from a flood of illegal migrants—even though some of them could be drug dealers, human traffickers, criminals, terrorists, and others who might do us harm. If these

Democratic leaders know that walls work, why won't they protect the American people and the American homeland with a wall? Why was one of Joe Biden's first acts as president to stop the construction of the border wall?

There are many reasons Progressives call for open borders. For some, it's a way of signaling their virtue and showing how enlightened they are. For others, it's an issue to run on, a way of generating political contributions and motivating voter turnout. For still others, illegal immigration is simply a source of cheap labor. And for many political strategists on the left, illegal immigration is a way of importing future citizens—and future Democratic voters.

Democrats like to portray unrestricted illegal immigration as a matter of compassion. But where is the compassion in importing a foreign-born underclass to do the work we won't do—or won't pay a decent wage to do? That's not compassion. That's exploitation—and it's a racist policy.

Spinning the Border Crisis

On March 1, 2021, Homeland Security Secretary Alejandro Mayorkas appeared with Jen Psaki at a White House press conference. A reporter asked Mayorkas, "Do you believe that right now there's a crisis at the border?"

"I think the answer is no," Mayorkas replied. "I think there is a challenge at the border that we are managing, and we have our resources dedicated to managing it."

The reporter pointed out that Mayorkas's predecessor in the Obama era, Jeh Johnson, said that a thousand border crossings a day constituted a crisis that overwhelms the system—and that Customs and Border Protection officials estimated that there were

3,000 to 4,000 daily border crossings at that time, adding, "How is this not a crisis?"

"I have explained that quite clearly," Mayorkas said. "We are challenged at the border. The men and women of the Department of Homeland Security are meeting that challenge. It is a stressful challenge, and that is why, quite frankly, we are working as hard as we are."

The word *crisis* suggests a situation out of control. *Challenge* suggests a problem that is manageable and solvable. *Spin*, of course, is the art of portraying a crisis as a challenge—and Mayorkas was spinning like a windmill in a hurricane. The most unforgivable spin Mayorkas engaged in was when he tried to shift the blame for the crisis to the previous administration.

Mayorkas claimed that he was having to "rebuild the system from scratch" and that "the prior administration dismantled our nation's immigration system in its entirety. . . . Quite frankly, the entire system was gutted." Nonsense. There was no crisis at the border when Joe Biden took office on January 20, 2021. But when Mayorkas gave his press conference on March 1, the border was out of control. You can't pin that on the previous administration.

The Trump White House left Biden and Mayorkas a functioning and well-run immigration and homeland security system. In June 2019, the United States and Mexico reached an agreement in which Mexico stepped up its immigration enforcement and took in migrants awaiting asylum hearings in the United States. And in September 2019, the United States and Honduras reached an agreement that ended caravans of asylum seekers traveling through Central America to the United States. By the end of the Trump administration, problems at the border had settled down considerably.

Then Joe Biden walked into the Oval Office, pen in hand, and blew it all up. The crisis at the border is Joe Biden's crisis, 100 percent. He owns it—lock, stock, and unfinished wall.

In the press conference, Alejandro Mayorkas went on to compound the problem even further. He said to people who were considering crossing the border, "They need to wait. . . . We need individuals to wait, and I will say that they will wait with a goal in mind, and that is our ability to rebuild as quickly as possible a system so that they don't have to take the dangerous journey, and we can enable them to access humanitarian relief from their countries of origin."[186]

Mayorkas didn't say, "Don't come." He said, "Wait. . . . Wait with a goal in mind." With a wink and a nod, he signaled to families and minors, to drug smugglers and human traffickers, and even to criminals and terrorists: The border will be open—we just want an orderly stampede. Soon we will help you reach your goal.

A Nation of Immigrants

America is a nation of immigrants and has been since it was founded. The key to America's greatness has always been our unique combination of cultural diversity and national unity, as expressed in the motto *E Pluribus Unum*, "Out of Many, One."

Progressives like to recite the saying, "We're a nation of immigrants," without distinguishing between legal and illegal immigration. They like to quote, without context, the message of the Statue of Liberty, composed by Emma Lazarus in 1883:

> Give me your tired, your poor,
> Your huddled masses yearning to breathe free,
> The wretched refuse of your teeming shore.

Send these, the homeless, tempest-tost to me,
I lift my lamp beside the golden door!

Those are beautiful words, and all of us, whether liberal or conservative, believe those words to the core of our being. The difference between those on the left and those on the right is that we conservatives believe that the huddled masses should come through a legal process and that we should know who they are—and we should exclude anyone coming to our golden door who wishes us harm.

The poem by Emma Lazarus sets forth a beautiful ideal. It's not an immigration policy, but it is an expression of the compassionate, welcoming heart of America toward immigrants. But notice that Emma Lazarus also uses the image of a golden door. A door is a barrier that swings on hinges to allow certain people in—and shut other people out. This is why we have a legal immigration policy. We need to know who wants to pass through that golden door—and why. And we need to be able to shut criminals and terrorists out.

The Legal Immigration Nightmare

At the second Democratic debate in Miami, June 27, 2019, the moderator asked for a show of hands of candidates who would support government-run healthcare for illegal immigrants at taxpayer expense. Shockingly, all the candidates on the stage raised their hands, including Joe Biden and Kamala Harris. When Joe Biden was vice president, his boss, President Barack Obama, pointedly assured the nation that Obamacare would not cover illegal immigrants. Biden, however, reversed Obama's policy, claiming, "You have to [cover illegal immigrants]. It's the humane thing to do." And when Pete Buttigieg said in the debate that illegal immigrants should have a pathway to citizenship, no one on the stage disagreed.[187] After Joe Biden was inaugurated, he proceeded to implement these views as policy.

One of the strangest quirks of our chaotic immigration system is that we frequently treat *illegal* immigrants as welcomed guests while treating legal immigrants as criminals. Take, for example, the case of Patricia Audrey Peters, who came to America legally from the United Kingdom in 2001. She worked for a venture capital firm, purchased a home, paid substantial taxes, and never broke the law. Yet she was forced to spend years in costly litigation with the U.S. Citizenship and Immigration Services (USCIS), which denied her a permanent resident green card and spent three years trying to deport her.

When Ms. Peters's case reached the Ninth Circuit Court of Appeals, the three-judge panel quickly became confused by the shifting claims of the government attorneys. At first, USCIS attorneys claimed that Ms. Peters had submitted an outdated form. Then they claimed the agency had "appropriately rejected" her green card application because of incorrect filing fees. When one judge asked the government attorneys to explain the filing fees problem, the attorney went into a long and convoluted explanation—and it turned out that the U.S. government was trying to deport Ms. Peters because she had overpaid the agency $5. The government attorneys insisted that the government's position was "substantially justified." The exasperated judge called the government's persecution of Ms. Peters a "nightmare of bureaucracy" and ordered the government to issue the green card and leave the woman alone.[188]

But illegal immigration is another matter altogether. Progressives expect America to welcome all comers, regardless of the strain on social services, the economy, the justice system, and the wages of our citizens. Every nation on earth considers it a matter of national security to know who is coming across its borders and for what purpose. In all the world, only the United States is held to a different standard and expected to completely open its borders.

Kids in Cages

We can't have an honest national conversation about illegal immigration because we don't have an honest national media. They won't give you the honest facts in the *New York Times* or the *Washington Post* or on ABC, NBC, CBS, or CNN. The illegal immigration issue has been reduced to name-calling. If you support the border wall or if you want a rational border policy, the media will label you a racist. The racist card has been so overplayed that it has lost all meaning.

We should be having a fact-based, reasonable national conversation about how many immigrants we should permit into the country every year, under what circumstances, where they should come from, and how they should be vetted. We should have a conversation about whether to create a path to citizenship for the undocumented immigrants who are already here. We can't have these conversations because the Democrats and their media allies are too busy vilifying anyone who wants a sane immigration policy.

Meanwhile, the Biden-Harris administration is making policies that create incentives for a migrant onslaught at our southern border. When President Biden's own words and executive actions create a predictable crisis at the border, his administration's only response is to blame the previous administration. How did the Biden White House not foresee all of this? What did President Biden think would happen when he made such an ostentatious show of canceling the border wall and reversing the Trump immigration agenda?

Joe Biden's reckless knee-jerk impulse to overturn everything Trump accomplished has resulted in death and tragedy at the border. The Biden-Harris administration's migrant youth detention facilities are overcrowded, and they are keeping kids longer than the three days permitted by law. And yes, they are keeping them in the very cages that Progressive leaders and the media castigated the Trump administration for.

On June 30, 2018, candidate Kamala Harris said, "When we have kids in cages, crying for mommies and daddies, we know we are better than this." And California Senator Dianne Feinstein said, "This is the United States of America. It isn't Nazi Germany, and there's a difference, and we don't take children from their parents until now." And Democratic Representative Alexandria Ocasio-Cortez of New York doubled down on the obnoxious Nazi comparison: "The U.S. is running concentration camps on our southern border. . . . I want to talk to the people that are concerned enough with humanity to say that 'never again' means something."

Clearly, Progressives are so ideologically misguided, so blinded by their own Trump derangement, that they cannot see what the rest of us see all too clearly: When you signal to the world that America's borders are a thing of the past, you can expect uncontrollable masses of poor people to stream in. Not only have Joe Biden and his fellow Progressives committed a political blunder of epic proportions, but they have also perpetrated a tragic humanitarian crisis, with children as the victims.

Why has the Biden-Harris administration been so focused on a "challenge" involving children?

First, children draw on our sympathies—as they should. We all want migrant children to be treated humanely and compassionately. Second, political opportunists like to play on our sympathies and exploit children for their own political advantage. This is why dishonest politicians and media figures used the "children in cages" mantra as a bludgeon against the Trump administration. It works. Third, I believe that these politicians are planning ahead. Joe Biden's immigration plan offers a path to citizenship in eight years.[189] So if the Biden-Harris administration allows children ages 10 and up to flood into the country, the Democrats can expect to have an army of new Democratic voters a mere eight years from now. The Biden-Harris folks know exactly what they're doing.

A Policy Based on a Failed Ideology

The president of Mexico, Andrés Manuel López Obrador, expressed his frustration with Biden's policies, saying that poor people and criminal cartels in Latin America see Joe Biden as the "migrant president." López Obrador added, "We need to work together to regulate the flow" of immigrants from Central America through Mexico. He pointed to specific Biden policies that are giving the Mexican government headaches, including the fast track to citizenship for undocumented immigrants in America.

Criminal cartels keep close tabs on U.S. laws, and they have developed sophisticated tracking systems using computer-coded wristbands to track their human cargo—and their profits. One Mexican official says that the cartels began implementing these systems "from the day Biden took office."[190]

Cartel profits are skyrocketing thanks to the Biden-Harris administration's hasty and ill-conceived move to undo every Trump-era border security measure. Just as Biden's thoughtless day one cancellation of the Keystone XL Pipeline damaged relations with Canada, his thoughtless cancellation of Trump-era border policies has strained our relationship with Mexico.

Biden's allies in the corporate media have become the public relations arm of the Democratic Party. A 2018 *Washington Post* story on the Trump-era migrant facilities was headlined, "The American Tradition of Caging Children," and spoke of "the horror going on at the border."[191] In February 2021, the *Washington Post* ran a story on the Biden border facilities—facilities that were opened by the Trump administration in 2019—but this time the headline read, "First Migrant Facility for Children Opens under Biden." Under the headline, instead of "the horror going on at the border," we read about the "bright blue hospital tent with white bunk beds inside" and the entryway festooned with "flowers, butterflies and handmade posters."[192]

What neither the Biden-Harris administration nor the *Washington Post* will tell you is that there is a good and compassionate reason that the Obama, Trump, and Biden-Harris administrations have kept migrant children behind protective fences. Many of these children have been sex trafficked or otherwise abused and exploited by smugglers and others. These so-called cages and concentration camps are designed to keep these kids *safe* until they can be reunited with their families.

President Biden's reflexive decision to sweep away the Trump border policies has generated a full-blown crisis. All the hyperbolic, condescending rhetoric about kids in cages has met the reality on the ground. The Biden-Harris administration is forced to use the same measures the previous administration used—and it's amusing to see Jen Psaki and Alejandro Mayorkas trying to spin their way out of this crisis.

What is not amusing—what is, in fact, heartbreaking—is the human tragedy caused by a border policy based on a failed Progressive ideology and sheer Trump derangement. The face of this tragedy is 23-year-old Yesenia Cardona, who dreamed of becoming a lawyer but was lured to her death by the false promises of the Biden border agenda.

15

Defunding Our Defenders

In February 2021, a meme began circulating on the internet made up of a series of actual news headlines in chronological order:

- June 26, 2020, National Public Radio: "Minneapolis Council Moves to Defund Police, Establish 'Holistic' Public Safety Force"[193]
- July 21, 2020, *New York Times*: "Minneapolis Police Experience Surge of Departures in Aftermath of George Floyd Protests"[194]
- September 15, 2020, Minnesota Public Radio: "With Violent Crime on the Rise in Minneapolis, City Council Asks: Where Are the Police?"[195]

- September 16, 2020, *New York Post*: "Minneapolis City Council Alarmed by Surge in Crime Months after Voting to Defund the Police"[196]
- September 28, 2020, *The Hill*: "Some Minneapolis City Council Members Would Like a Redo on Defunding the Police"[197]
- February 13, 2021, Associated Press: "Minneapolis to Spend $6.4 Million to Recruit More Police Officers"[198]

Once the Minneapolis City Council began to defund the police, any rational human being could have predicted this sequence of events. You have to be an ideologically crazed Progressive not to see this coming.

We all remember the protests that began in Minneapolis in May 2020 after the death of George Floyd under the knee of police officer Derek Chauvin. In just the first three nights of protests, rioting, and looting, May 27 to May 29, Minneapolis suffered the destruction of its Third Precinct police building and damage to or destruction of some 1,300 properties in the city. Neighboring Saint Paul had 37 buildings heavily damaged or destroyed.

The response of the Minneapolis City Council was largely to appease and side with the demonstrators and rioters. On June 4, Council Member Jeremiah Ellison tweeted, "We are going to dismantle the Minneapolis Police Department. And when we're done, we're not simply gonna glue it back together. We are going to dramatically rethink how we approach public safety and emergency response. It's really past due."[199]

Three days later, on June 7, nine of the thirteen City Council members stood before a crowd at Powderhorn Park and made a vow to dismantle the city's police department. One member told the crowd, "It is clear that our system of policing is not keeping our communities safe. Our efforts at incremental reform have failed, period."[200] Two council members disagreed with the pledge and did not attend the rally.

The radical majority on the Minneapolis City Council made good on their pledge to disband the police—and the news head-lines cited earlier chronicled the results of that decision.

Our elected leaders have sworn to uphold the law and the Constitution. When they panic in the face of an angry mob, this is what happens. They act hastily, failing to think through the consequences of their actions. Mob violence and civil disorder spread. Businesses and police stations burn. People lose their live-lihoods—and their lives.

We see this same tendency to appease the mob in the policies of Joe Biden and Kamala Harris.

Joe Biden's Confused Messaging

The protests and riots spread across the nation in 2020's "Summer of Rage." As the rioting spread, so did the cowardice of civic lead-ers. In New York, Philadelphia, Baltimore, Washington, DC, San Francisco, Los Angeles, and other American cities, cowardly mayors and city councils rushed to appease the protesters and defund their police departments. By August 2020, New York City had cut a bil-lion dollars from its police budget. In Los Angeles, where Mayor Eric Garcetti had been planning to increase the budget for the LAPD, he reversed himself and announced a cut of up to $150 million.

In the midst of this law enforcement chaos came candidate Joe Biden, who courageously took a stand on both sides of the issue. His campaign staff stated firmly, "Biden does not believe that police should be defunded." In an interview, when asked if funding should be redirected away from police departments, Biden replied, "Yes, absolutely." A few days later, after a poll was released showing that 81 percent of African Americans wanted to *maintain or increase* police presence in their neighborhoods, Joe Biden called for *increased* funding for the police so that they could handle the "God-awful problems" in minority neighborhoods.[201]

Clearly, Joe Biden stands for defunding the police . . . or not.

Actually, he's for *increased* funding for police . . . or not.

His answer depends on what day you ask him. And on what the latest polls say.

Joe Biden prides himself on his cozy relationship with union members, including the rank-and-file cops in the police unions. But Biden's confused messaging during the summer of 2020 included support for the rights of protesters and calls for more stringent oversight and reforms of policing, and no mention was made of police officers killed and wounded by protesters and rioters. Biden seemed to be switching sides, and his new messaging left many in law enforcement embittered toward their once-reliable ally Joe Biden.

Bill Johnson, executive director of the National Association of Police Organizations, expressed the frustration of many cops toward Joe Biden:

> Clearly, he's made a lot of changes the way candidates do during the primary process, but he kept moving left and fell off the deep end. For Joe Biden, police are shaking their heads because he used to be a stand-up guy who backed law enforcement. But it seems in his old age, for whatever reason, he's writing a sad final chapter when it comes to supporting law enforcement.

And Jim Pasco, executive director of the Fraternal Order of Police, said:

> On law-and-order issues, Biden was right of center: the '94 crime bill, the Brady law and enhanced penalties. But as time has gone by, his positions have moderated, moderated, moderated to where we are today, where he would not be considered a law-and-order guy in the sense that law enforcement sees it.[202]

The man behind the Resolute Desk is a man the Joe Biden of 10, 20, or 30 years ago would not recognize.

Kamala Harris's Confused Messaging

At the beginning of her primary campaign for president, Kamala Harris touted her career as a prosecutor and attorney general of California as a qualification for president. She called herself a "top cop." When the political winds began to change in the summer of 2020 and cops fell in disfavor with Progressives, Kamala Harris tried to reinvent herself as a criminal justice reformer and an ally of Black Lives Matter.

Massaging her message has always been a challenge for Kamala Harris. In an effort to straddle the fence between "soft on crime" and "tough on crime," she has tried to persuade voters that she is "smart on crime." What she has most often been, however, is confused on crime—and on police reform.

In her political autobiography, *The Truths We Hold*, she wrote, "We must speak truth about police brutality, about racial bias, about the killing of unarmed black men. Police brutality occurs in America, and we have to root it out wherever we find it."[203]

Yet when she was attorney general of California and she had an opportunity to root out police brutality, she was AWOL. She declined to use her authority to investigate charges of police and prosecutorial misconduct, even when the facts were difficult to ignore. She fought to keep people in prison who had almost certainly been wrongfully convicted. *The Guardian* reports:

> Jeff Adachi, the public defender of San Francisco, twice urged Harris to open a civil rights investigation into the San Francisco police department, once after police were caught sending racist and homophobic text messages and again [after] a string of high-profile killings of young people of color by police. "I never received a response," Adachi said in an email.
>
> In 2016, numerous male officers across the Bay Area became embroiled in a sexual exploitation scandal. . . . A federal judge said the Oakland police department's investigation into its own officers was "wholly inadequate," but Harris did not launch her own investigation. The inaction was particularly shameful and hypocritical given her stated commitments on fighting trafficking and protecting exploited youth, activists said.
>
> "We pleaded with her and pressured her to at least investigate, if not prosecute, some of the local police departments who had killed African American men and Latino men," said Anne Butterfield Weills, a local civil rights lawyer. "She ignored us."[204]

During media appearances in the summer of 2020, she was often asked her views on defunding the police. On MSNBC, she said:

The status quo has been to determine and create policy around the idea that more police equals more safety. And that's just wrong. You know what creates greater safety? Funding our public schools, so that, currently, two-thirds of our public school teachers don't have to come out of their own back pocket to pay for school supplies.

This sounds like she favors defunding police and giving the money to teachers and schools.

Wanted: A Clear Set of Moral Principles

Appearing on ABC's *Good Morning America*, Harris supported the decision of LA Mayor Eric Garcetti to defund the LAPD by $150 million. She said:

We've got to reexamine what we're doing with American taxpayer dollars and ask the question: are we getting the right return on our investment? Are we actually creating healthy and safe communities? That's a legitimate conversation, and it requires a really critical evaluation. I applaud Eric Garcetti for doing what he's done.[205]

(Harris typically avoids answering questions by saying we need to have a conversation without actually taking a position.)

Kamala Harris also appeared on ABC's *The View* in June 2020. Cohost Meghan McCain asked Harris, "Are you for defunding the police?"

Harris countered, "How are you defining 'defund the police'?"

McCain referred to a tweet by radical Democratic Congresswoman Ilhan Omar, who attended the disband-the-police rally in Minneapolis. "I'm at the community meeting at Powderhorn Park in Minneapolis," Omar had tweeted, "where City Council members just unveiled a mission statement for reimagining policing." McCain explained that to her, "defund the police" meant exactly what it sounded like, "removing the police."

Kamala Harris declined to answer yes or no. Instead, she said, "We need to reimagine public safety in America," and she added that there is a conversation we should have about spending less on police and putting more resources into public schools, job training, and job creation.[206]

The problem with Kamala Harris is not her position regarding defunding the police. The real problem is that she won't take positions or answer questions. Trying to get a straight answer is like trying to nail Jell-O to the wall. She has no core convictions—and that's a dangerous quality in a leader.

If the nation is again gripped by a "defund-the-police" mania as it was in the summer of 2020, there is every likelihood that Kamala Harris will be swept along with the tide of radical voices in the streets and in the media. Like the Minneapolis City Council, she's liable to make a poorly thought-out, unprincipled decision in the heat of the moment—a decision that both she and the rest of us will live to regret.

Matters of policing and criminal justice should not be decided by people who lack a strong inner core. They should be decided by people who will readily, openly state a set of clear moral convictions—people who believe in justice, fairness, and what's best for the American people, not merely what's in the political best interest of Kamala Harris.

A Future without Police?

Although most Americans never heard the slogan "defund the police" before the Black Lives Matter protests began in May 2020, the idea of abolishing police departments, prisons, and the entire criminal justice system has been around for a long time. Civil rights author W. E. B. Du Bois, one of the cofounders of the NAACP, laid the intellectual groundwork for the abolition of prisons and police forces in *Black Reconstruction* (1935). In the 1960s, radical Marxist Professor Angela Davis called for the dismantling of what she called the "prison-industrial complex."

In 2017, sociologist Alex S. Vitale published *The End of Policing*, which Politico described as "a manual of sorts for the defund movement." Interviewed on NPR, Vitale said:

> I'm certainly not talking about any kind of scenario where tomorrow someone just flips a switch and there are no police. What I'm talking about is the systematic questioning of the specific roles that police currently undertake and attempting to develop evidence-based alternatives so that we can dial back our reliance on them.[207]

But there are some defund-the-police advocates who are perfectly willing to flip that switch. Activist and community organizer Mariame Kaba has long advocated for the abolition of the police and prisons. Her June 12, 2020, opinion piece in the *New York Times* was headlined, "Yes, We Literally Mean Abolish the Police." A subhead added, "Because Reform Won't Happen."

What used to be a fringe proposal relegated to radical cells on university campuses is now being openly debated by elected officials and media figures. Some deny that *defunding* equates to *dismantling*. Others are very enthusiastic about a future without police, even though we've already seen how that experiment would turn out.

In New York City in July 2020, Mayor Bill de Blasio supported a City Council vote to cut the police budget by $1 billion. How did that work out? In September 2020, New York had 152 shootings versus 67 the previous September. Murders jumped from 29 to 51 and burglaries increased from 912 to 1,255.

Democratic City Councilman Robert Holden said:

> Defunding the police is perhaps the worst idea in NYC government history. We can't legislate using fashionable slogans that fit on protest signs. It hurts every New Yorker. The NYPD are the gold standard for law enforcement around the world. Any issues that need to be addressed require more training, which costs money.

The Defunders Are Not Going Away

Mayor DeBlasio's wife, Chirlane McCray, strongly advocated for the City Council's defunding proposal in July 2020. Eight months later, distressed by rising crime rates in the city, she took to Twitter and asked New Yorkers to intervene whenever they saw violence on city streets. She tweeted:

> As attacks on Asian American communities continue, we're asking New Yorkers to show up for their neighbors and intervene when witnessing hateful violence or harassment. I know that can be frightening when you aren't sure what to do or say, but you can learn.

In a follow-up tweet, she added, "Fear is a normal feeling when stepping into a confrontation, but being prepared can help."[208]

Then she suggested a five-step approach to confronting and deescalating street violence (step one should be "Carry plenty of life insurance"). When New York City decided to defund the police, the city was left with a soaring crime rate and a series of ridiculous tweets from New York's first lady calling on New Yorkers to become amateur cops.

Much of the leftist eagerness to eradicate police comes from a naive belief that human nature is perfectible. All we have to do is educate (or indoctrinate) people early enough and create social programs, guaranteed income programs, and public housing to remove the incentives for people to commit crimes. You and I know that this utopian vision is a pipe dream—but Progressives are convinced that if they can achieve enough power and control over our lives, they can create a heaven on earth.

The defund-the-police movement will be around for a long time to come. The anti-cop radicals aren't going anywhere. We can expect mayors, city councils, and perhaps even a president and vice president to try to appease their way out of the next defund-the-police uprising. We have to be ready to rise up as well and to call a halt to those who would abolish our criminal justice system and our civilization.

16

The Assault on the Constitution

THERE HAS BEEN A lot of controversy over the question, Does Joe Biden plan to pack the Supreme Court? Biden's hero and role model, Franklin Delano Roosevelt, proposed the first court-packing scheme as part of the Judicial Procedures Reform Bill of 1937. Roosevelt was frustrated because the Supreme Court had ruled against many of his New Deal proposals. He wanted to reshape the court to do his bidding. The Constitution does not specify how many justices should serve on the court, so Roosevelt planned to appoint additional justices ("pack the court") until there were enough FDR appointees to rubber-stamp his agenda.

Leaders of both parties and even Vice President John Nance Garner were horrified by FDR's scheme. The reform bill died in Congress.

Throughout the 2020 campaign, Biden dodged the question of whether he would pack the court, saying, "Whatever position I take, that will become the issue. . . . I'm not gonna answer the question." That's nonsense. The whole idea of running for president is that you state your positions on the issues, those positions become part of a national conversation, and the voters decide if they like your agenda or not. That's how democracy works. In the 2016 election, then-candidate Trump released a list of judges from which he would choose to fill a Supreme Court vacancy if he were elected president. The goal was to give voters a strong sense of where he stood on the court and the types of judges he would appoint.

During a campaign stop in Phoenix, Biden said, "You'll know my opinion on court packing when the election is over." The next day, in Las Vegas, a reporter asked Biden if voters deserved to know if he would pack the court. Biden's testy reply: "No, they don't deserve—I'm not going to play his [President Trump's] game."

Candidate Biden was asked the most important question of the 2020 election: Would he expand the Supreme Court? He dismissed it as a game. The question involves a fundamental restructuring of the Supreme Court. Undoing the nine-justice composition of the court would trample a tradition that has stood since 1869.

Packing the court would set off a judicial arms race: Biden raises the number of justices to 15, a Republican successor raises it to 21, and on and on until the Supreme Court becomes a black-robed mob that can barely fit into Nationals Park. A candidate who thinks the American people don't deserve an answer to this question doesn't deserve to be elected.

Packing the Commission

At the first Trump-Biden presidential debate, moderator Chris Wallace asked Biden, "Are you willing to tell the American people tonight whether or not you will support . . . packing the court?" Biden lamely ducked the question, saying, "Whatever position I take on that, that will become the issue. The issue is the American people should speak. You should go out and vote." He wanted people to vote, but he refused to tell them what they were voting *for*.

After his inauguration, President Biden created a supposedly bipartisan commission to make recommendations about reforms to the judiciary. The commission would report to the president in roughly six months. To head the commission, Biden chose Bob Bauer, a career Democrat and Biden's former campaign lawyer.

One of the first members Bauer selected for the panel was Caroline Fredrickson, past president of the liberal American Constitution Society. She once said, "I often point out to people who aren't lawyers that the Supreme Court is not defined as [a] 'nine-person body' in the Constitution, and it has changed size many times."[209]

The panel consists of 36 members. Four members are conservatives or libertarians, included to prop up the claim that the commission is bipartisan. The other members tilt way to the left. A bipartisan commission with 32 leftists and 4 conservatives seems designed to arrive at a predetermined conclusion. Did Bauer pack the commission to steamroll any dissent from the four conservatives?

As the *Wall Street Journal* observed, "The threat of court-packing is intended to make the [Supreme Court] Justices think twice about rulings that progressives dislike. . . . The Biden commission has more than a whiff of the executive branch telling the judicial branch how to do its job."[210]

Do you think the fix might be in? So do I.

Who Stole the Courts?

Former Senator Russ Feingold, president of the far-left American Constitution Society, once said, "There's a real understanding that the courts have been stolen by the right."[211] And Aaron Belkin, director of Take Back the Court, said, "The entire agenda of what needs to get done is in jeopardy thanks to stolen federal courts. We know that court expansion is the only strategy to allow the administration to solve the problems facing the country."[212]

What's this? Someone *stole* the courts? When did this happen?

The fact is, it never happened. Nobody stole the courts. Donald Trump was elected president, and he filled vacancies on the courts.

Barack Obama appointed 55 federal appeals court judges during his two terms in office. He left office with more than a hundred federal court vacancies unfilled, including 17 seats on the appeals courts and one Supreme Court seat. The Obama administration felt no urgency about filling those vacancies. After all, the polls showed that Hillary Clinton would win handily over that upstart real-estate-developer-turned-reality-show-star. Hillary's administration would become Barack Obama's third term, and the court vacancies would be filled with Progressive judges soon enough.

But Hillary lost—and elections have consequences. President Donald Trump proceeded to fill the vacancies left by his predecessor. Trump appointed 234 federal judges, including 3 Supreme Court justices and 54 federal appeals court judges (almost as many in four years as Obama appointed in eight). Democrats must accept blame because, as *Bloomberg Law* observed, "Neither the

White House nor Senate Democrats moved quickly enough to fill vacancies during the Obama years."[213]

Democrats also can blame the late Justice Ruth Bader Ginsburg. Following repeated battles with cancer, she resisted pleas from Democratic leaders that she retire. She remained on the bench until her death at age 87 during the final year of the Trump administration.

Some Progressives claim Senate Majority Leader Mitch McConnell stole a Supreme Court seat after the death in 2016 of Justice Antonin Scalia. McConnell blocked confirmation of Barack Obama's nominee, Merrick Garland, saying that it was an election year and the next Supreme Court justice should be chosen by the new president (President Trump later chose Neil Gorsuch for that vacancy).

The left cried foul again in 2020, another election year, when Ruth Bader Ginsburg died and President Trump nominated Amy Coney Barrett to replace her. McConnell supported the Barrett nomination, making a subtle distinction that during the Garland confirmation process, the Senate and White House were controlled by different parties while during the Barrett confirmation, the Senate and White House were both controlled by the same party.

But the simple reason McConnell could block the confirmation of Merrick Garland and facilitate the confirmation of Amy Coney Barrett is that the Constitution and rules of the Senate allowed it. When a Supreme Court vacancy opens up, a president has a constitutional right to nominate a replacement justice—and the Senate has a constitutional right to withhold consent. That's not stealing the courts. That's playing by the rules.

Those same rules are still in place, and Republicans are currently at a disadvantage. Not only did the Republicans lose the

White House, but they lost control of the Senate. Again, elections have consequences.

When Progressives openly claim that the federal courts have somehow been stolen by the Republicans, you can bet they'll go to any lengths to steal it back. Their plan to steal back the Supreme Court: a return to FDR's court-packing scheme.

Recruiting Activist Judges

Progressives have a plan to radicalize the rest of the federal court system under the guise of diversity. For this purpose, they've invented a new category of diversity: *professional diversity.* On December 22, 2020, incoming White House Counsel Dana Remus sent a letter to Democratic senators asking them to recommend judicial nominees who are diverse not merely in the usual categories of race, religion, gender, and disability but also diverse in the area of law they practice.

"With respect to U.S. District Court positions," Remus wrote, "we are particularly focused on nominating individuals whose legal experiences have been historically underrepresented on the federal bench, including those who are public defenders, civil rights and legal aid attorneys, and those who represent Americans in every walk of life."[214] In other words, the Biden-Harris administration is eager to recruit activists to the federal bench.

In contrast to President Trump, who released his list of likely Supreme Court nominees before he was elected, Joe Biden has refused to name names. A conservative organization called the "Article III Project" studied the lists of candidates being proposed by Progressive groups, especially a far-left organization called "Demand Justice." And CNN Supreme Court reporter Ariane de Vogue also published a list of likely Biden court nominees.[215]

Let's look at some of the names on these two lists, beginning with candidates promoted by the radical "dark money" group Demand Justice, headed by former Hillary Clinton Press Secretary Brian Fallon. (*Dark money* is political spending by nonprofit organizations that are not required to disclose their donors; they can funnel unlimited funds to influence elections without accountability to voters.)

Demand Justice, a project of the hard-left Sixteen Thirty Fund, spent millions fighting Brett Kavanaugh's Supreme Court confirmation and attacking his reputation and was involved in a smear campaign against DC Circuit Court Judge David Griffith.[216] The homepage of the Demand Justice website (demandjustice.org) states, "The Supreme Court is broken. We can restore balance by adding seats." And the "About Us" page says, "Why we fight: The Supreme Court has been hijacked and democracy is at stake." Demand Justice–approved nominees include:

- Xavier Becerra, former attorney general of California, an implacable foe of the unborn who sued the Trump administration 62 times over illegal immigration, sanctuary cities, the border wall, the census, abortion policy, and more. His referral from Demand Justice undoubtedly helped him land his current gig as secretary of Health and Human Services.
- Brigitte Amiri, deputy director of the ACLU Reproductive Freedom Project and one of the leading pro-abortion attorneys in the nation. As an ACLU lawyer, she has aggressively sued the Little Sisters of the Poor and assorted Catholic hospitals.
- James Forman, Jr., a Yale Law School professor who canceled class so that his students could protest the Brett

Kavanaugh nomination. Forman delivered the U.C. Irivine
Fall 2017 Distinguished Critical Race Theory Lecture and
an address at the Critical Race Theory Conference at UCLA
Law School in 2010.

- Melissa Murray, an NYU School of Law professor, a Yale
  Law School grad who also taught at U.C. Berkeley, special-
  izing in reproductive rights and social justice issues. She
  once told an interviewer (speaking of motherhoood), "You're
  a host. I can't be more plain than that. You are a host."[217]
  In other words, to Murray, an unborn human being is a
  parasite.

- Judge Cornelia "Nina" Pillard, a DC circuit judge and one
  of the few Demand Justice selections who is a real sitting
  judge. (Sitting judges leave a trail of decisions that can derail
  Senate confirmation; law professors and advocacy attorneys
  are harder to scrutinize.) A legal expert who knew Pillard for
  more than a quarter century described her as "the most left-
  wing judge in the history of the Republic."[218]

- Zephyr Rain Teachout, Fordham Law School professor. In
  the fall of 2011, Teachout joined the anarchist Occupy Wall
  Street movement in Manhattan, participating in the nightly
  General Assemblies, the Spokes Council administrative
  body, and the Occupy Wall Street Activist Legal Working
  Group.[219] In 2018, Teachout ran unsuccessfully for New
  York state attorney general, endorsed by the *New York Times*.
  She pledged to prosecute President Trump for corruption
  and force him to divest his business holdings. Teachout
  was so strident that she drew a rebuke from left-of-center
  political scientist Brendan Nyhan, who tweeted: "Democrats
  should not rationalize Zephyr Teachout's behavior—what if

the [New York attorney general] was a Republican who ran on investigating President Hillary Clinton? We must not go down this road. The powers of prosecutors are vast and easily abused."[220]

- Sherrilyn Ifill, NAACP Legal Defense and Educational Fund president and former chair of the board of George Soros's Open Society Foundations. She is a proponent of racial quotas and wants to force police officers to attend critical race theory–based anti-bias training.[221] In one of her books, she acknowledges the influence of Derrick Bell, the originator of critical race theory, on her thinking.[222]

- Pamela S. Karlan, Stanford Law School professor. When Justice David Souter retired in 2009, Progressives wanted President Obama to nominate Karlan. Obama thought she was too extreme and picked Sonia Sotomayor instead. Karlan believes the Constitution should *evolve*. Her testimony at the first Trump impeachment hearing caused an uproar: "While the president can name his son Barron, he can't make him a baron." She was forced to apologize for dragging the president's 13-year-old son into the proceedings—though it was an obnoxious apology: "I wish to apologize for what I said earlier about the president's son. It was wrong of me to do that. I wish the president would apologize, obviously, for the things that he's done that's wrong."[223] Fun fact: The Trump-deranged Karlan once crossed the street rather than walk past the Trump International Hotel in Washington, DC.[224]

Here are some other names on Biden's short list of radical activist jurists (some you will recognize; others you should watch for in coming months): U.S. District Court Judge Ketanji Brown Jackson; U.S. District Court Judge J. Michelle Childs; Stacey Abrams (after losing her 2018 race for governor of Georgia which she has not conceded and claims was stolen, she led the successful 2021 effort to flip Georgia's two Senate seats from Republican to Democrat); U.S. District Court Judge Leslie Abrams Gardner (sister of Stacey Abrams); Professor Leah Litman; ACLU attorney Rochelle Garza; California Supreme Court Justice Leondra Reid Kruger; Professor Melissa Murray; Professor Suzette Malveaux; Deepak Gupta (reportedly the only private-practice attorney on Biden's list); Cheri Beasley (chief justice of the Supreme Court of North Carolina); and Dale Ho (director of the ACLU's Voting Rights Project).

A Critical Race Critique

If we could take a deep dive into the writings and thoughts of these Progressive jurists, we would find the pervasive presence of critical race theory. This destructive movement originated in the mid-1970s in the writings of Harvard Law Professor Derrick Bell. Over the decades, critical race theory came to dominate the nation's law schools and then quietly infiltrated American higher education. From there, it spread unseen like a cancer on America.

Critical race theory now dominates all the strongholds of American society—academia, the news media, the entertainment media, social media platforms, and the government. It has even made deep inroads into the military, public schools, the corporate world, and Catholic and Protestant Christianity. But critical race theory is most dominant where it began—in the legal community.

Critical race theory is a Marxist framework that examines the law as it impacts race relations, social issues, and political power. It teaches that the great institutions of Western civilization, including the U.S. Constitution and our system of laws, are founded on "white supremacy." This all-pervasive system of white supremacy maintains its power through the law. To achieve racial equity for oppressed races and other oppressed groups (such as LGBTQ+ people), systems of white supremacy and white privilege must be torn down.

Advocates of critical race theory have rejected Martin Luther King's vision of a colorblind society, trading it for a "get even" society of endless racial grievance and revenge. Critical race theory rejects Western values of evidence, reason, objective truth, the nuclear family, and achievement through hard work, claiming that these are tools of oppression. James Lindsay, a liberal university professor and leading critic of the woke radical movement, described eight reasons why critical race theory is a failed approach to ending racism:

Critical Race Theory . . .

- believes racism is present in every aspect of life, every relationship, and every interaction and therefore has its advocates look for it everywhere.
- relies upon "interest convergence" (white people only give black people opportunities and freedoms when it is also in their own interests) and therefore doesn't trust any attempt to make racism better.
- is against free societies and wants to dismantle them and replace them with something its advocates control.
- only treats race issues as "socially constructed groups," so there are no individuals in Critical Race Theory.
- believes science, reason, and evidence are a "white" way of knowing and that storytelling and lived experience are a

"black" alternative, which hurts everyone, especially black people.

- rejects all potential alternatives, like colorblindness, as forms of racism, making itself the only allowable game in town (which is totalitarian).
- acts like anyone who disagrees with it must do so for racist and white supremacist reasons, even if those people are black (which is also totalitarian).
- cannot be satisfied, so it becomes a kind of activist black hole that threatens to destroy everything it is introduced into.[225]

Scientific theories explain reality in ways that can be confirmed by evidence and logic. But critical race theory has more in common with a fanatical religion than a scientific theory. It has creeds and dogmas that no one may question. Anyone who disagrees is a heretic. Whiteness is its original sin. White supremacy is its devil and the all-encompassing explanation for society's ills. If a white person denies being a racist (especially by claiming to be color-blind), the denial is seen as proof of racism. Your only hope of salvation is to confess that you are a racist and convert to becoming an anti-racist (as defined by critical race theory). But don't expect forgiveness, even if you convert. You are condemned by the color of your skin.

The Origin of "Wokeness"

Is racism still a problem in twenty-first-century America? Yes. Do blacks face greater challenges than other Americans in employment, education, and interactions with the police? Tragically, yes—and we need to keep working to solve those problems. But is it fair to say that America, our founding documents, and our economic system are based on white supremacy? Is it fair to say that white people are incurable racists because of the color of their skin? Absolutely not. Racism is a cancer, but you cure cancer with a surgeon's scalpel, not a shotgun.

Critical race theory claims that victims of white oppression have been lulled into a false consciousness. They are so enmeshed in the systemically racist culture that they don't know they are victims. This idea derives from Marxism. Karl Marx predicted that oppressed workers would throw off their chains and revolt against their oppressors. When the workers' revolution didn't happen, Marxist thinkers of the 1930s, led by Herbert Marcuse of the Frankfurt School of philosophy, put forth the notion that the oppressed masses suffered from false consciousness.

Forty years later, Derrick Bell at Harvard took the class-based critical theory of Herbert Marcuse, inserted race in place of class as the basis of oppression, and critical race theory was born. In critical race theory, people of color are so enmeshed in the white supremacist culture that they don't know they're oppressed. To revolt against their oppressors, they must achieve *critical consciousness*. They must become woke.

Derrick Bell's "Wild Tangent"

Black conservative economist Thomas Sowell, senior fellow at the Hoover Institution at Stanford, recalled a long conversation with Derrick Bell in the 1980s. He found Bell's views very troubling. Sowell said:

> There is this ideological intolerance that Bell has. While he's fighting against the whites, ostensibly, he's also fighting against those blacks who don't agree with him. He really has

a sort of totalitarian mindset. . . . He's not a stupid man. But you have to understand, Derrick Bell was put in an impossible position. He was hired as a full professor at Harvard Law School when he himself said that [he was not qualified].[226]

Sowell recounted that when Bell came to Stanford Law School as a visiting professor, his lectures were so unsatisfactory that students complained that they weren't getting anything out of his constitutional law course. So, without telling Bell, Stanford created a parallel series of lectures to give students what Professor Bell's course lacked.

Bell knew he was out of his depth. He couldn't earn the respect of his Harvard Law colleagues and students with his lackluster credentials. So he chose a different path to win respect. He decided to (as Sowell put it) pursue a "wild tangent of his own, and appeal to a radical racial constituency on campus and beyond." That wild tangent was critical race theory.

Sowell found Bell's writings on critical race theory to be filled with "an extremist hostility to white people." Sowell was familiar with Bell's earlier writings and found them to be the ideas of "a sensible man saying sensible things about civil rights issues." But after inventing critical race theory, Bell began writing "all sorts of incoherent speculations and pronouncements, the main drift of which was that white people were the cause of black people's problems."[227]

Today we are living with the consequences of Derrick Bell's wild tangent, the product of his racial hostility and intellectual inadequacy (which Bell himself admitted). Black Lives Matter is the political and organizational bulwark of that wild tangent. The woke anti-white radicalism in the media, academia, and leftist politics is the viral infection of that wild tangent. The protests, riots, and looting of the 2020 "Summer of Rage" are the predictable outcome of that wild tangent. And the list of radical jurists on President Joe Biden's desk is a roster of lawyers and scholars immersed in Derrick Bell's wild tangent.

Derrick Bell's original idea has spread like a cancer until it now threatens the existence of the United States. This is why you and I must take a stand for a sane, colorblind society. In the final pages of this book, we'll discuss what we can all do to make a difference.

17

The American Media
Disgrace, Part 1

PRESIDENT BIDEN HELD AN informal press briefing on Monday, January 25, 2021. Questioning of the president was carefully managed by Biden's handlers. After Biden's opening remarks, a White House staffer called on specific reporters from the AP, NBC, Reuters, the *Washington Post*—all reliable allies of the Democrats.

As White House aides were about to shoo reporters out of the room, Biden spotted Peter Doocy of Fox News and said, "Wait, wait, wait. I know he always asks me tough questions, and [they] always have an edge to them, but I like him anyway. So go ahead and ask the question." Fair and polite as always, Doocy asked Biden to explain two seemingly contradictory statements about the COVID-19 pandemic.[228]

Notice that President Biden singled Doocy out for asking tough questions with an edge to them. Isn't that what *all* reporters are supposed to do? The press certainly asked plenty of tough, even insulting, questions during the Trump era. But at noon on Inauguration Day 2021, the entire White House press corps retracted its fangs and became all warm and cuddly toward the White House—with the sole exception of polite-but-earnest Peter Doocy.

The difference between President Trump's relationship with the press and President Biden's was the subject of a number of tweets by reporters at the briefing. Real Clear News reporter Philip Wegmann tweeted, "A White House handler is calling on reporters by name and by outlet one-by-one to ask Biden a question, unlike Trump who called on reporters as the [spirit] moved him." And Joe Concha, columnist for *The Hill*, tweeted, "This continues to be profoundly odd and a painfully obvious attempt to protect him [Biden] from those suspected of having the audacity to ask a challenging question."

It's ironic that President Trump, who had the most adversarial press coverage in history, was the most *media-accessible* president in American history. Meanwhile, Biden gets the most glowing coverage of any president in American history—yet his handlers stage-manage his rare appearances with paranoid vigilance. What are they so afraid of?

Publicists and Propagandists

In June 2020, President Trump delivered the commencement address at the U.S. Military Academy at West Point. After the speech, he walked down a ramp in a manner that some in the media described as slow or unsteady. Reporters seized on that scene to suggest that President Trump was in ill-health, and they hammered the narrative relentlessly. Candidate Joe Biden also piled on, mocking, "Look at how he steps, and look how I step. Watch how I run up ramps and he stumbles down ramps."[229]

President Trump didn't stumble or fall. He simply stepped with care down a ramp without a handrail—yet the biased, Trump-deranged media were all too eager to turn the incident into a full-blown presidential health crisis. CNN's resident spin doctor, Dr. Sanjay Gupta (who is a neurologist), told Alisyn Camerota, "I talked to a bunch of neurologists over the weekend, a lot of people talking about this. People always have something to say and weighing in on this."[230] In short, he delivered a word salad designed to *imply* that a bunch of neurologists were concerned for the president, but upon examination, Gupta's words don't actually mean anything.

Fast-forward to February 9, 2021. President Joe Biden is climbing the steps to *Air Force One*—and he stumbles, catching himself with the help of the handrail. Then he continues on up the steps. Are reporters worried about President Biden's neurologic or physical health at age 78? Not at all! If Biden trips, it just makes him more relatable. In fact, CBS White House reporter Kathryn Watson (@kathrynw5) was so eager to cover for Biden that she tweeted, "I'm glad no one is filming me constantly because I trip over my own shoes on a regular basis."

On March 19, Biden again stumbled on the steps to *Air Force One*—this time falling *three times*, the final time landing painfully on both knees. Compare CNN's headlines of the Trump-on-the-ramp story and the Biden-on-his-knees story: June 15, 2020: "Why the Donald Trump West Point Ramp Story Actually Matters," and March 19, 2021: "White House Says Biden Is '100% Fine' after He Tripped Boarding Air Force One."

The difference in coverage is easy to explain: The media views Trump as an enemy to be destroyed. But journalists view Biden as one of their own, so they shield him from criticism.

Case in point: MSNBC's Stephanie Ruhle and her sycophantic interview with Jared Bernstein of Biden's Council of Economic Advisers on January 15, 2021. The subject was Biden's $1.9 trillion COVID-19 stimulus plan. Ruhle allowed Bernstein to deliver a long, uninterrupted infomercial for the Biden plan. At the end of the segment, Bernstein thanked Ruhle for the softball interview.

"Your help has been extremely important," Bernstein said, "because not only have you continued to amplify some of the things that we're trying to do here, but you've been in the weeds and you've talked about the very policies that have been knocking around for a long time and that we finally have been able to get together and put into a plan. So I want to thank you for your advocacy as well." Did you catch that? "I want to thank you for your *advocacy*."

Any true journalist should be ashamed to be publicly thanked for shilling for the politicians he or she is supposed to cover. But not Stephanie Ruhle. She gushed, "Well, Jared, if you're going to compliment me, there's always more time for that in our show. We're going to continue to cover this. Do you know why? Because policy matters. That's how people's lives change." (By the way, that interview is posted on the MSNBC website—but the chummy exchange at the end is edited out.)

People in the news media view themselves as part of the same team as Joe Biden and his administration. They're not *covering* the Biden White House. They're *flacking* for it. They're not an independent press. They're publicists and propagandists.

A Crisis of Media Bias

Recent Gallup polls show that the American press has squandered the trust and respect of the American people. An August 2020 poll conducted by Gallup and the Knight Foundation revealed that 86 percent of Americans believe that media outlets are politically biased (37 percent say there's "a fair amount" of bias; 49 percent say "a great deal" of bias). The poll found that 73 percent of Americans see biased reporting as a "major problem" (an increase from 65 percent in 2017). Most significant of all, 84 percent agree that "the media [are] to blame for political division in this country."[231]

Another Gallup poll, released in December 2020, found that 40 percent of Americans trust the media (9 percent say they have a "great deal" of trust; 31 percent have a "fair amount" of trust). Fully 60 percent of Americans distrust the media (33 percent have "no trust at all," and 27 percent have "not very much" trust).[232]

In March 2021, Judge Laurence Silberman delivered a minority opinion in a federal appeals case—an opinion that has a lot do with the crisis of media bias in our nation. Silberman was nominated by President Ronald Reagan to the U.S. Court of Appeals in 1985 and has been short-listed as a potential Supreme Court nominee three times, so he's an intellectual heavyweight. His opinion matters. He delivered his minority opinion in a libel case involving officials from the African nation of Liberia who claimed that an American media company had falsely accused them of taking bribes. In his partial dissent, Judge Silberman argued that the Supreme Court's 1964 *New York Times v. Sullivan* decision had expanded the power of the media in a dangerous direction. He wrote:

There can be no doubt that the *New York Times* case has increased the power of the media. . . . The increased power of the press is so dangerous today because we are very close to one-party control of these institutions. Our court was once concerned about the institutional consolidation of the press leading to a "bland and homogeneous" marketplace of ideas. . . . It turns out that *ideological* consolidation of the press (helped along by economic consolidation) is the far greater threat. . . .

Two of the three most influential papers (at least historically), the *New York Times* and the *Washington Post*, are virtually Democratic Party broadsheets. And the news section of the *Wall Street Journal* leans in the same direction. . . . Nearly all television—network and cable—is a Democratic Party trumpet. Even the government-supported National Public Radio follows along.

As has become apparent, Silicon Valley also has an enormous influence over the distribution of news. And it similarly filters news delivery in ways favorable to the Democratic Party. . . . Ideological homogeneity in the media—or in the channels of information distribution—risks repressing certain ideas from the public consciousness just as surely as if access were restricted by the government. . . .

The first step taken by any potential authoritarian or dictatorial regime is to gain control of communications, particularly the delivery of news. It is fair to conclude, therefore, that one-party control of the press and media is a threat to a viable democracy. It may even give rise to countervailing extremism. The First Amendment guarantees a free press to foster a vibrant trade in ideas. But a biased press can distort the marketplace. And when the media has proven its willingness—if not eagerness—to so distort, it is a profound mistake to stand by unjustified legal rules that serve only to enhance the press' power.[233]

Judge Laurence Silberman summed it up well. This is the disgraceful—and dangerous—state of American journalism in the twenty-first century.

No Ifs, Ands, or Buts

On Inauguration Day, President Joe Biden stood before a bank of flat screens for a virtual swearing-in ceremony of the White House staff. He told the staffers via Zoom:

> I am not joking when I say this. If you are ever working with me and I hear you treat another colleague with disrespect . . . talk down to someone, I promise you I will fire you on the spot. On the spot. No ifs, ands, or buts. Everybody . . . everybody is entitled to be treated with decency and dignity. That's been missing in a big way the last four years.[234]

That same day, January 20, 2021, White House Deputy Press Secretary T. J. Ducklo put President Biden's warning to the test. Ducklo was romantically involved with Axios political reporter Alexi McCammond, who had been covering the Biden campaign. Such relationships pose a conflict of interest by undermining a reporter's appearance of fairness. The Ducklo-McCammond relationship, while an open secret in Beltway media gossip circles, had received no publicity. But it was about to.

On Inauguration Day, January 20, a male writer for Politico left a message for Ducklo saying that Politico was running a story on Ducklo and McCammond and asking if Ducklo wanted to comment. After hearing the message, Ducklo called a Politico editor, hoping to quash the story. The editor told Ducklo to call the reporter who had left the message. But Ducklo didn't do that. He had a different plan.

Ducklo apparently learned from Alexi McCammond that she had been contacted about the story by a female Politico reporter, Tara Palmeri. So Ducklo called Palmeri and told her he wanted to talk to her off the record, setting a ground rule that nothing he said was for publication and that his name couldn't be used. Once Palmeri agreed, Ducklo proceeded to threaten her, demanding she kill the story. "I will destroy you," he said, adding that he would ruin her reputation if the story was published. His threats were laced with offensive language, misogynistic insults, and demeaning accusations. As Ducklo ranted, Palmeri took notes.

The next day, after Palmeri disclosed the conversation to her editors, Politico contacted the White House to discuss Ducklo's threats. It was day two of the Biden-Harris administration, and senior White House officials were facing their first scandal. Press Secretary Jen Psaki, Communications Director Kate Bedingfield, and Senior Advisor Anita Dunn agreed that Ducklo was out of line. They promised Politico that Ducklo would send Palmeri a note of apology.

Wait—a note of apology? What happened to Biden's promise to fire you on the spot?

It gets worse. Psaki, Bedingfield, and Dunn accused Palmeri of wrongdoing by breaking her off-the-record agreement with Ducklo. But first, Palmeri did not write about the incident itself, and second, the subject of a story doesn't get to cry foul when off the record is invoked to conceal threats and abusive behavior.

(Ironically, Alexi McCammond was well aware of this principle. After interviewing retired NBA star Charles Barkley in 2019, she broke their off-the-record agreement when Barkley reportedly told her, "I don't hit women, but if I did, I would hit you.")

Politico asked Ducklo and McCammond for comment in late January—then sat on the story for weeks. On February 8, in order to get ahead of the Politico piece, Duklo and McCammond pre-emptively leaked their relationship to *People* magazine, which published a breezy puff piece on the Ducklo-McCammond relationship, full of sunshiny quotes from the happy couple. The *People* piece knocked the wind out of the Politico piece, which appeared the following day.[235] If the Trump administration had made a similar play to undermine a Politico story, the media hue and cry would have been deafening. But no one in the media uttered a word of complaint about the White House arrangement with *People*.

Failing the Test

On February 12, *Vanity Fair* broke the story about Ducklo's threatening call to Palmeri. That same day, Jen Psaki tried to lay the matter to rest, announcing that Ducklo had apologized to Palmeri. With approval from White House Chief of Staff Ron Klain, Psaki had placed Ducklo on a one-week unpaid suspension. "In addition," Psaki added, "when he returns, he will no longer be assigned to work with any reporters at Politico."[236]

What was that again? He'll no longer talk to *any* reporters at Politico? You might think the White House was punishing Ducklo and doing Politico a favor. In reality, the White House gave Ducklo a tap on the wrist while *punishing* Politico with lack of access.

Stories erupted in the *Washington Post* and *New York Magazine*, on Fox News and CNN, and elsewhere asking why President Biden hadn't carried out his promise to fire offenders on the spot. In the midst of the uproar, Jen Psaki held a press briefing in which a reporter asked, "Was the president involved in this discussion at all?" Psaki replied, "No, I have not discussed it with the president. It was a decision I made, and with the approval of the chief of staff."[237]

That statement set off alarm bells in my mind. Psaki had not discussed the Ducklo matter with President Biden? The incident had occurred on January 20, and this was February 12, more than three weeks later. Ducklo was not some underling—he had been the top press official in Biden's campaign and was the number two person in the White House press office. Yet Jen Psaki and Chief of Staff Ron Klain had kept the president completely out of the loop?

On Saturday morning, February 13, T. J. Ducklo resigned. I honestly feel bad for him. I know first hand what it is like to screw up very publicly and ask for forgiveness. He's in treatment for stage IV cancer, he made an embarrassing mistake that made headlines, and he said some awful things he wishes he could take back. Plus, in March, his girlfriend, Alexi McCammond, accepted a new job as *Teen Vogue*'s editor in chief, only to resign days later when some racially insensitive tweets she had made in 2011 (when she was only 17) resurfaced on social media. It's been quite a fall from grace for this Washington press corps power couple. I certainly don't excuse Ducklo's abusive behavior toward the Politico reporter—but I don't want to kick him when he's down.

The important take-away from the Ducklo-McCammond fiasco is not criticism of T. J. Ducklo or Jen Psaki. What we should learn from this incident is that the Biden-Harris administration, in its first ethical test, fumbled a fairly minor crisis. President Biden was kept in the dark about the scandal. His promise to fire anyone who broke his rules—on the spot, no ifs, ands, or buts—was ignored. And someone made a very poor decision to punish Politico instead of the real offender, T. J. Ducklo.

So we have to wonder: What will the Biden-Harris White House do when a *real* calamity rears its head? Who will make the decision? And will anyone tell the president?

18

The American Media
Disgrace, Part 2

IN JANUARY 2017, DAYS before Trump's inauguration, CNN ran a lurid story from the infamous (and discredited) Steele dossier featuring a bizarre claim that Trump had hired prostitutes to pee on a hotel bed that President Obama had once slept in. It was the kind of preposterous nonsense no grownup but James Comey would believe. In fact, former FBI Director Comey revived the fake story for his April 2018 book tour, prompting CNN to rehash the story 77 times in a five-day period, according to the Media Research Center.[238]

The Trump presidency was dogged by fake stories about Trump-Russia collusion. In December 2017, Brian Ross of ABC News reported a false Russian collusion story that spread like a prairie fire and sent the stock market tumbling. The story was proved false, and Ross's blunder ended his career at ABC News. Over at CNN, Brian Stelter peddled Russia conspiracy theories like this one: "Trump's odd behavior with Vladimir Putin is compelling so many people to ask: 'What does Putin have on Trump? Has Trump been compromised?' All of those people, those experts, those reporters, they are looking at the fact pattern and seeing something strange, even sinister."[239]

All the fake news of the Trump era could fill several books: CNN's Don Lemon accusing Trump of treason, MSNBC's Lawrence O'Donnell claiming to have evidence of Trump business loans cosigned by Russian oligarchs, and many reporters (including Joy Reid of MSNBC, Boris Sanchez of CNN, and Tom Costello of NBC) twisting Trump's words to claim that he had called the COVID-19 pandemic a hoax.[240]

President Trump used to rile up the members of the White House press corps by labeling them fake news. He struck a sensitive nerve with the press because he was right—and they knew it. They weren't just sloppy at their jobs. They were consciously shaping a fake narrative by editing out important facts, inserting insinuations and outright lies, and churning out an endless stream of propaganda around the narrative that President Trump was unfit for office.

The once-great *Washington Post* covered itself in shame with its January 9, 2021, story on President Trump's December 23 phone call to the Georgia elections investigation chief. The story contained fabricated quotations, surrounded by quotation marks, attributed to President Trump. Those fake quotations were used by House Democrats as part of their impeachment case. Two months later, the Georgia secretary of state released a recording of the call, and the *Post* was forced to correct its story—after the damage was done.[241]

I remember when the *Washington Post* adopted its pompous slogan, "Democracy Dies in Darkness," in February 2017, one month after the Trump inauguration. We have to wonder: If democracy dies in darkness, why does the *Post* keep pulling down the shade?

Bad News from the Border

One huge story the *Washington Post* lowered the shade on is the Biden border crisis. On March 15, 2021, as the border was being overrun by migrants from Mexico, Central America, Haiti, and other parts of the world, the *Post* ran a story headlined, "Migrants Are Not Overrunning US Border Towns, Despite the Political Rhetoric."

This is a straight news story, not an opinion piece, and it opens, "The way many Republicans describe it, President Biden has thrown open the border between Mexico and the United States so that anyone who wants to come into the country can do so, illegally or legally." The writer quoted Congressman Steve Scalise as saying that President Biden had "sent a message around South and Central America that our border is open."

The reporter must have had a hard time finding a highly placed official to contradict Republican claims. The only person quoted for an opposing view was a Hidalgo County judge, who said, "There's no open borders here. The border is shut down to most everyone."[242]

Even though the *Washington Post* was unable to find border towns overrun by migrants, other news outlets had no problem finding towns in crisis. For example, the *New York Times* talked to Don McLaughlin, Jr., mayor of Uvalde, Texas (population 16,000). "I would call it a crisis with an exclamation point," McLaughlin said. "We changed administrations, we changed the policies and it's like the floodgates have opened."[243]

The *Washington Examiner* talked to Bruno Lozano, the Democratic mayor of Del Rio, Texas (population 36,000). Lozano is furious with the Biden-Harris administration for turning a blind eye to the crisis in the border towns. His message to President Biden: "You're going to sit here and do a catch and release for unlawful entry that's not contributing to my local taxes, but you won't let persons that have a legal visa in Mexico, who just want to come to the United States and shop or visit their families, because of COVID-19 restrictions."[244]

And the Associated Press went to Gila Bend, Arizona (population 2,000), where Mayor Chris Riggs declared a state of emergency over the influx of migrant families. The town has no shelter or hospital; yet federal agents brought six families to Gila Bend, dropped them off at a park, and drove away. "I've got nothing here . . . nowhere to put them," Riggs said. "Literally, they'd be sleeping at the park, and I'm not going to do that to little children." So the mayor and his wife borrowed vans and drove the families to a shelter in Phoenix, 60 miles away.[245]

The migrant crisis in the border towns was easy for those other news organizations to find, but the *Washington Post* declared all this crisis talk to be mere political rhetoric. The crisis is real, but the *Post* just lowered the shade and refused to look.

Even though the Associated Press reported on the crisis at Gila Bend, the news organization has warned reporters not to use the word *crisis*. AP Vice President John Daniszewski sent a memo to staffers that they were to follow the Biden-Harris administration's lead in denying there was a crisis at the border. Daniszewski's memo, titled, "From the Standards Center: A Note About the Current Increase in Border Entrances," urged AP writers to use "accurate and neutral language." The situation at the border is "problematic" for border agents, a "political challenge" for Biden, and even a "dire situation" for the migrants—but "it does not fit the classic dictionary definition of a crisis." I can't help noting that the AP was not so prissy about the classic dictionary definition of a crisis during the previous administration.[246]

The Media Misplaces the Blame

Three months into his presidency, President Biden had a full-blown humanitarian disaster on his hands: Thousands of children jammed into holding facilities built to house a few hundred, all sleeping on gym mats with foil sheets, many coughing and with no social distancing, going days without showers or exercising outdoors. The Biden-Harris administration tried to hide these horrors from the American people, but photos leaked out. Those photos made the so-called kids in cages narrative from prior administrations seem like a day at Disneyland.

Clearly, Joe Biden's lax immigration policies were like the Pied Piper, luring thousands of migrant children to America. But who did the mainstream media blame for the crisis? At CNN, on March 15, reporter Lucy Kafanov was eager to assure viewers that this crisis was not Joe Biden's fault, saying, "There's no denying that this is an incredibly complex humanitarian issue that's, of course, made even more difficult by the fact that we're dealing with this in the midst of a pandemic." The same day, over at MSNBC, host Kasie Hunt said, "Obviously, this is a problem that the Biden-Harris administration inherited from the Trump administration."[247] Oh, obviously.

When Donald Trump was in the White House, reporters blamed border problems on Donald Trump. Now that Joe Biden is president, reporters still blame Trump. At least they're consistent.

Clearly, this crisis belongs 100 percent to President Joe Biden. He promised throughout the campaign to reverse President Trump's border policies—and he delivered on that promise on day one. Word spread throughout Latin America that the border was open—and people came in droves.

On March 21, 2021, ABC News *This Week* aired correspondent Martha Radditz's report from Casa Alitas, a Catholic shelter in Tucson. One man had come from Brazil with his wife and three children. Radditz asked him, "Would you have tried to do this [cross the border] when Donald Trump was president?"

"Definitely not," the man replied. "We had the chance, you know. The same violence that's going on [in Brazil] today was there last year."

"So," Radditz said, "did you come here because Joe Biden was elected president?"

"Basically. Basically," the man said. "The main thing was the violence in my country. And the second thing I think was Joe Biden."[248]

The "Cheat Sheet" Press Conference

On March 25, 2021, a record-setting 64 days after his inauguration, Joe Biden finally held his first solo press conference. Three days before the press conference, *Washington Post* scribe Margaret Sullivan (who has called for Fox News to be defunded and abolished[249]) warned the White House press corps to go easy on old Joe and avoid focusing on that awkward little problem at the border. Journalists, she said, should resist the "temptation to play to the crowd . . . just to show how tough we are."[250]

She needn't have worried. The White House press corps was as docile as a basket of kittens.

President Biden seemed to be working from a prepared script, using a cheat sheet with photos and names of journalists that were numbered in the order they were to be called. Back in the day, when he was the chair of the Senate Foreign Relations Committee, Joe Biden was famed for his encyclopedic knowledge of global events. At this press conference, however, he was reduced to reading his answers verbatim from his notes.

The first reporter in line was Zeke Miller of the Associated Press. He tossed Biden a Nerf-ball question: How did Biden plan to "deliver on your promise to Americans on issues like immigration reform, gun control, voting rights, climate change" in the face of "stiff united opposition from Republicans?"

The second questioner, the partially taxpayer-financed Yamiche Alcindor of PBS, was even more fawning and dewy-eyed, attributing the crisis at the border *not* to Biden's chaotic messaging and immigration policies (which is the truth) but to "the perception of you that got you elected as a moral decent man," and that is "why a lot of immigrants are coming to this country and entrusting you with unaccompanied minors."

Biden picked up the false premise and ran with it: "Well, look, I guess I should be flattered [that] people are coming because I'm the nice guy. That's the reason why it's happening, that I'm a decent man or however it's phrased, that's why they're coming, because they know Biden's a good guy."

He went on to blame his predecessor (of course) and to claim that the border crisis was merely the annual springtime surge of migrants (even though migrants have told reporters on camera that they are coming because of Biden's promises; many wear T-shirts with the Biden campaign logo and the words "Biden, please let us in!"). And while it's true that illegal immigration surges annually in the springtime, the surge traditionally comes in April and May, not February and March. The Biden border crisis is a direct response to the president's chaotic policies and rhetoric.

Biden's Big Malarky

The Biden press conference was a hot mess of evasions, distortions, unanswered questions, and outright lies. The worst lie Biden perpetrated was in response to a question from Cecilia Vega of ABC News. She told a story about a nine-year-old boy named Yossell who had walked to the United States from Honduras. Vega said the boy's mother told her that she sent Yossell to the United States because she believed (correctly) that Biden would not deport him.

During the Trump era, illegal immigrants, whether adults, families, or unaccompanied minors, were expelled from the country under the public health authority of Title 42 of the U.S. Code. The U.S. government would either fly the migrants to their home countries at taxpayer expense or deliver them safely to the Mexican government. But Joe Biden created an exemption to Title 42 that forbids the deportation of unaccompanied minors. And this is why little Yossell walked all the way from Honduras to Texas— because his mother correctly interpreted Joe Biden's immigration policy.

Under Trump, Yossell would have been flown back home to be reunited with his mother. But under Biden, he gets to be locked up in an overcrowded detention facility, alone and scared, separated from his family. In answering Cecilia Vega's question, Biden put up a verbal smokescreen to misdirect reporters and viewers from the cruel insanity of his policy toward minors. That was bad enough—but then he delivered the Big Malarky: "Look," he said, "the idea that I'm going to say—which I would never do—'if an unaccompanied child ends up at the border, we're just going to let him starve to death and stay on the other side'—no previous administration did that either, except Trump."

Wait, did he really say, "Except Trump"?

Yes, Joe Biden actually claimed that President Trump sent little children across the border to starve to death in the desert. Even if you are a never-Trumper, such a brazen. outrageous lie against your country and its government should make your blood boil.

But none of the reporters who were called on offered any pushback. And that's a disgrace.

Weird and Worrisome Moments

Asked about China, Biden launched into a lengthy story about his years-long relationship with Chairman Xi Jinping. To be fair, Biden laid out a fairly sound approach to China, saying:

> I made it clear to [Chairman Xi] . . . that we're not looking for confrontation, although we know there will be steep, steep competition. . . . We'll insist that China play by the international rules: fair competition, fair practices, fair trade. . . . I made it clear that no American President . . . [will] ever back down from speaking out on what's happening to the Uighurs, what's happening in Hong Kong, what's happening in country [by the way, I edited out one of Biden's many cheap shots at his predecessor].

Biden concluded:

> China has an overall goal, and I don't criticize them for the goal, but they have an overall goal to become the leading

country in the world, the wealthiest country in the world, and the most powerful country in the world. That's not going to happen on my watch because the United States are going to continue to grow and expand.

Biden hasn't always been that forceful on China—and the business dealings of his son Hunter in China make me doubt his sincerity. But I hope he carries through with this new tough approach.

Perhaps the most worrisome moment of the press conference came when a reporter asked President Biden about the filibuster. He seemed ready to knock this question out of the park. He began confidently, "I'm going to say something outrageous: I have never been particularly poor at calculating how to get things done in the United States Senate. So the best way to get something done, if you—[he paused, his expression changing from forceful to confused as he tripped over his words]—if you hold near and dear to you that you, um, like to be able to—[another pause]—anyway—[he looked down at the lectern for three embarrassing seconds and then finished lamely]—I, uh, we're ready to get a lot done."

Anyone can have a senior moment—but I worry about how President Biden's senior moment was received in Beijing and the Kremlin. It would be a mistake for conservatives to underestimate Joe Biden and his hard-left plan for America. And it would be dangerous for the world if our adversaries concluded that America had a weak or ineffectual leader in the Oval Office.

A Disgrace to the First Amendment

Biden didn't call on Emerald Robinson of Newsmax or Steve Doocy of Fox News. The 10 reporters he did call on never asked a truly hard-hitting question. No one asked him to explain why the nation's public schools aren't open (as the CDC guidelines say they should be), why he nixed the Keystone XL Pipeline (killing good union jobs), or what he thinks of statehood for the District of Columbia. There was not a single question about COVID-19, not one about a pandemic that the entire globe is dealing with. CNN's Chief White House Correspondent Kaitlin Collins did, however, ask three questions about whether he would seek reelection. Way to go CNN. The White House press corps gave Biden a pass—and at times a big smooch—for simply not being Donald Trump.

President Biden's first official press conference is emblematic of his entire relationship with our dysfunctional media. The First Amendment says, "Congress shall make no law . . . abridging the freedom of speech, or of the press." Why is freedom of the press important? Because a free press is supposed to hold our leaders accountable. The behavior of the White House press corps, since Inauguration Day, and especially at Biden's first press conference, is a disgrace to the First Amendment and a disservice to the American people.

As Americans and as consumers of the news, we deserve better—and we must *demand* better.

19

The Future
of the Nation

O<small>N</small> M<small>ARCH</small> 2, 2021, President Joe Biden held a secret after-noon meeting with liberal historians in the East Room of the White House. The president and the invited scholars sat around a long table. Opening a black-covered notebook, Biden jotted down thoughts as the historians told him who, among Biden's White House predecessors, they most admired and why.

Among the liberal historians present were Jon Meacham (author of the Pulitzer Prize–winning *American Lion: Andrew Jackson in the White House*), Michael Beschloss (far-left author of nine books on the presidency), Michael Eric Dyson (biographer of figures ranging from Malcolm X to Barack Obama), Yale historian Joanne B. Freeman (an expert on Alexander Hamilton), Princeton historian Eddie Glaude, Jr. (a *Huffington Post* contributor with a focus on

African American studies), Harvard historian Annette Gordon-Reed (author of *Thomas Jefferson and Sally Hemings: An American Controversy*), Walter Isaacson (author of biographies on Leonardo da Vinci, Benjamin Franklin, and Steve Jobs), and Doris Kearns Goodwin (biographer of Lyndon Johnson, the Kennedys, and Abraham Lincoln).

No conservative historians were present. The eminent David Pryce-Jones could have offered a wise counterweight to the leftist bias in the room—but he wasn't invited. Richard Brookhiser could have offered an alternative view of Hamilton—but he wasn't invited either. The brilliant classicist Victor Davis Hanson—an expert on why empires rise and fall—could have warned against the debt and inflation consequences of massive spending projects—but he, too, was uninvited.

Why does it matter if a historian is liberal or conservative? Aren't historical facts simply a matter of record? Do the political leanings of a historian have any impact on his or her view of history? They certainly do.

When historians rank the best and worst presidents, both liberals and conservatives generally agree that the top two presidents of all time were Washington and Lincoln. Washington invented the presidency as we know it today. Lincoln used the power of the presidency to hold the Union together.

But beyond Washington and Lincoln, liberal historians and conservative historians divide sharply on their views of presidents and the presidency. Liberal historians tend to favor presidents like Theodore Roosevelt, Woodrow Wilson, and Franklin D. Roosevelt. Why? Because they all constructed imperial presidencies that expanded the intrusive role of "Big Government" in our lives. Never mind that Teddy Roosevelt was an interventionist and an imperialist, that Woodrow Wilson imposed segregation on a racially integrated U.S. military and expanded federal police powers, or that FDR's New Deal programs delayed America's recovery from the Great Depression. Liberal historians love presidents who make Big Government even bigger.

Conservative historians prefer presidents like Calvin Coolidge and Ronald Reagan—presidents who reduced the size of government, who cut taxes and cut spending, and who, by doing so, expanded individual freedom and prosperity. And that's why no conservative historians were invited that day.

Go Big and Do It Now

According to some reports, Joe Biden appears to be thinking of his place in history—and that's why he seems hell bent on accomplishing big things in a big hurry. Mike Allen of Axios, who broke the story about Biden's secret meeting, called it a "discussion of how big is too big—and how fast is too fast—to jam through once-in-a-lifetime historic changes to America." Allen also called the secret meeting a "for-the-history-books marker of the think-big, go-big mentality that pervades his West Wing."

The historians reportedly told Biden exactly what he wanted to hear: Forget bipartisanship and playing by the rules. Now is the time to bulldoze anything that stands in your way, including such bipartisan niceties as the filibuster. Joe Biden, who ran for president as a bipartisan healer and a uniter, has unmasked himself as a sharply partisan, hard-left strongman president. Right now, his party has total control of the Congress—which could end with the midterm elections of 2022. So, during this two-year window of opportunity, he is ready to shove the levers of government as far to the left as they will go.

And the leftist historians agreed: Go big, and do it *now.*

They confirmed Joe Biden's worst instincts, urging him to spend big, grow the size of government, expand the power of government, and become another FDR. As Axios observed, Joe Biden "loves the growing narrative that he's bolder and bigger-thinking than President Obama."

In that meeting, Michael Beschloss filled Biden's ears with the classic Progressive myth that FDR saved the nation from chaos and economic despair with his big-spending New Deal programs. So Joe Biden is determined to ram through Congress what Axios calls "a $5 trillion-plus overhaul of America, and vast changes to voting, immigration and inequality."[251] If achieving an FDR-sized legacy means wrecking the rules and traditions of the U.S. Senate, so be it. Joe Biden will pass his agenda without bipartisan compromise, without Republican votes, and without looking back.

The Fool the People Act

In the weeks following Joe Biden's inauguration, our nation began debating the so-called For the People Act, also known as H.R.1. I suggest calling it the "Fool the People Act" because it would chill speech, change and nationalize voting laws, and alter the enforcement of campaign finance laws in ways that would strongly favor the Democratic Party. This 791-page piece of legislation was originally introduced by Democratic Congressman John Sarbanes on January 3, 2019, as the first bill of the 116th Congress. The House passed H.R.1 on March 8, 2019, by a straight party-line vote, all Democrats, no Republicans. Senate Majority Leader Mitch McConnell blocked it from consideration in the then-Republican-controlled Senate.

The Democrats reintroduced it as H.R.1 and S.1 in the 117th Congress in March 2021. It passed the House on a near-party-line vote (Democratic representative Bennie Thompson of Mississippi joined Republicans, fearing the bill would eliminate majority-black congressional districts like his). The bill now goes to the evenly split Senate, where Vice President Harris holds the tie-breaking vote. But Senate Republicans can still block H.R.1/S.1 with the filibuster. The problem for the Republicans is that Democrats, including President Biden, are openly calling for the end of the filibuster. The problem for the Democrats is that Democratic Senators Joe Manchin of West Virginia and Kyrsten Sinema of Arizona have expressed opposition to ending the filibuster—at least for now.

A little over a month after Joe Biden's inauguration, Congressman Jim Jordan of Ohio was a guest on *Spicer & Co.* I told Congressman Jordan, "This H.R.1 bill scares me. The right to vote is the most sacred right of every American—and we're basically blowing up any requirement to ensure the integrity of the election."

Jordan said:

Sean, the left wants to cancel Newsmax, they want to cancel President Trump, and now they want to cancel fair elections. This bill nationalizes elections, nationalizes all the problems we saw in the last election. It's going to attack the First Amendment and disclose political donors so they can be harassed and canceled. It creates a speech czar at the Federal Election Commission. And maybe the most egregious thing is that it requires taxpayers to pay for elections. Think about it: People in western Ohio, which I represent, people in rural Georgia, people in east Texas will have their tax dollars used to re-elect Chuck Schumer, Nancy Pelosi, and Alexandria Ocasio-Cortez and the Squad. That's just wrong.

Ironically, Democrats are trying to blow up the very democracy their party is named after. Let's look at the hidden provisions of the deceptively named For the People Act, H.R.1, so that we can better understand how Democrats plan to impose permanent one-party rule on all Americans.

H.R.1 and the Speech Czar

On February 9, 2021, nine former commissioners of the Federal Election Commission (FEC) sent a letter to congressional leaders urging Congress not to pass the For the People Act. These nine former commissioners were unanimous in saying that the bill would destroy the bipartisan character of the FEC and undermine public confidence in the commission.

The FEC is currently a bipartisan six-member commission with exclusive jurisdiction over the enforcement of campaign finance law. It was specifically designed to have an even number of members to prevent one party from taking control of the commission. In order for the FEC to issue a new rule or conduct an investigation, at least four members have to agree—and that means that there must be genuine bipartisan agreement. Democrats claim that the FEC is ineffective because votes are often a 50-50 partisan stalemate. But the even-numbered membership is the genius of the FEC because it forces members to make fair compromises and seek bipartisan consensus.

H.R.1 would change all that. The Democrats are pushing this bill now, while they control the White House and both houses of Congress, because they want to eliminate the bipartisan structure of the FEC, put themselves in charge, and use the FEC as a tool to achieve the election results they want. Instead of an occasional three-three stalemate vote, there would always be a three-two party-line split, with Democrats in the majority. According to H.R.1, the FEC would be led by the chair of the commission, hand-picked by the president.

Conservatives call this new role for the commission chair a "speech czar" because the chair would have an array of new and far-reaching powers, including the power to appoint and remove the general counsel and staff director and the power to issue subpoenas, compel testimony, and punish political speech. Currently, the FEC chair and vice chair must be from different parties, but under H.R.1, they can come from the *same* party—further concentrating power in the hands of the majority party.

Under H.R.1, the power of the general counsel is expanded so that he or she may launch an investigation and issue subpoenas without the bipartisan concurrence of commission members. H.R.1 concentrates all the power to find candidates guilty or innocent of campaign finance violations in the hands of one party. In effect, this legislation turns the FEC into a formidable weapon for partisan political advantage.

Even the ACLU Is Horrified

H.R.1 also contains disclosure requirements that would chill political speech. It would require organizations that make campaign disbursements of more than $10,000 in an election cycle to publish a list of donors who contributed $10,000 or more. In today's out-of-control cancel culture, you can imagine how that list would be used by political opponents. A *National Review* editorial cautioned:

New disclosure rules would treat huge amounts of speech and advertising on matters of public concern as if they were campaign contributions, including any advertisement urging viewers to contact elected officials to support or oppose a program, policy, or law. This would require donors to, say, the AARP to be identified as supporters of any candidate if the AARP demands that the candidate keep a promise to protect Social Security. The cumulative effect is to further burden citizen rights to petition and further insulate the government from criticism.[252]

The disclosure requirement is so scary that even the ACLU opposes it. In a letter to the House of Representatives, the ACLU's national political director and senior legislative counsels wrote, in part:

The American Civil Liberties Union, on behalf of its 3 million members, supporters and activists, opposes H.R.1 . . . in its current form, and urges you to vote "no" on final passage. . . . While some of our concerns have been addressed or mitigated since introduction, the bill, in its current form, would still unconstitutionally burden speech and associational rights. . . . We therefore urge you to vote "no" on final passage of H.R.1.[253]

For the first time in living memory, the Democrats have ignored the concerns of their long-time ally, the ACLU. Another Democratic constituency, however, will love H.R.1: trial attorneys. The anti–free speech provisions of H.R.1 will generate years of court-clogging litigation.

A Naked Power Grab

H.R.1 is a brazen assault on our democratic process. Currently, each state enacts and enforces its own election laws, and the federal government only intervenes to correct serious violations of voting rights. H.R.1 would abolish state control and federalize elections to a shocking degree. It would nullify the laws enacted by the 50 states, as well as bipartisan federal election laws passed in 1993 and 2002.

The bill bars states from confirming the identity of voters against a list of registered voters, requires Election Day voter registration, requires name and address changes on Election Day, and forbids states from treating these potentially fraudulent ballots as provisional ballots to be checked later. Clearly, Democrats want voter fraud to be easy to commit and impossible to detect.

The law requires states to provide online voter registration without safeguards against fraud and hacking. It requires automatic voter registration for anyone released from prison; anyone who applies for unemployment benefits, Medicaid, or Obamacare; and anyone who enrolls in college. In an op-ed for the *Daily Signal* on March 3, 2021, former Vice President Mike Pence warned:

> [H.R.1] would force states to adopt universal mail-in ballots, early voting, same-day voter registration, online voter registration, and automatic voter registration for any individual listed in state and federal government databases, such as the Department of Motor Vehicles and welfare offices, ensuring duplicate registrations and that millions of illegal immigrants are quickly registered to vote.
>
> States would be required to count every mail-in vote that arrives up to 10 days after Election Day. States must also

allow ballot harvesting—where paid political operatives collect absentee ballots from places such as nursing homes—exposing our most vulnerable voters to coercion and increasing the risk that their ballots will be tampered with.

At the same time, state and local election officials would be stripped of their ability to maintain the accuracy of voter rolls, barred from verifying voter eligibility, and voter IDs would be banned from coast to coast.[254]

That's right, the bill bans voter ID requirements. You just show up at the poll on Election Day and make a sworn statement that you are who you claim to be (say you're Mickey Mouse, if you like, and the poll worker *must* let you vote). The bill makes permanent the vast use of mail-in voting that was supposedly a temporary measure during the COVID-19 pandemic (as Democrats love to say, "Never let a crisis go to waste"). States are forbidden to employ anti-fraud measures to secure the integrity of the vote.

And yes, ballot harvesting—currently a crime in almost every state—would become a protected practice under H.R.1. The bill also compels all 50 states to permit ballot drop boxes, curbside voting, and 15 days of early voting.

Since the founding of the United States of America, the drawing of congressional districts has been conducted by the legislatures of the individual states. H.R.1 would upend that tradition and put the responsibility in the hands of a so-called independent commission. Illegal immigrants would be counted and represented on the same basis as lawful U.S. citizens.

H.R.1, the "Fool the People Act," is an in-your-face attempt to politicize the currently nonpolitical Federal Election Commission and to weaponize it to establish perpetual one-party rule. It's a naked power grab by a political machine that has shown itself willing to discard any tradition, break any rule, and ignore any constitutional safeguard to crush the opposition. And the people who brought you H.R.1 have even bigger power grabs planned for the future.

It's up to all of us—both our elected leaders and We the People—to stop those plans and defend our Republic from this assault.

A State Called DC?

Another assault on our nation's future is the Democrats' push to make the District of Columbia a state. The people who live in DC pay taxes but have no voting representatives, so one of the slogans for DC statehood is "No taxation without representation." Susan Rice, President Biden's director of the Domestic Policy Council, has even said that DC statehood would end "the enduring oppression of the citizens of the District of Columbia."[255]

Democrats argue DC statehood on the grounds of racial justice. Congresswoman Ayanna Pressley said:

> The state of Washington, DC, would be 46 percent black, which would make it the state with the highest percentage of black people in the entire country. . . . Uplifting black political power must be a part of the conversation. We cannot allow electoral justice for the people of Washington, DC, to be denied any longer. . . . I'm going to make it plain: DC statehood is a racial justice issue. And racism kills.[256]

Congresswoman Pressley is probably sincere, but she's also sincerely wrong. And her fellow Democrats don't see DC statehood as an issue of justice. They see it as an issue of raw political power.

In the 2020 presidential election, voters in the District of Columbia cast 92.2 percent of their votes for Biden-Harris and 5.4 percent for Trump-Pence. That incredibly lopsided result tells you all you need to know about the real motives of the Democrats. DC statehood would create a perpetually blue state and add two more U.S. senators to the Democratic column. This is why the issue has only partisan Democratic support. Both sides know what this is really all about—political power.

The framers of the Constitution intentionally set aside a special district to allow the federal government to operate independently. Article I, Section 8, Clause 17 of the Constitution explicitly provides for a "District (not exceeding ten Miles square) as may, by Cession of particular States, and the Acceptance of Congress, become the Seat of Government of the United States." The Founders believed that the seat of government should not be part of any state, nor should it be treated as a state. Instead, the seat of government should be located in a special district where legislators from every state could gather on neutral ground and conduct the people's business.

The Founding Fathers worried that if the seat of government were located in a state, that state would have too much influence over the federal government. They also worried that if the seat of government were its own state, the people there would vote to expand federal power. The framers explicitly made the seat of government a unique district, neither located within a state nor a state in its own right, when they ratified the Constitution in 1788. DC was formed by taking parts of Maryland and Virginia. As time went on, a chunk of land was given back to Virginia (which is why it is no longer a perfect square). If areas of DC are no longer needed as part of the federal government, then they should be given back to Maryland and Virginia, respectively.

Getting around the Constitution

DC statehood is plainly unconstitutional, full stop, period, right? Not so fast. The Democrats think they've figured a way around the framers' intent.

H.R.51, a 2019 bill passed by the House, gerrymanders the District of Columbia, isolating the Capitol, the White House, the Supreme Court, the National Mall, and other federal buildings as the seat of government. The surrounding neighborhoods of the District of Columbia would become a state. The advocates of this legislation point out that the framers of the Constitution set a maximum size for the district, not to exceed 10 miles square. They didn't say anything about a minimum size.

So the Democrats think they can carve out a new blue state without spending the time and trouble to amend the Constitution. Will they get away with it? Will the Supreme Court agree with their scheme?

It may depend on whether the case is decided by the nine Supreme Court justices we have today—or the unknown number of justices in Joe Biden's packed court.

What will that mean for the future of the nation? Stay tuned.

20

A Conservative Action Agenda

O<small>N</small> F<small>EBRUARY</small> 22, 2021, two House Democrats, Anna G. Eshoo and Jerry McNerney, both of California, wrote letters to the heads of a dozen cable TV and tech companies urging them to cancel three conservative-leaning TV networks: Newsmax, Fox News, and One America News Network (OANN). The letters went to AT&T, Amazon, Apple, Comcast, Verizon, Roku, Charter, Dish, Cox, Altice, Alphabet, and Hulu. It was an authoritarian power play by two politicians with no respect for the First Amendment.

Eshoo and McNerney blamed the three networks for inciting the Capitol riot on January 6, 2021, and for spreading misinformation about COVID-19. They demanded answers to a series of question designed to silence conservative speech, including:

What moral or ethical principles (including those related to journalistic integrity, violence, medical information, and public health) do you apply in deciding which channels to carry or when to take adverse actions against a channel? . . .

Do you require, through contracts or otherwise, that the channels you carry abide by any content guidelines? If so, please provide a copy of the guidelines. . . .

How many of your subscribers tuned in to Fox News, Newsmax, and OANN on [name of company] for each of the four weeks preceding the November 3, 2020, elections and the January 6, 2021, attacks on the Capitol? Please specify the number of subscribers that tuned in to each channel. . . .

Are you planning to continue carrying Fox News, Newsmax, and OANN on [name of company] both now and beyond any contract renewal date? If so, why?[257]

Do Eshoo and McNerney *really* think that Newsmax, Fox News, and OANN caused the Capitol breach or helped spread COVID-19? If so, shouldn't MSNBC and CNN and the other "alphabet networks" be deplatformed for spreading the Russia collusion hoax? Shouldn't those media outlets be canceled for encouraging the rioting, looting, and murder during the 2020 "Summer of Rage"? Shouldn't CNN anchor Chris Cuomo be canceled for supporting mob violence when he said, "Please, show me where it says protesters are supposed to be polite and peaceful"?[258] (Didn't he read in the First Amendment in law school that the people have the right to assemble "peaceably"?)

Shouldn't the Biden-Harris administration be canceled for undermining trust in the coronavirus vaccine? In September 2020, candidate Joe Biden and running mate Kamala Harris accused President Trump of dangerously rushing the approval process for the vaccine, prompting the Kaiser healthcare organization to headline its KHN Morning Briefing, "Biden Raises Fears Trump Will Rush Unsafe Vaccine for Political Gain."[259] An October 2020 CNN poll showed that the percentage of Americans willing to take the vaccine fell from 66 percent in May to 51 percent in October[260] as Biden and Harris stoked irrational fears. Shouldn't Eshoo and McNerney cancel them, too?

They're Coming for Your Rights

Brendan Carr, a member of the Federal Communications Commission, responded to the Eshoo-McNerney letters:

> The Democrats are sending a message that is as clear as it is troubling—these regulated entities will pay a price if the targeted newsrooms do not conform to Democrats' preferred political narratives. This is a chilling transgression of the free speech rights that every media outlet in this country enjoys.
>
> Debate on matters of public interest should be robust, uninhibited, and wide open. More speech is better than less. Yet the concerted effort by Democrats to drive political dissent from the public square represents a marked departure from these First Amendment norms.[261]

On February 24, two days after the Democrats' poison-pen letters went out, the House Energy and Commerce Committee held a hearing on disinformation and extremism in right-wing media. Democratic Congressman Mike Doyle of Pennsylvania seemed to have Brendan Carr's statement ("More speech is better than less") in mind when he said, "More free speech just isn't winning the day over the kind of speech that we're concerned about."[262] With that statement, Doyle tipped his hand. He and the other Democrats on the committee planned to suppress speech they disapproved of.

The Democrats devised a clever ruse for targeting conservative speech. Democratic Chairman Frank Pallone, Jr., said, "We're all staunch defenders of the First Amendment and its mandate that 'Congress make no law abridging the freedom of speech, or of the press.' The First Amendment prohibits us from passing laws that inappropriately limit speech—even when it is controversial or overly partisan." So far, so good, then: "But that does not mean that we should ignore the spread of misinformation that causes public harm."[263]

That's the catch. By defining conservative speech as "misinformation that causes public harm," Democrats plan to cancel Newsmax, Fox News, and OANN. At no time in the hearing did any witness or committee member demonstrate a cause-and-effect relationship between specific content on those networks and any public harm. They simply stated that the breach of the Capitol happened and people died from the coronavirus, and then they blamed conservative networks without offering any evidence.

Anti-freedom momentum is building on the radical left and in the shadowy recesses of "Big Tech." We saw it beginning when Twitter censored President Trump's tweets and when Twitter and Facebook banned President Trump from their platforms. Following the Capitol riots, Apple, Google, and Amazon simultaneously deplatformed Parler, a social media app popular among conservatives. The tech giants claimed that rioters used Parler to coordinate with each other during the Capitol breach (arresting documents indicate that rioters preferred Facebook).

It sounds like a bizarre conspiracy theory, but it's literally true: The Democrats are coming for your First Amendment rights.

Radical Struggle Sessions

In September 2020, the Trump administration instructed government agencies to end federal employee indoctrination programs based on critical race theory. A memo from Office of Management and Budget Director Russell Vought banned programs that teach "(1) that the United States is an inherently racist or evil country or (2) that any race or ethnicity is inherently racist or evil."[264] On his inauguration, Joe Biden reinstated those indoctrination programs.

The anti-racism indoctrination business is booming. Robin DiAngelo wrote the textbook for many of these programs, *White Fragility*. Here's a sample: "I believe that the white collective fundamentally hates blackness for what it reminds us of: that we are capable and guilty of perpetrating immeasurable harm and that our gains come through the subjugation of others. We have a particular hatred for 'uppity' blacks, those who dare step out of their place and look us in the eye as equals."[265] DiAngelo has reportedly made more than $2 million from the sale of this neo-racist drivel, plus she charges corporations such as Levi's, Amazon, and Goldman Sachs $30,000 to $40,000 to conduct a single corporate "training" session.

These sessions have replaced old notions of multiculturalism and diversity with divisive accusations of privilege and equity. These training sessions are much like the "struggle sessions" conducted by the Chinese Communist Party under Mao, which used public humiliation, verbal abuse, accusations of wrong attitudes, and obligatory confessions to impose the ideology. Even the socialist magazine *Jacobin* warns against these training sessions:

> Anti-racism trainings—particularly of the "white fragility" sort—demand access to workers' thoughts and feelings on highly charged topics, usually in the presence of their supervisors, and evaluate those workers' responses, often with the explicit goal of generating discomfort. No wonder, then, that they often backfire.[266]

If you work in a corporate or government environment, you will probably be subjected to this abusive training. You don't have to accept it. The next few pages will provide an action agenda to help you stand against Progressive pressure and help you fight the Biden-Harris assault on our rights, our faith, our economy, and our American way of life.

1. Fight Back against Cancel Culture

In George Orwell's *Nineteen Eighty-Four*, the totalitarian regime invented a language, Newspeak, to control the people's thinking. In Newspeak, a person executed by the government was not just dead but an "unperson," completely erased from memory. This is the goal of today's cancel culture—to erase all opponents from memory.

If you oppose the woke radicals, you will not merely be criticized. They will destroy your reputation and force you out of your career. Your social media accounts may be terminated. It is already happening to people in business, academia, government, and the media.

Culture critic Helen Pluckrose created a website to help people deal with "critical social justice" (including critical race theory) in the workplace. The website, CounterweightSupport.com, offers resources to protect you from wokeness in the workplace. It offers resources for both employers and employees, including videos, talking points, mental health resources, and example letters you can use to opt out of mandatory training sessions. Counterweight promotes individual rights, viewpoint diversity, and the free exchange of ideas.

If you're a student or faculty member whose free speech rights have been attacked, visit the nonpartisan Foundation for Individual Rights in Education (FIRE) website at TheFIRE.org. You'll find news, media, student and faculty rights materials, a FIRE speakers' database, a First Amendment library, and a contact page for submitting your case for assistance.

If you need legal representation to protect your constitutional rights, you can turn to the Pacific Legal Foundation (PLF) at PacificLegal .org. PLF is a nonprofit organization that represents Americans free of charge against government overreach.

The Goldwater Institute at GoldwaterInstitute.org seeks "to defend and strengthen the freedom guaranteed to all Americans in the constitutions of the United States and all fifty states." Established in 1988, the Goldwater Institute maintains a litigation service, the Scharf-Norton Center for Constitutional Litigation, that defends civil liberties against government abuse.

The website CriticalRace.org, created by conservative Cornell Law School Professor William Jacobson, seeks to educate parents and students about critical race theory indoctrination on campus. The website features a database of more than 200 colleges and universities that promote critical race theory.

2. Hold Big Tech Accountable

Ryan Anderson is president of the Ethics and Public Policy Center, a conservative think tank. He is also the author of the 2018 book, *When Harry Became Sally: Responding to the Transgender Moment*, which focuses on transgender issues and the surge in the number of girls seeking irreversible sex-reassignment procedures.

The *Washington Post* trashed the book in a review titled, "Ryan Anderson's Book Calling Transgender People Mentally Ill Is Creating an Uproar." The *Post* stated, "Anderson makes an inflammatory claim—that transgender people are mentally ill." Anderson contacted the *Post* and asked the editors to quote a single sentence from his book that called transgender people mentally ill. They couldn't—so the following day, the story appeared on the *Post* website, reheadlined and rewritten with the false claims deleted.

Fast-forward to 2021. Amazon.com, owned by Jeff Bezos (who also owns the *Washington Post*), quietly deleted *When Harry Became Sally* from its web pages. Later, when Republican senators asked Amazon to explain its book-banning decision, the company replied: "We have chosen not to sell books that frame LGBTQ+ identity as a mental illness."[267]

Unlike the *Washington Post*, Amazon refused to reconsider its position, even though Anderson's book makes no such claim. Amazon doesn't have to reconsider its position because, as a literary agent told the *Wall Street Journal*, "They own the system." As Anderson wrote in a *Wall Street Journal* op-ed:

> Why would Amazon exercise its unrivaled market power to banish my book? Because the book is changing minds in a continuing debate about how best to help patients who experience gender dysphoria. *When Harry Became Sally* has been

praised by medical and legal experts—and that's what makes it unacceptable to the woke. . . . No good comes from shutting down a debate about important matters on which reasonable people disagree.[268]

How can we, as conservatives and consumers, persuade Big Tech companies to respect the free exchange of ideas? Well, we can get vocal. When you see a company attack free speech, write to the CEO and chairman of the board. Be courteous and respectful, never insulting. Let the company know that you are committed to free speech. Be concise, and make sure that your facts are correct. Speak out on social media about constitutional and moral principles.

Should Private Companies Obey the First Amendment?

Big Tech platforms like Amazon, Twitter, and Facebook will tell you that they don't have to obey the First Amendment. Unlike the government, they are free to censor speech they disapprove of. And that's true—Big Tech isn't bound by the First Amendment. But a basic respect for the free exchange of ideas is essential to a free society. Once our institutions adopt the notion that they can cancel speech and individuals they dislike, even our First Amendment protections against *government* censorship begin to erode. Soon, members of Congress begin calling for networks like Newsmax to be canceled. It has to stop.

One of my favorite statements about book banning came from a February 25, 2021, tweet by biotech entrepreneur Vivek Ramaswamy (@VivekGRamaswamy), founder of Roivant Sciences. He tweeted, "Name *one* time in human history when the group fighting to ban books and censor speech were the good guys. I'll wait." Let's urge Big Tech to be the good guys and permit free speech on their platforms.

Organize with other people who share your concerns and agree together to put pressure on companies that threaten free speech. You and your conservative friends may want to consider whether to continue using platforms like Facebook, Instagram, and Twitter. There are other social media services that are friendlier to conservative voices. On the other hand, you may want to remain on the mainstream platforms so that you can continue to influence your leftist friends.

Making your voice heard, holding corporations accountable— these are small actions, but they are not insignificant, especially if you join with other conservatives. Corporate Progressivism didn't become this arrogant and abusive overnight. It will take time and effort to make a difference. But if everyone reading this book will write one email or blog post or tweet per day, or even per week, we can influence Big Tech for the better.

3. Hold Companies Accountable on China

Communist China engages in human slavery, genocide, and the brutal suppression of human rights. The regime lied about COVID-19 and unleashed a pandemic on the world. China cheats on international agreements, steals intellectual property, and is bent on world domination. Yet many U.S. companies bow the knee to China.

In 2019, the videogame company Blizzard removed a professional gamer from one of its tournaments, took away his prizes, and banned him from tournament play for a year. Why? Because he voiced support for the Hong Kong protest movement.[269]

That same year, Houston Rockets General Manager Daryl Morey tweeted support for Hong Kong protesters. The National Basketball Association issued a groveling apology to Communist China. Morey later issued an apology of his own, probably as a condition of keeping his job. It's a disgrace that an American citizen had to beg China's forgiveness for supporting democracy and freedom.[270]

Companies with a China Problem

Many U.S. companies are so enmeshed with Communist China that they now face a choice between supporting human rights and obeying a slaveholding regime. Disney, Nike, Apple, Microsoft, Google, LinkedIn, and many other U.S. companies have a serious China problem. We need to let these companies know that we are watching.

The Walt Disney Company has the biggest China problem of all. In 2020, Disney released its live-action film *Mulan*. In the closing credits, Disney gave special thanks to eight units of the Communist Party's Public Security Bureau, including the Xinjiang Public Security Bureau in Turpan—the agency that operates Uighur slave camps in Xinjiang. The U.S. State Department sanctioned that agency for human rights abuses a year before *Mulan*'s release. *Mulan* was partially filmed in Xinjiang, where Uighurs, Tibetans, Christians, and other minorities are imprisoned for counterrevolutionary thought. Disney also allowed Communist Party "consultants" to change the storyline of the movie to conform to Communist propaganda.[271]

Two of Disney's six theme park resorts are located in Communist China—one in Hong Kong and the other in Shanghai. Disney looks to China as a major source of revenue. But Disney's soft-on-genocide stance in the *Mulan* debacle, along with heightening tensions between the United States and the People's Republic of China, spells trouble ahead. American consumers must pressure Disney to choose human rights over blood-stained profits.

Disney's China problem skews the news we consume. Throughout the COVID-19 pandemic, Disney has shown a disturbing tendency to adhere to the Communist Party line. Compare and contrast two stories by two American news organizations about the origin of the COVID-19 pandemic.

On March 28, 2021, Leslie Stahl of the CBS News *60 Minutes* program did a thorough investigation into the badly misman-aged Wuhan Institute of Virology. The *60 Minutes* report made it clear that the COVID-19 virus almost certainly escaped from the Wuhan laboratory—and the Chinese government covered it up.[272]

Two days later, on March 30, Disney-owned ABC News ran its version of the same story—and came to the opposite conclusion. The ABC News story didn't even mention the Wuhan Institute of Virology by name but merely parroted the Communist Party's position that the laboratory accident scenario was extremely unlikely.[273] Why did CBS News and ABC News cover the same story so differently? Perhaps it's because Disney, ABC's parent company, owns theme parks in Communist China.

We need to let Disney's CEO and board of directors know that we expect Disney to stop supporting the genocidal regime of Communist China.

4. Get Up to Speed on Free-Market Economics

Joe Biden has launched a $5 trillion-plus transformation of America. What will such a massive infusion of government spending do to the American economy? Will it send inflation soaring? And what about the mountain of debt we are inflicting on our children and grandchildren?

I urge you to read four great books on free-market economics. Start with something short and simple: *Economics in One Lesson*, by Henry Hazlitt. Then proceed to *Basic Economics: A Common Sense Guide to the Economy*, by Thomas Sowell. Then advance to *Capitalism and Freedom*, by Milton Friedman, for an understanding of how capitalism promotes social progress and freedom. For a satisfying, enlightening, but more challenging read, tackle *The Road to Serfdom*, by Friedrich Hayek. These four books will make you an expert on free-market economics. Another place to educate yourself on free-market economics (and other conservative issues and values) is PragerU at PragerU. com, founded in 2009 by Allen Estrin and Dennis Prager. Search especially for these videos: *The Market Will Set You Free*, *Can the Government Run the Economy?*, and *Is Capitalism Moral?*

Once you understand economics, you can become an advocate for the free market in your everyday life—with your kids, with coworkers in the lunchroom, and through your engagement on social media.

5. Be Bold but Respectful in Defending Your Values

If you have Progressive friends and relatives, you know that they aren't shy about expressing their opinions on Facebook or over Thanksgiving dinner. They'll tell you exactly what they think of your political beliefs, your religious convictions, the news channels you watch—and never worry about offending you.

You don't have to start a fight with them. You can defend your beliefs, boldly but respectfully. When Progressives accuse conservatives of being bigoted people who lack compassion for the poor, calmly say, "That's a cartoon-villain stereotype of conservatives. We conservatives are full of compassion, and we show it through our acts of service to others and our generous donations to charities. We don't think it's compassionate to expand the welfare state and make generations of people dependent on government handouts. We believe in shrinking the size of government and lowering taxes to grow the economy, create jobs, and strengthen families."

Progressives are no match for a reasonable, well-informed conservative. We have the facts and moral principles on our side. We can point to the moments in history—under Calvin Coolidge, Ronald Reagan, and Donald Trump—when the government cut taxes, reduced spending and regulations, and prosperity exploded.

Don't let Progressives get away with the old canard that conservatives are selfish and bigoted. A strong economy is a compassionate economy. The best way to help the poor is by creating jobs. We want the best for every American, regardless of race, class, or religion—and we believe in principles of liberty and equality that make it possible for everyone to pursue the American dream.

6. Stay in Touch with Your Elected Representatives

Your calls and emails to your elected representatives make a difference. Become informed about the issues affecting your city, your county, your state, and your nation. Then contact your representatives at every level. Attend city council meetings and school board meetings. Encourage your friends to get involved as well.

Put the phone numbers of your elected representatives in your phone—then, instead of reading a year-old magazine in the waiting room of your doctor's office, use that time to call your representatives and influence your government. Sometimes elected officials will talk to you personally. But whether you talk to a legislator or an aide, you will make a difference. Your calls remind politicians that they must earn your vote every day.

Call to encourage your representatives when they do something right. They like to hear, "I support your position on that legislation. I know you're getting a lot of pressure, but hang in there. I'm praying for you. You're doing a great job." Your representatives will fight all the harder for conservative principles when they know that you have their back.

7. Defend Religious Liberty

The First Amendment doesn't *grant* you religious liberty. You are *endowed by your Creator* with the unalienable right to freely practice your religion and your conscience. The First Amendment requires the government to respect a right that is *naturally* yours and granted to you by God.

If the government infringes on your religious liberty, submit your case to an organization like the American Center for Law and Justice (ACLJ.org), the Becket Fund for Religious Liberty (BecketLaw.org), the Alliance Defending Freedom (ADFLegal .org), or First Liberty (FirstLiberty.org). Inform the media, tell your story on social media, and post it on YouTube. As you state your case, be as accurate, reasonable, and persuasive as possible.

Practice your faith by giving generously to religious organizations that serve the poor, such as Catholic Charities, Little Sisters of the Poor, the Salvation Army, and Samaritan's Purse. Dollar for dollar, these organizations do far more for the needy than the welfare state.

Pray for the healing of our nation. Pray for national repentance. Pray for our leaders, including the leaders of the Democratic Party. Pray for them to awaken to God's truth and to seek God's wisdom.

8. Defend Life

The right to life is not just a moral issue. It's a matter of scientific evidence. Those who say we should follow the science about climate change or the coronavirus often ignore what science tells us about the unborn. Medical science shows that a fetus can feel pain at 14 weeks' gestation and possibly as early as 8 weeks. We need to encourage people to follow the science as well as the moral and ethical pro-life argument. We need to make everyone aware that the Biden-Harris administration is the most radically pro-abortion, pro-infanticide administration in history.

Teach pro-life values to your adolescents and teenagers. Tell them that you'll always love them and that they can come to you with any problem, even an unplanned pregnancy, and that abortion is never the solution. Adoption is always an option, and there are great resources available from the National Council for Adoption at AdoptionCouncil.org. Encourage young people to get involved with a local 40 Days for Life group (learn more at 40DaysForLife .com, and find a local chapter at www.40DaysForLife.com/en/ vigil-search.aspx).

How is sex education taught at your children's school? Talk to teachers and principals. Attend school board meetings. Make sure that abstinence is positively and clearly presented to your student.

Support your local crisis pregnancy center with your time and donations (including baby clothes and maternity clothing). Pray for your nation, for legislators and judges, and for women with crisis pregnancies. Pray that those who work in abortion facilities will find their conscience and get out of this industry of death. Be active, vocal, and prayerful.

Visit 2ndVote at 2ndvote.com and learn which corporations support traditional Judeo-Christian values—and how to defund corporations that support abortion, critical race theory, Marxism, attacks on the Second Amendment, and more. The 2ndVote website says, "Your first vote is cast at the ballot box, hoping to make a difference. Your second vote is in the checkout line." At 2ndVote, you'll also learn why buying stock in companies that respect your values pays a higher return on investment. 2ndVote Advisers actually administers two funds (EGIS and LYFE) that only invest in non-woke companies.

9. Protect Your Children from Radical Indoctrination

President Biden's secretary of education, Miguel Cardona, implemented mandatory critical race theory courses in Connecticut high schools,[274] so you know that critical race training is coming to a public school near you. The education establishment has bought into the woke radical lie that America was founded on racism and slavery and that all the institutions of American society are designed to perpetuate white supremacy. Propaganda materials such as those produced by The 1619 Project are already being used to indoctrinate your children and grandchildren. How will you protect these impressionable young minds from a corrosive Progressive education?

You have options for educating your children—options that require a sacrifice of both time and money. One of the best things you can do for your children is to put them in a good private or parochial school. If you are a grandparent and you have the financial means, consider donating to send your grandchildren to a private school.

Another option, homeschooling, requires a major investment of time and energy and should only be undertaken if you have thoroughly studied what is involved. Consider starting a home-school co-op with other parents in your church or neighborhood. In a co-op, homeschooling families gather to provide educational and social activities. Each family contributes time and resources. Some homeschool co-ops pool resources to hire an experienced teacher.

Talk to local and state political candidates and ask them about their education priorities. We should be concerned not only about our own children but also about what our neighbors' children are learning about America. The riots during the summer of 2020 were a direct result of the lies fed to a generation of young people in public schools and universities. If we want our civilization to endure, we have stop the woke education agenda in its tracks.

Encourage your young people to get involved with Turning Point USA (TPUSA.com), founded in 2012 by Charlie Kirk to "educate, train, and organize students to promote freedom." Or invite them to join the Young Americas Foundation (YAF.org), founded in 1969 to ensure that "young Americans understand and are inspired by the ideas of individual freedom, a strong national defense, free enterprise, and traditional values." YAF owns and maintains Ronald Reagan's Santa Barbara, California, ranch, Rancho del Cielo.

10. Become a Skeptical News Consumer

On my Newsmax show, *Spicer & Co.*, my cohost, Lyndsay Keith, and I try to bring you the news the other networks won't talk about. We provide the curiosity the mainstream media lacks. We work hard to get our facts right every time—and if we make a mistake, we correct it. If you haven't watched the show, try it. You may find that it's more informative and entertaining than most of the news shows on the alphabet networks.

We all need to be skeptical news consumers. We need to fact-check most of what we see and hear in the news before making up our minds. We need to look for the bias, the spin, the hidden agenda, the missing information. And when we see biased reporting, whether on a local news channel or on a national network, we need to hold those news outlets accountable.

Contact the editors and respectfully explain why you found their coverage to be inaccurate or unfair. Write about it on social media—and be scrupulously honest in everything you write. Provide links and sources—and never pass along unconfirmed internet rumors (that's the fastest way to destroy your credibility). Within your circle of influence, help people learn how to spot bias and dishonesty in the news.

Get acquainted with the Media Research Center at MRC .org—America's most reliable media watchdog. Visit the MRC site, donate, and subscribe to MRC's informative newsletter, and you will quickly learn to spot bias and left-wing propaganda all around you.

Freedom Is a Fragile Thing

These are tough times for America and for the conservative movement. But you and I are tough people. The Biden-Harris administration is determined to impose a radical agenda on us all. Joe Biden, in his fixation on building an FDR-sized legacy, is determined to transform our "One Nation under God" into a dystopian "Radical Nation." The Biden-Harris administration is bent on violating our religious liberty, indoctrinating our children, opening our borders, and committing us to an uncertain windmills-and-sunshine energy future while spending America into bankruptcy.

Progressives are on offense now, and we are on defense. But there's always another election, and in the meantime, you and I have work to do. Our children and grandchildren are counting on us. As Ronald Reagan so wisely said, "Freedom is a fragile thing, and it's never more than one generation away from extinction. It is not ours by way of inheritance; it must be fought for and defended constantly by each generation, for it comes only once to a people."[275]

This is our time. This is our fight. We refuse to hand down a radical nation to our children and grandchildren. We are committed to leaving them the same heritage of liberty that was entrusted to us, the same Declaration of Independence and Constitution, the same free-market economic system, and the same faith in God. There's no guarantee that we will win, but I do guarantee this: You and I will keep fighting for our beliefs and our freedom.

God bless you in this righteous fight.

Notes

1 Jake Tapper, @jaketapper, Twitter.com, January 20, 2021, https://twitter.com/ jaketapper/status/1352035862121484291.
2 Alex Kalman, "The Letters That Outgoing Presidents Wrote to Their Successors," *The Atlantic*, November 14, 2020, https://www.theatlantic.com/culture/ archive/2020/11/letters-presidents-their-successors/617089/.
3 *Economist* Staff, "Orderly Transfers of Power Occur Less Often Than You Might Think," *The Economist*, October 16, 2020, https://www.economist.com/ graphic-detail/2020/10/16/orderly-transfers-of-power-occur-less-often-than -you-might-think.
4 Rachelle Hampton, "'I Think My Gmail Has Crashed': The Teacher Who Made Bernie Sanders' Mittens on Watching Them Go Viral," Slate.com, January 21, 2021, https://slate.com/human-interest/2021/01/bernie-sanders-inauguration -mittens-vermont-teacher-interview.html.
5 Daniel K. Hall-Flavin, "What Is Passive Aggressive Behavior? What Are Some of the Signs?," MayoClinic.org, https://www.mayoclinic.org/healthy-lifestyle/ adult-health/expert-answers/passive-aggressive-behavior/faq-20057901.
6 Jamie Ehrlich, "Maxine Waters Encourages Supporters to Harass Trump Administration Officials," CNN.com, June 25, 2018, https://www.cnn.com/ 2018/06/25/politics/maxine-waters-trump-officials/index.html.

7 Paul Crookston, "Booker Tells Activists to 'Get Up in the Face of Some Congresspeople,'" *Washington Free Beacon*, July 25, 2018, https://freebeacon.com/politics/booker-tells-activists-get-face-congresspeople/.

8 Douglas Ernst, "Nancy Pelosi Wonders Why There 'Aren't Uprisings' across Nation: 'Maybe There Will Be,'" *Washington Times*, June 14, 2018, https://www.washingtontimes.com/news/2018/jun/14/nancy-pelosi-wonders-why-there-arent-uprisings-acr/.

9 NBC News, *Meet the Press*, October 14, 2018, https://www.nbcnews.com/meet-the-press/meet-press-october-14-2018-n919956.

10 Jason Hancock, "'I Hope Trump Is Assassinated,' Missouri Lawmaker Writes—and Quickly Regrets," *Kansas City Star*, August 17, 2017, https://www.kansascity.com/news/politics-government/article167755572.html.

11 Veronica Stracqualursi, "Biden Says He Would 'Beat the Hell' Out of Trump If in High School," CNN.com, March 21, 2018, https://www.cnn.com/2018/03/21/politics/joe-biden-donald-trump/index.html.

12 NBC News Exit Poll Desk, "NBC News Exit Poll: Support for Trump Increased among Black and Hispanic Voters," NBCNews.com, January 6, 2021, https://www.nbcnews.com/politics/2020-election/live-blog/election-day-2020-live-updates-n1245892/ncrd1246327#blogHeader.

13 Joseph R. Biden, Jr., "Inaugural Address by President Joseph R. Biden, Jr.," WhiteHouse.gov, January 20, 2021, https://www.whitehouse.gov/briefing-room/speeches-remarks/2021/01/20/inaugural-address-by-president-joseph-r-biden-jr/.

14 Bernie Sanders (@BernieSanders), Twitter.com, February 3, 2016, https://twitter.com/BernieSanders/status/694967235333484544.

15 Daisy, "Equality and Equity," Social Change UK, March 29, 2019, https://social-change.co.uk/blog/2019-03-29-equality-and-equity.

16 Karl Marx, *Critique of the Gotha Programme* (1875), Marxists.org, https://www.marxists.org/archive/marx/works/1875/gotha/ch01.htm.

17 Bari Weiss, "The Self-Silencing Majority," *Deseret News*, March 2, 2021, https://www.deseret.com/indepth/2021/3/2/22309605/the-silenced-majority-bari-weiss-new-york-times-cancel-culture-free-speech-democrat-republican.

18 Ellie Bufkin, "Biden Faces Backlash over Vow to Prioritize Minority-Owned Businesses," KATV.com, January 12, 2021, https://katv.com/news/nation-world/biden-faces-backlash-over-vow-to-prioritize-minority-owned-businesses.

19 Nicolas Loris, "Staying in Paris Agreement Would Have Cost Families $20K," Heritage.org, November 5, 2019, https://www.heritage.org/environment/commentary/staying-paris-agreement-would-have-cost-families-20k.

20 *New York Times Magazine,* "The 1619 Project," NYTimes.com, August 14, 2019, https://www.nytimes.com/interactive/2019/08/14/magazine/1619-america-slavery.html.

21 Juliet Eilperin, Brady Dennis, and Darryl Fears, "Biden to Place Environmental Justice at Center of Sweeping Climate Plan," *Washington Post*, January 27, 2021, https://www.washingtonpost.com/climate-environment/2021/01/26/biden-environmental-justice-climate/.

22 Morgan Phillips, "Biden Has 'Bigger Issues' to Worry About Than Following Own Mask Mandate: Psaki," Fox News, January 21, 2021 (updated January 22, 2021), https://www.foxnews.com/politics/biden-bigger-issues-mask-mandate -psaki.

23 Abigail Shrier, "Joe Biden's First Day Began the End of Girls' Sports," *Wall Street Journal*, January 22, 2021, https://www.wsj.com/articles/joe-bidens-first -day-began-the-end-of-girls-sports-11611341066.

24 Editorial Board, "Ease Up on the Executive Actions, Joe," *New York Times*, January 27, 2021, https://www.nytimes.com/2021/01/27/opinion/biden -executive-orders.html.

25 Lawrence H. Summers, "Opinion: The Biden Stimulus Is Admirably Ambitious. But It Brings Some Big Risks, Too," *Washington Post*, February 4, 2021, https:// www.washingtonpost.com/opinions/2021/02/04/larry-summers-biden-covid -stimulus/.

26 Jeff Cox, "Raising Minimum Wage to $15 Would Cost 1.4 Million Jobs, CBO Says," CNBC.com, February 8, 2021, https://www.cnbc.com/2021/02/08/ raising-minimum-wage-to-15-would-cost-1point4-million-jobs-cbo-says.html.

27 Based on calculations using NerdWallet's Cost of Living Calculator at https:// www.nerdwallet.com/cost-of-living-calculator.

28 Andrew Kerr, "Democrats' $15 Minimum Wage Bill Would Eliminate 1.3 Million Jobs, CBO Finds," Daily Caller, July 8, 2019, https://dailycaller.com/ 2019/07/08/democrats-15-minimum-wage-bill-jobs-cbo/.

29 Thomas Catenacci, "Corporations That Support the $15 Minimum Wage Can Afford It. Here's Who Can't," Daily Caller, January 30, 2021, https://dailycaller .com/2021/01/30/corporations-minimum-wage-amazon-mcdonalds-national -federation-independent-business/.

30 Susan Collins, "Group of 10 Republican Senators Outline COVID-19 Relief Compromise, Request Meeting with President Biden," press release, January 31, 2021, https://www.collins.senate.gov/newsroom/group-10-republican-senators -outline-covid-19-relief-compromise-request-meeting-president.

31 The White House, "Statement by White House Press Secretary Jen Psaki on President Joe Biden and Vice President Kamala Harris' Meeting with Republican Senators," WhiteHouse.gov, February 1, 2021, https://www .whitehouse.gov/briefing-room/statements-releases/2021/02/01/statement-by -white-house-press-secretary-jen-psaki-on-president-joe-biden-and-vice -president-kamala-harris-meeting-with-republican-senators/.

32 Alexander Bolton and Amie Parnes, "GOP Says Ron Klain Pulling Biden Strings," *The Hill*, March 1, 2021, https://thehill.com/homenews/ administration/540782-gop-says-ron-klain-pulling-biden-strings?rl=1.

33 Air.TV, "Ron Klain on 'Covid Relief' Bill: 'Most Progressive Domestic Legislation in a Generation,'" Air.TV, February 27, 2021, https://www.air.tv/ watch?v=DbhKgCQKT6WyKQncmWW4-Q, embedded video.

34 NBC News, "Full Biden: I Would Be 'Most Progressive' President in History | Meet The Press | NBC News," YouTube.com, February 16, 2020, https:// www.youtube.com/watch?v=uOYcXsIKoyg, remarks begin at the 8:59 mark of the video.

35 GOP War Room, "Sen. Kamala Harris Compares ICE to the KKK," YouTube .com, November 15, 2018, https://www.youtube.com/watch?v=KM -4PROZkUM&t=197s.

36 Eugene Daniels, "Biden Makes Harris the Point Person on Immigration Issues amid Border Surge," Politico, March 24, 2021, https://www.politico.com/ news/2021/03/24/kamala-harris-immigration-border-surge-477810.

37 Lauren Egan and Mike Memoli, "Confusion Clouds Harris Immigration Role," NBC News, April 10, 2021, https://www.nbcnews.com/politics/white-house/ confusion-clouds-harris-immigration-role-n1263671.

38 Lia Eustachewich, "Man Twice Bailed Out by Kamala Harris-Backed Fund— Gets Arrested Again," New York Post, February 3, 2021, https://nypost.com/ 2021/02/03/man-twice-bailed-out-by-harris-supported-fund-arrested-again/.

39 Holly Honderich and Samanthi Dissanayake, "Kamala Harris: The Many Identities of the First Woman Vice-President," BBC News, November 7, 2020, https://www.bbc.com/news/election-us-2020-53728050.

40 Adam Cancryn and Carla Marinucci, "What Kamala Harris Believes: Key Issues, Policy Positions and Votes," Politico.com, August 11, 2020, https:// www.politico.com/news/2020/08/11/what-kamala-harris-believes-key-issues -positions-and-votes-393807.

41 GovTrack, "Vice President Kamala Harris," GovTrack.us, https://www.govtrack .us/congress/members/kamala_harris/412678; GovTrack, "Sen. Kamala Harris's 2020 Report Card," GovTrack.us, https://www.govtrack.us/congress/members/ kamala_harris/412678/report-card/2020.

42 Tim Levin, "'We Do Have Two Systems of Justice in America': Kamala Harris Slams Trump Administration's Denials of Systemic Racism," MSN.com, September 6, 2020, https://www.msn.com/en-us/news/politics/we-do-have -two-systems-of-justice-in-america-kamala-harris-slams-trump-administration -s-denials-of-systemic-racism/ar-BB18LvD8.

43 Jasmine Wright, "Demonstrators Say Public Safety Reimagined Is a Future without Police," CNN.com, June 21, 2020, https://www.cnn.com/2020/06/21/ us/demonstrators-reimagine-public-safety-without-police/index.html.

44 Steven Greenhut, "Kamala Harris Reimagines Herself as a 'Progressive Prosecutor,'" Orange County Register, July 5, 2019, https://www.ocregister.com/ 2019/07/05/kamala-harris-reimagines-herself-as-a-progressive-prosecutor/.

45 Lara Bazelon, "Kamala Harris Was Not a 'Progressive Prosecutor,'" New York Times, January 17, 2019, https://www.nytimes.com/2019/01/17/opinion/ kamala-harris-criminal-justice.html.

46 Molly Redden, "The Human Costs of Kamala Harris' War on Truancy," Huffington Post, March 27, 2019 (updated March 29, 2019), https:// www.huffpost.com/entry/kamala-harris-truancy-arrests-2020-progressive -prosecutor_n_5c995789e4b0f7bfa1b57d2e.

47 Breakfast Club Power 105.1 FM, "Kamala Harris Talks 2020 Presidential Run, Legalizing Marijuana, Criminal Justice Reform + More," YouTube.com, February 11, 2019, https://www.youtube.com/watch?v=Kh_wQUjeaTk.

48 Fox News, "Harris' Dad Slams His Daughter's Use of 'Identity Politics,'"
    YouTube.com, February 21, 2019, https://www.youtube.com/watch?v=qRqXK
    wwZ08I.

49 Kamala Harris (@KamalaHarris), tweeted on November 1, 2020, retweeted by
    Liz Cheney (@Liz_Cheney), https://twitter.com/liz_cheney/status/132301797
    3863428106?lang=en. Liz Cheney tweet by Tom Fitton (@TomFitton), https://
    twitter.com/TomFitton/status/1323068769950961664.

50 CNN Transcripts, "Jake Tapper Hosts Kamala Harris (D-CA) in Des Moines,
    IA," January 28, 2019, Transcripts.CNN.com, http://transcripts.cnn.com/
    TRANSCRIPTS/1901/28/se.01.html.

51 Oversight Hearing before the Subcommittee on Energy and Mineral Resources
    of the Committee on Natural Resources, U.S. House of Representatives,
    "Climate Change: Preparing for the Energy Transition," One Hundred
    Sixteenth Congress, First Session, Tuesday, February 12, 2019, https://www
    .govinfo.gov/content/pkg/CHRG-116hhrg35198/html/CHRG-116hhrg35198
    .htm.

52 Jason Lemon, "Kamala Harris Partners with Alexandria Ocasio-Cortez to
    Address Climate Equity as Senator Vies for Biden's VP Spot," *Newsweek*, August
    6, 2020, https://www.msn.com/en-us/news/politics/kamala-harris-partners
    -with-alexandria-ocasio-cortez-to-address-climate-equity-as-senator-vies-for
    -biden-s-vp-spot/ar-BB17EQzB.

53 Ibid.

54 Kipp Jones, "Biden and Harris Both Called for Mandatory Buyback of 20
    Million 'Assault Weapons,' Here's What Happens When People Obey,"
    Western Journal, March 25, 2021, https://www.westernjournal.com/biden-harris
    -called-mandatory-buyback-20-million-assault-weapons-happens-people-obey/.

55 Eric Boehm, "The *Washington Post* Tried to Memory-Hole Kamala Harris' Bad
    Joke about Inmates Begging for Food and Water," *Reason*, January 22, 2021,
    https://reason.com/2021/01/22/the-washington-post-memory-holed-kamala
    -harris-bad-joke-about-inmates-begging-for-food-and-water/.

56 Ibid.

57 Patrick Goodenough, "Leaked WH Memo Reportedly Tells Federal Agencies
    to Refer to 'Biden-Harris Administration,'" CNSNews, March 24, 2021,
    https://www.cnsnews.com/article/washington/patrick-goodenough/leaked-wh
    -memo-reportedly-tells-federal-agencies-refer-biden; Bradford Betz, "White
    House Lists 'Biden Harris Administration' on Official Website," Fox News,
    March 29, 2021, https://www.foxnews.com/politics/white-house-lists-biden
    -harris-administration-on-official-website.

58 Adam Kredo, "State Dept Spox: 'Largest Threat to U.S. National Security Are
    U.S. Cops,'" *Washington Free Beacon*, January 30, 2021, https://freebeacon.com/
    biden-administration/state-dept-spox-largest-threat-to-u-s-national-security-are
    -u-s-cops/.

59 Evie Fordham, "Biden State Department Spokesperson Jalina Porter Who Said
    Police Are 'Largest' National Security Threat Responds," Fox News, February 2,
    2021, https://www.foxnews.com/politics/biden-state-department-jalina-porter
    -police.

60   Steven Nelson, "Biden 'Proud' of Team after China Mocks US at Alaska Summit," *New York Post*, March 19, 2021, https://nypost.com/2021/03/19/biden-proud-of-team-after-china-mocks-us-at-alaska-summit/.

61   Jalina Porter, "Department Press Briefing—March 19, 2021," U.S. State Department, March 19, 2021, https://www.state.gov/briefings/department-press-briefing-march-19-2021/.

62   Bradford Betz, "Consulting Firm Linked to Biden's Cabinet Scrubs China Work from Website," Fox News, December 2, 2020, https://www.foxnews.com/politics/consulting-firm-biden-cabinet-scrubs-china-website; WestExec Advisors, Strategic Advisory Firm, "Managing China-Related Risk in an Era of Strategic Competition," Internet Archive Wayback Machine, page captured July 16, 2020, https://web.archive.org/web/20200716000825/https://westexec.com/.

63   Antony J. Blinken, Secretary of State, "Secretary Antony J. Blinken, National Security Advisor Jake Sullivan, Director Yang and State Councilor Wang at the Top of Their Meeting," U.S. State Department, March 18, 2021, https://www.state.gov/secretary-antony-j-blinken-national-security-advisor-jake-sullivan-chinese-director-of-the-office-of-the-central-commission-for-foreign-affairs-yang-jiechi-and-chinese-state-councilor-wang-yi-at-th/.

64   Tristan Justice, "No One Really Knows Where Susan Rice Stands on Domestic Policy. That Makes Her the Perfect Pick for VP," *The Federalist*, August 10, 2020, https://thefederalist.com/2020/08/10/no-one-really-knows-where-susan-rice-stands-on-domestic-policy-that-makes-her-the-perfect-pick-for-vp/.

65   Annie Karni, "Taking on a New Role, Susan Rice Is Asserting Herself," *New York Times*, March 5, 2021, https://www.nytimes.com/2021/03/05/us/politics/susan-rice-domestic-policy-council.html.

66   Eli Lake, "Top Obama Adviser Sought Names of Trump Associates in Intel," Bloomberg, April 3, 2017, https://www.bloomberg.com/opinion/articles/2017-04-03/top-obama-adviser-sought-names-of-trump-associates-in-intel.

67   Chuck Grassley and Lindsay Graham, "Grassley, Graham Uncover 'Unusual Email' Sent by Susan Rice to Herself on President Trump's Inauguration Day," Grassley.Senate.gov, February 12, 2018, https://www.grassley.senate.gov/news/news-releases/grassley-graham-uncover-unusual-email-sent-susan-rice-herself-president-trump-s.

68   Angelica Stabile, "Grenell: Susan Rice Will Be 'Shadow President' in Biden Administration," Fox News, January 17, 2021, https://www.foxnews.com/politics/grenell-susan-rice-shadow-president-biden-administration.

69   Steven Nelson, "Biden Picks Buttigieg for Transportation Secretary: Reports," *New York Post*, December 15, 2020, https://nypost.com/2020/12/15/biden-picks-buttigieg-for-transportation-secretary-reports/.

70   Mark Moore, "Team Biden Deletes Old Campaign Ad Criticizing Pete Buttigieg," *New York Post*, December 17, 2020, https://nypost.com/2020/12/17/team-biden-deletes-ad-blasting-buttigieg-after-cabinet-nomination/.

71   S222 Congressional Record—Senate, "CREC-2021-02-02-pt1-PgS222.pdf," February 2, 2021, https://www.congress.gov/117/crec/2021/02/02/CREC-2021-02-02-pt1-PgS222.pdf.

72 Jordan Liles, "Did Pete Buttigieg Stage a Bike Ride after Riding in SUV?," Snopes.com, April 3, 2021, https://www.snopes.com/fact-check/pete-buttigieg -bike-suv/.

73 Alex Pappas, "John Kerry Slammed for 'Shameful' Shadow Diplomacy after Admitting to Meetings with Iran," Fox News, September 13, 2018, https:// www.foxnews.com/politics/john-kerry-slammed-for-shameful-shadow -diplomacy-after-admitting-to-meetings-with-iran.

74 Sam Dorman, "John Kerry Took Private Jet to Iceland for Environmental Award, Called It 'Only Choice for Somebody like Me,'" Fox News, February 3, 2021, https://www.foxnews.com/politics/john-kerry-private-jet-iceland-climate -award.

75 Sam Dorman, "John Kerry Family Private Jet Emitted Estimated 116 Metric Tons of Carbon over Past Year," Fox News, January 29, 2021 (updated January 30, 2021), https://www.foxnews.com/politics/john-kerry-family-private-jet -emissions.

76 David Kamp, "Joe Biden on Having Few Assets, and Why He Wishes He'd Had a Republican Child," *Vanity Fair*, November 8, 2017, https://www.vanityfair.com/ culture/2017/11/joe-biden-book-assets.

77 Adam Entous, "Will Hunter Biden Jeopardize His Father's Campaign?," *The New Yorker*, July 8–15, 2019 issue, posted July 1, 2019, https://www.newyorker .com/magazine/2019/07/08/will-hunter-biden-jeopardize-his-fathers-campaign.

78 BBC, "Hunter Biden: What Was He Doing in Ukraine and China?," BBC News, December 10, 2020, https://www.bbc.com/news/world-54553132.

79 Brie Stimson, "Hunter Biden Got $83G per Month for Ukraine 'Ceremonial' Gig: Report," FoxNews.com, October 19, 2019, https://www.foxnews.com/ politics/hunter-biden-paid-80g-per-month-while-on-board-of-ukranian-gas -company-report; Emily Jacobs, "Hunter Biden Received $3.5M from Russian Billionaire: Report," NYPost.com, September 23, 2020, https://nypost.com/ 2020/09/23/hunter-biden-received-3-5m-from-russian-billionaire-report/; Mairead McArdle, "Hunter Biden Offered $10 Million Annually by Chinese Energy Firm for 'Introductions Alone,' Email Shows," MSN.com, October 15, 2020, https://www.msn.com/en-us/news/politics/hunter-biden-offered-2410 -million-annually-by-chinese-energy-firm-for-e2-80-98introductions-alone-e2 -80-99-email-shows/ar-BB1a3pj8; BBC, "Hunter Biden: What Was He Doing in Ukraine and China?," BBC News, December 10, 2020, https://www.bbc.com/ news/world-54553132.

80 Joe Biden, *Promises to Keep: On Life and Politics* (New York: Random House, 2007), 59.

81 Ben Schreckinger, "Biden Inc.," Politico.com, August 2, 2019, https://www .politico.com/magazine/story/2019/08/02/joe-biden-investigation-hunter -brother-hedge-fund-money-2020-campaign-227407/.

82 Ibid.

83 Ibid.

84 Ibid.

85 Ibid.

86 Adam Entous, "Will Hunter Biden Jeopardize His Father's Campaign?," *The New Yorker*, July 8–15, 2019 issue, posted July 1, 2019, https://www.newyorker.com/magazine/2019/07/08/will-hunter-biden-jeopardize-his-fathers-campaign.

87 Ibid.

88 Steven Nelson and Bruce Golding, "Hunter Biden Still 'Working to Unwind His Investment' in Chinese Firm," *New York Post*, February 5, 2021, https://nypost.com/2021/02/05/hunter-biden-working-to-unwind-investment-in-chinese-firm/; U.S. State Department, "Press Briefing by Press Secretary Jen Psaki and Council of Economic Advisers Member Jared Bernstein," State.gov, February 5, 2021, https://www.whitehouse.gov/briefing-room/press-briefings/2021/02/05/press-briefing-by-press-secretary-jen-psaki-and-council-of-economic-advisers-member-jared-bernstein-february-5-2021/.

89 Ibid.

90 Chuck Ross, "Ex-Hunter Biden Business Partner Confirms Authenticity of Email, Says Biden 'Aggressively Leveraged' Family Name," Daily Caller, October 22, 2020, https://dailycaller.com/2020/10/22/hunter-biden-joe-biden-tony-bobulinski/.

91 Jon Levine and Mary Kay Linge, "Hunter Biden and China: A Timeline of His Business Ties to the Far East," *New York Post*, December 19, 2020, https://nypost.com/article/hunter-biden-china-timeline-business-ties/.

92 AsiaNews/Agencies, "By Order of Xi Jinping, Powerful Businessman Ye Jianming Is Arrested," AsiaNews.it, March 1, 2018, http://www.asianews.it/news-en/By-order-of-Xi-Jinping,-powerful-businessman-Ye-Jianming-is-arrested-43239.html.

93 Council on Foreign Relations, "Joe Biden on Defending Democracy," YouTube.com, January 23, 2018, https://www.youtube.com/watch?v=Q0_AqpdwqK4&t=3109s.

94 Bethania Palma, "Does a C-SPAN Video Show Joe Biden 'Confessing to Bribery'?," Snopes.com, October 9, 2019, https://www.snopes.com/fact-check/c-span-video-joe-biden-ukraine/.

95 U.S. Senate Committee on Finance, "HSGAC-Finance Joint Report 2020.09.23.pdf," Finance.Senate.gov, September 18, 2020, https://www.finance.senate.gov/imo/media/doc/HSGAC-Finance Joint Report 2020.09.23.pdf.

96 Jon Levine and Mary Kay Linge, "Hunter Biden and China: A Timeline of His Business Ties to the Far East," *New York Post*, December 19, 2020, https://nypost.com/article/hunter-biden-china-timeline-business-ties/.

97 Matt Taibbi, "With the Hunter Biden Expose, Suppression Is a Bigger Scandal Than the Actual Story," TK News by Matt Taibbi, October 24, 2020, https://taibbi.substack.com/p/with-the-hunter-biden-expose-suppression-136.

98 Andrew Restuccia, "Biden Says China Will 'Eat Our Lunch' on Infrastructure," *Wall Street Journal*, February 11, 2021, https://www.wsj.com/articles/biden-says-china-will-eat-our-lunch-on-infrastructure-11613063295.

99 The White House, "Remarks by President Biden before Meeting with Senators on the Critical Need to Invest in Modern and Sustainable American Infrastructure," WhiteHouse.gov, February 11, 2021, https://www.whitehouse

.gov/briefing-room/speeches-remarks/2021/02/11/remarks-by-president-biden
-before-meeting-with-senators-on-the-critical-need-to-invest-in-modern-and
-sustainable-american-infrastrucutre/; Amanda Macias, "Biden Warns China
Is Going to 'Eat Our Lunch' If US Doesn't Get Moving on Infrastructure,"
CNBC.com, February 11, 2021, https://www.cnbc.com/2021/02/11/biden
-says-china-will-eat-our-lunch-on-infrastructure.html.

100 Stephen Johnson, "Virgin Hyperloop Completes World's First Human Test,"
BigThink.com, November 12, 2020, https://bigthink.com/technology
-innovation/hyperloop-test.

101 Michelle Baran, "Virgin's Hyperloop Could Mean a 30-Minute New York-
to-DC Journey," *Afar magazine*, October 8, 2020, https://www.afar.com/
magazine/virgins-hyperloop-now-closer-to-becoming-a-reality.

102 Joseph R. Biden, "Letter to His Excellency António Guterres," WhiteHouse.gov,
January 20, 2021, https://www.whitehouse.gov/briefing-room/statements
-releases/2021/01/20/letter-his-excellency-antonio-guterres/.

103 Jeremy Page, Chao Deng, and Drew Hinshaw, "Coronavirus Likely Came from
Animal, Not Leaked from Laboratory, WHO Says," *Wall Street Journal*,
February 9, 2021, https://www.wsj.com/articles/coronavirus-most-likely
-spilled-over-to-humans-through-intermediate-animal-says-who-11612868217.

104 *Real Time with Bill Maher,* "Heather Heying and Bret Weinstein: The Lab
Hypothesis | Real Time (HBO)," January 29, 2021, https://www.youtube.com/
watch?v=ZMGWLLDSA3c.

105 Marlow Stern, "Bill Maher Pushes Steve Bannon Wuhan Lab COVID
Conspiracy," *Daily Beast*, January 30, 2021, https://www.thedailybeast.com/
bill-maher-pushes-bonkers-steve-bannon-wuhan-lab-covid-conspiracy.

106 Josh Rogin, "Opinion: State Department Cables Warned of Safety Issues at
Wuhan Lab Studying Bat Coronaviruses," *Washington Post*, April 14, 2020,
https://www.washingtonpost.com/opinions/2020/04/14/state-department
-cables-warned-safety-issues-wuhan-lab-studying-bat-coronaviruses/.

107 Javier C. Hernández, "Trump Slammed the WHO over Coronavirus. He's
Not Alone," *New York Times*, April 8, 2020, updated May 29, 2020, https://
www.nytimes.com/2020/04/08/world/asia/trump-who-coronavirus-china.html.

108 Ibid.

109 Robert Gates, *Duty: Memoirs of a Secretary at War* (New York: Knopf, 2014), 288.

110 Michael R. Pompeo, Secretary of State, Press Statement: "Determination of the
Secretary of State on Atrocities in Xinjiang," U.S. State Department, January
19, 2021, https://2017-2021.state.gov/determination-of-the-secretary-of-state
-on-atrocities-in-xinjiang/index.html.

111 Open Doors USA, "China—Open Doors USA," OpenDoorsUSA.org, no date,
https://www.opendoorsusa.org/christian-persecution/world-watch-list/china/.

112 Lily Kuo, "In China, They're Closing Churches, Jailing Pastors—and Even
Rewriting Scripture," *The Guardian*, January 13, 2019, https://www.theguardian
.com/world/2019/jan/13/china-christians-religious-persecution-translation
-bible.

113 Joel Gehrke, "Blinken Endorses Pompeo's Genocide Charge against China and
Vows Tough Approach to Asian Power," *Washington Examiner*, January 19,

2021, https://www.msn.com/en-us/news/politics/blinken-endorses-pompeo-s
-genocide-charge-against-china-and-vows-tough-approach-to-asian-power/
ar-BB1cU3YM.

114 Michael Pillsbury, *The Hundred-Year Marathon: China's Secret Strategy to Replace
America as the Global Superpower* (New York: Saint Martin's Press, 2015), 52.

115 Ibid., 92.

116 Ibid., 1–4.

117 H. R. McMaster, "Opinion: Biden Would Do the World a Favor by Keeping
Trump's China Policy," *Washington Post*, January 18, 2021, https://www
.washingtonpost.com/opinions/2021/01/18/mcmaster-biden-trump-china/.

118 The White House, "Inaugural Address by President Joseph R. Biden, Jr.,"
WhiteHouse.gov, January 20, 2021, https://www.whitehouse.gov/briefing
-room/speeches-remarks/2021/01/20/inaugural-address-by-president
-joseph-r-biden-jr/.

119 The White House, "Statement by President Biden on the Attack on the Right
to Vote in Georgia," WhiteHouse.gov, March 26, 2021, https://www.whitehouse
.gov/briefing-room/speeches-remarks/2021/03/26/statement-by-president
-biden-on-the-attack-on-the-right-to-vote-in-georgia/.

120 Glenn Kessler, "Biden Falsely Claims the New Georgia Law 'Ends Voting Hours
Early,'" *Washington Post*, March 30, 2021, https://www.washingtonpost.com/
politics/2021/03/30/biden-falsely-claims-new-georgia-law-ends-voting-hours
-early/.

121 ESPN, "President Joe Biden Speaks about Fans Returning to Stadiums,
Vaccination Progress | SportsCenter," YouTube.com, March 31, 2021, https://
www.youtube.com/watch?v=gvWwBHk3lRg.

122 Fay Vincent, "Rob Manfred's All-Star Error," *Wall Street Journal*, April 6, 2021,
https://www.wsj.com/articles/rob-manfreds-all-star-error-11617726664?mod
=opinion_lead_pos6.

123 Fox News, "Georgia Minority Owned Businesses Desperately Needed MLB
Tourism to Rebound from Pandemic: Jobs Expert," Fox News, April 5, 2021,
https://video.foxnews.com/v/6246675356001#sp=show-clips.

124 Maggie Haberman, "They're Going to Put Y'All Back in Chains" (updated),
Politico's *Burns and Haberman Blog*, August 14, 2012, https://www.politico.com/
blogs/burns-haberman/2012/08/theyre-going-to-put-yall-back-in-chains
-updated-132073; David Emery, "Did Joe Biden Tell a Racially Mixed Audience
That Republicans Would 'Put Y'All Back in Chains'?," Snopes.com, May 15,
2019, https://www.snopes.com/fact-check/joe-biden-put-yall-back-in-chains/.

125 The White House, "Remarks by President Biden at Pfizer Manufacturing Site,
Kalamazoo, Michigan," WhiteHouse.gov, February 19, 2021, https://www
.whitehouse.gov/briefing-room/speeches-remarks/2021/02/19/remarks-by
-president-biden-at-pfizer-manufacturing-site/.

126 Mary Ellen Cagnassola, "Fact Check: Is Only 9% of Joe Biden's COVID
Stimulus Plan Going to Public Health?," *Newsweek*, February 18, 2021,
https://www.newsweek.com/fact-check-only-9-joe-bidens-covid-stimulus
-plan-going-public-health-1570369.

127 Aimee Picchi, "Child Tax Credit: Millions of Parents Could Soon Get Up to $3,600 per Child," CBS News, March 17, 2021, https://www.cbsnews.com/news/child-tax-credit-stimulus-covid-relief-bill-2021-03-16/.

128 Tom Kertscher, "Fact Check: Do Minority Farmers Receive a 'Bonus' in the COVID-19 Relief Bill?," PolitiFact.com, March 31, 2021, https://www.statesman.com/story/news/politics/politifact/2021/03/31/politifact-check-covid-relief-minority-farmers-past-discrimination-not-bonus/4819776001/.

129 Casey B. Mulligan and Stephen Moore, "How Many Jobs Will the 'Stimulus' Kill?," *Wall Street Journal*, February 26, 2021, https://www.wsj.com/articles/how-many-jobs-will-the-stimulus-kill-11614295867.

130 Steven Pearlstein, "In Democrats' Progressive Paradise, Borrowing Is Free, Spending Pays for Itself, and Interest Rates Never Rise," *Washington Post,* March 3, 2021, https://www.washingtonpost.com/business/2021/03/03/democrats-stimulus-spending-inflation/.

131 Ibid.

132 Tyler Olson, "Biden's Two Dollars T Spending Plan, Billed as Infrastructure Bill, Spends Less Than Half on Infrastructure," Fox News, April 2, 2021, https://www.foxnews.com/politics/biden-spending-plan-billed-as-infrastructure-bill-spends-non-infrastructure.

133 Glenn Kessler, "Biden's Pitch That the Economy 'Will Create 19 Million Jobs' If Infrastructure Is Passed," *Washington Post*, April 6, 2021, https://www.washingtonpost.com/politics/2021/04/06/bidens-pitch-that-economy-will-create-19-million-jobs-if-infrastructure-is-passed/.

134 Tamar Lapin, "'Unicorns Are Infrastructure': Sen. Gillibrand Mocked for Definition of Biden Plan," *New York Post*, April 7, 2021, https://nypost.com/2021/04/07/sen-gillibrand-mocked-for-renaming-bidens-infrastructure-plan/.

135 Ibid.

136 George Orwell, *Nineteen Eighty-Four* (New York: Knopf, 1992), 6.

137 The Independent Counsel, Starr Report: Narrative, *Nature of President Clinton's Relationship with Monica Lewinsky* (Washington, DC: U.S. Government Printing Office, May 19, 2004), https://web.archive.org/web/20001203073600; http://icreport.access.gpo.gov/report/6narrit.htm#N_1091_.

138 Ronn Blitzer, "Biden Aims to Redefine Word 'Bipartisan' as Dems Work to Push Spending Bill without Any GOP Votes," Fox News, April 12, 2021, https://www.foxnews.com/politics/biden-redefine-bipartisan-dems-push-spending-bill-without-gop-votes; Michael D. Shear, Emily Cochrane, and Jim Tankersley, "To Build Support for Plan, Biden Offers His Own Take on 'Bipartisan,'" *New York Times*, April 1, 2021 (updated April 7, 2021), https://www.nytimes.com/2021/04/01/us/politics/biden-infrastructure-plan.html.

139 Beckett Adams, "To Defend Biden, Media and Democrats Simply Redefine 'Court Packing,'" *Washington Examiner*, October 12, 2020, https://www.washingtonexaminer.com/opinion/to-defend-biden-media-and-democrats-simply-redefine-court-packing.

140 Reagan McCarthy, "Nadler Claims Democrats' Court Packing Scheme Is Actually 'Unpacking,'" Townhall.com, April 15, 2021, https://townhall.com/

tipsheet/reaganmccarthy/2021/04/15/dems-horrible-court-packing-plan
-n2587961.

141 George Orwell, "Politics and the English Language," in *Politics and the English
Language and Other Essays* (1946), FadedPage.com, February 16, 2018, https://
www.fadedpage.com/books/20180223/html.php.

142 James Brooks, "Municipality of Anchorage Will Pay $100,001 to Settle
Transgender Discrimination Lawsuit Involving Homeless Shelter," *Anchorage
Daily News*, October 1, 2019, https://www.adn.com/alaska-news/anchorage/
2019/10/01/municipality-of-anchorage-will-pay-100001-to-settle-transgender
-discrimination-lawsuit-involving-homeless-shelter/; Associated Press, "Alaska
Shelter Can Turn Away Transgender Women Following City Decree," NBC
News, October 1, 2019, https://www.nbcnews.com/feature/nbc-out/shelter-says
-it-beat-back-rule-it-take-transgender-women-n1060721.

143 Bonnie Horgos, "The Vatican Draws a Line on Gender, and Transgender
Catholics Push Back," *Religion & Politics*, July 30, 2019, https://
religionandpolitics.org/2019/07/30/the-vatican-draws-a-line-on-gender-and
-transgender-catholics-push-back/.

144 Robert Barnes, "In Major Supreme Court Case, Justice Department Sides with
Baker Who Refused to Make Wedding Cake for Gay Couple," *Washington Post*,
September 7, 2017, https://www.washingtonpost.com/politics/courts_law/
in-major-supreme-court-case-justice-dept-sides-with-baker-who-refused-to
-make-wedding-cake-for-gay-couple/2017/09/07/fb84f116-93f0-11e7-89
fa-bb822a46da5b_story.html.

145 Office of the Attorney General, "Memorandum for All Executive Departments
and Agencies," Subject: Federal Law Protections for Religious Liberty, October
6, 2017, https://www.justice.gov/opa/press-release/file/1001891/download.

146 Ibid.

147 Nathan Skates, "The Biden Plan on Abortion, Religious Freedom, Firearms, and
COVID," Falkirk Center, November 13, 2020, https://www.falkirkcenter.com/
2020/11/13/the-biden-plan-on-abortion-religious-freedom-firearms-and-covid/.

148 Becca Coon, "Biden's Left Turn Threatens Religious Liberty," *Decision*, July 1,
2020, https://decisionmagazine.com/bidens-left-turn-threatens-religious-liberty/.

149 Barack Obama, "Presidential Proclamation—Religious Freedom Day, 2013,"
The White House, January 16, 2013, https://obamawhitehouse.archives.gov/
the-press-office/2013/01/16/presidential-proclamation-religious-freedom-day.

150 Gerhard Casper and Kathleen M. Sullivan, eds., *Landmark Briefs and Argu-
ments of the Supreme Court of the United States: Constitutional Law*, 2013 Term
Supplement (Bethesda, MD: ProQuest LLC, 2014), 344.

151 Terence P. Jeffrey, "Kamala Harris' Crusade against Freedom of Religion," CNS
News, March 6, 2019, https://www.cnsnews.com/commentary/terence-p
-jeffrey/kamala-harris-crusade-against-freedom-religion.

152 Ryan Colby, *Little Sisters of the Poor v. Commonwealth of Pennsylvania*,
BecketLaw.org, The Becket Fund for Religious Liberty, no date, https://
www.becketlaw.org/case/commonwealth-pennsylvania-v-trump/.

153 Jordan Davidson, "*Washington Post* 'Fact Check' Claims Becerra Never Sued Nuns," *The Federalist*, February 26, 2021, https://thefederalist.com/2021/02/26/washington-post-fact-check-claims-becerra-never-sued-nuns/.

154 Ibid.

155 Christine Rousselle, "At Hearing, Becerra Won't Name Single Abortion Restriction He Favors," Catholic News Agency, February 24, 2021, https://www.catholicnewsagency.com/news/at-hearing-becerra-wont-name-single-abortion-restriction-he-favors.

156 Kate Scanlon, "Former HHS Official: Xavier Becerra Could Promote Abortion Internationally," *National Catholic Register*, February 25, 2021, https://www.ncregister.com/cna/former-hhs-official-xavier-becerra-could-promote-abortion-internationally.

157 Devin Watkins, "Pope to Pro-Life Movement: 'Politicians Should Place Defense of Life First,'" Vatican News, February 2, 2019, https://www.vaticannews.va/en/pope/news/2019-02/pope-francis-pro-life-movement-politicians-defend-life.html.

158 Heidi Przybyla, "Joe Biden's Long Evolution on Abortion Rights Still Holds Surprises," NBC News, June 5, 2019, https://www.nbcnews.com/politics/2020-election/biden-s-long-evolution-abortion-rights-still-holds-surprises-n1013846.

159 Joe Biden, *Promises to Keep* (New York: Random House, 2007), 104–105.

160 Gustaf Kilander, "Dad Says COVID Lockdown Was behind 12-Year-Old Son's Suicide," *The Independent*, February 18, 2021, https://www.independent.co.uk/news/world/americas/brad-hunstable-hayden-covid-suicide-b1803754.html; Jordan Houston, "12-Year-Old Boy Hangs Himself after Struggle with COVID Isolation, Dad Says," Heavy.com, February 14, 2021, https://heavy.com/news/texas-boy-hangs-himself-covid/.

161 FAIR Health, "The Impact of COVID-19 on Pediatric Mental Health," A FAIR Health White Paper, March 2, 2021, https://s3.amazonaws.com/media2.fairhealth.org/whitepaper/asset/The%20Impact%20of%20COVID-19%20on%20Pediatric%20Mental%20Health%20-%20A%20Study%20of%20Private%20Healthcare%20Claims%20-%20A%20FAIR%20Health%20White%20Paper.pdf (pages 2–3).

162 Erica L. Green, "Surge of Student Suicides Pushes Las Vegas Schools to Reopen," *New York Times*, January 24, 2021, https://www.nytimes.com/2021/01/24/us/politics/student-suicides-nevada-coronavirus.html.

163 Associated Press, "San Francisco Sues Schools, Citing High Number of Suicidal Students," *New York Post*, February 12, 2021, https://nypost.com/2021/02/12/san-francisco-sues-schools-cites-high-of-suicidal-students/.

164 Ibid.

165 Ira Stoll, "Day after Inauguration, Biden Welcomes Teachers Union Leaders to White House, Education Next," *Education Next*, January 22, 2021, https://www.educationnext.org/day-after-inauguration-biden-welcomes-teachers-union-leaders-white-house/.

166 Louis Casiano, "Biden Declines to Tell Chicago Teachers Refusing to Teach In-Person to Go Back to Work," Fox News, January 25, 2021, https://www.foxnews.com/politics/biden-chicago-teachers-in-person; Evie Fordham,

"Teachers Unions' Political Support for Biden Paying Off as He Takes Their Side in Reopening Battle," Fox News, February 3, 2021, https://www.foxnews .com/politics/teachers-unions-support-biden-reopening-schools-political.

167   CBS New York Team, "CDC: Schools Can Safely Reopen If Precautions in Place," CBS New York, January 27, 2021, https://newyork.cbslocal.com/ 2021/01/27/cdc-on-schools-reopening/; Cory Turner, Anya Kamanetz, and Tamara Keith, "CDC Offers Clearest Guidance Yet for Reopening Schools," NPR *All Things Considered*, February 12, 2021, https://www.npr.org/2021/ 02/12/967033554/cdc-offers-clearest-guidance-yet-for-reopening-schools; Jon Levine, "Powerful Teachers Union Influenced CDC on School Reopenings, Emails Show," *New York Post*, May 1, 2021, https://nypost.com/2021/05/01/ teachers-union-collaborated-with-cdc-on-school-reopening-emails/.

168   Cecily Myart-Cruz, "Special UTLA News Statement 3/01/2021," YouTube.com, March 1, 2021, https://www.youtube.com/watch?v=IrPAmgabpW8.

169   Deborah Netburn, Chris Megerian, and Howard Blume, "Here's the CDC's Advice for Reopening Schools Safely," *Los Angeles Times*, February 12, 2021, https://www.latimes.com/science/story/2021-02-12/heres-the-cdcs-advice-for -reopening-schools-safely.

170   Christopher F. Rufo, "Woke Elementary," *City Journal*, January 13, 2021, https://www.city-journal.org/identity-politics-in-cupertino-california -elementary-school.

171   Phil Shiver, "Sixth Grade Choir Teacher Separates Kids into 'Privileged' and 'Targeted' Groups in Lesson on 'Oppression,'" Blaze Media, March 3, 2021, https://www.theblaze.com/news/teacher-separates-students-priveleged-targeted -groups.

172   Gabe Kaminsky, "Illinois Teachers Shamed for Color of Their Skin in Taxpayer-Sponsored 'Antiracist' Training," *The Federalist*, March 5, 2021, https:// thefederalist.com/2021/03/05/illinois-teachers-shamed-for-color-of-their-skin -in-taxpayer-sponsored-antiracist-training/.

173   Andrew Mark Miller, "San Diego Teachers Required to Attend 'White Privilege' Training Where They Are Told 'You Are Racist': Report," *Washington Examiner*, December 4, 2020, https://www.washingtonexaminer.com/news/san-diego -teachers-required-to-attend-white-privilege-training-where-they-are-told-you -are-racist-report.

174   Selim Algar and Kate Sheehy, "NYC Public School Asks Parents to 'Reflect' on Their 'Whiteness,'" *New York Post*, February 16, 2021, https://nypost.com/ 2021/02/16/nyc-public-school-asks-parents-to-reflect-on-their-whiteness/.

175   Editorial Board, "The Political Making of a Texas Power Outage," *Wall Street Journal*, February 16, 2021, https://www.wsj.com/articles/the-political-making -of-a-texas-power-outage-11613518653.

176   *USA Today* Staff, "Read the Full Transcript from the First Presidential Debate between Joe Biden and Donald Trump," USAToday.com, September 30 and October 4, 2020, https://www.usatoday.com/story/news/politics/elections/ 2020/09/30/presidential-debate-read-full-transcript-first-debate/3587462001/.

177 Biden Campaign, "The Biden Plan for a Clean Energy Revolution and Environmental Justice," JoeBiden.com, no date, https://joebiden.com/climate -plan/.

178 Thomas Friedman, "Opinion—A Warning from the Garden," *New York Times*, January 19, 2007, https://www.nytimes.com/2007/01/19/opinion/19friedman. html.

179 Oversight Hearing before the Subcommittee on Energy and Mineral Resources of the Committee on Natural Resources, U.S. House of Representatives, "Climate Change: Preparing for the Energy Transition," One Hundred Sixteenth Congress, First Session, Tuesday, February 12, 2019, https://www .govinfo.gov/content/pkg/CHRG-116hhrg35198/html/CHRG-116hhrg35198 .htm.

180 David Montgomery, "AOC's Chief of Change," *Washington Post*, July 10, 2019, https://www.washingtonpost.com/news/magazine/wp/2019/07/10/feature/how -saikat-chakrabarti-became-aocs-chief-of-change/.

181 United States Environmental Protection Agency, "Global Greenhouse Gas Emissions Data," EPA.gov, September 10, 2020, https://www.epa.gov/ ghgemissions/global-greenhouse-gas-emissions-data.

182 Matt McGrath, "'Dodgy' Greenhouse Gas Data Threatens Paris Accord," BBC.com, August 7, 2017, https://www.bbc.com/news/science-environment -40669449.

183 Editorial Board, "Biden's Keystone Pipeline Kill," *Wall Street Journal*, January 20, 2021, https://www.wsj.com/articles/bidens-keystone-pipeline-kill -11611184519.

184 Canadian Association of Petroleum Producers (CAPP), "Oil and Natural Gas Pipelines," CAPP.ca, 2020, https://www.capp.ca/explore/oil-and-natural -gas-pipelines/.

185 *Los Angeles Times* and Chip Yost, "Cause of Imperial County Crash That Killed 13 Remains a Mystery; Officials Probe Why 25 People Were in SUV," KTLA .com, March 3, 2021, https://ktla.com/news/local-news/cause-of-imperial -county-crash-that-killed-13-remains-a-mystery-officials-probe-why-25-people -were-in-suv/; Associated Press, Chip Yost, and Carlos Herrera, "SUV Came through Hole in Border Fence Prior to Imperial County Crash That Killed 13," KTLA.com, March 3, 2021, https://ktla.com/news/california/investigation -into-possible-human-smuggling-launched-in-deadly-imperial-county-crash/; ABC 7 New York, "Father Mourns 23-Year-Old Daughter among 13 Killed in Crash Near US-Mexico Border: 'There Are No Words,'" ABC7NY.com, March 5, 2021, https://abc7ny.com/california-car-crash-yesenia-magali-melendrez -cardona-in-victims-us-mexico-border/10391362/; Joshua Rhett Miller, "Guatemalan Would-Be Lawyer Died in Mom's Arms in California SUV Crash," *New York Post*, March 5, 2021, https://nypost.com/2021/03/05/ guatemalan-woman-died-in-moms-arms-in-california-suv-crash/.

186 Rev.com Staff, "Press Secretary Jen Psaki White House Press Conference Transcript March 1," Rev.com, March 1, 2021, https://www.rev.com/blog/ transcripts/press-secretary-jen-psaki-white-house-press-conference-transcript -march-1.

187 Rachel Stoltzfoos, "Democrats Push Immigration Policies That Amount to Open Borders in Second Debate," Daily Caller, June 28, 2019, https://dailycaller.com/2019/06/28/democrats-immigration-open-borders-second-debate/.

188 Marinka Peschmann, "Judges Baffled by DHS Efforts to Deport Legal Immigrant," Breitbart.com, January 17, 2014, https://www.breitbart.com/politics/2014/01/17/dhs-kicking-out-legal-immigrants-including-a-professional-and-an-earthquake-engineer-judge-cites-fox-news/.

189 Michael D. Shear, "Biden's Immigration Plan Would Offer Path to Citizenship for Millions," *New York Times*, February 18 (updated March 8), 2021, https://www.nytimes.com/live/2021/02/18/us/joe-biden-news.

190 Elizabeth Elizalde, "'Migrant President': Mexico Says Biden Asylum Policies Boost Illegals, Cartels," *New York Post*, March 10, 2021, https://nypost.com/2021/03/10/mexico-says-biden-asylum-policies-boost-illegals-cartels/.

191 Valerie Strauss, "The American Tradition of Caging Children," *Washington Post*, October 10, 2018, https://www.washingtonpost.com/education/2018/10/10/american-tradition-caging-children/.

192 Silvia Foster-Frau, "First Migrant Facility for Children Opens under Biden," *Washington Post*, February 22, 2021, https://www.washingtonpost.com/national/immigrant-children-camp-texas-biden/2021/02/22/05dfd58c-7533-11eb-8115-9ad5e9c02117_story.html.

193 Vanessa Romo, "Minneapolis Council Moves to Defund Police, Establish 'Holistic' Public Safety Force," National Public Radio, June 26, 2020, https://www.npr.org/sections/live-updates-protests-for-racial-justice/2020/06/26/884149659/minneapolis-council-moves-to-defund-police-establish-holistic-public-safety-forc.

194 John Eligon, "Minneapolis Police Experience Surge of Departures in Aftermath of George Floyd Protests," *New York Times*, July 21, 2020, https://www.nytimes.com/2020/07/21/us/minneapolis-police-george-floyd-protests.html.

195 Brandt Williams, "With Violent Crime on the Rise in Minneapolis, City Council Asks: Where Are the Police?," Minnesota Public Radio, September 15, 2020, https://www.mprnews.org/story/2020/09/15/with-violent-crime-on-the-rise-in-mpls-city-council-asks-where-are-the-police.

196 Megan Henney, "Minneapolis City Council Alarmed by Surge in Crime Months after Voting to Defund the Police," *New York Post*, September 16, 2020, https://nypost.com/2020/09/16/minneapolis-city-council-alarmed-by-crime-surge-after-defunding-police/.

197 Alexandra Kelley, "Some Minneapolis City Council Members Would Like a Redo on Defunding the Police: Report," *The Hill*, September 28, 2020, https://thehill.com/changing-america/respect/diversity-inclusion/518564-some-minneapolis-city-council-members-would-like.

198 Associated Press, "Minneapolis to Spend $6.4 Million to Recruit More Police Officers," VOA News, February 13, 2021, https://www.voanews.com/usa/minneapolis-spend-64-million-recruit-more-police-officers.

199 Louis Casiano, "Minneapolis City Council President, Dem Jeremiah Ellison Claim They'll 'Dismantle' Police," Fox News, June 4, 2020, https://www.

foxnews.com/politics/jeremiah-ellison-minnesota-ag-keith-ellisons-son-disman-tle-minneapolis-police-department.

200 Associated Press, "Minneapolis Council Majority Backs Disbanding Police Force," NBC 29, June 7, 2020 (updated June 8), https://www.nbc29.com/2020/06/07/minneapolis-city-council-members-announce-intent-dismantle-police-department/.

201 Editorial Board, "Joe Biden's Doubletalk on 'Defund the Police,'" *New York Post*, August 9, 2020, https://nypost.com/2020/08/09/joe-bidens-doubletalk-on-defund-the-police/.

202 Marc Caputo and Natasha Korecki, "Police Groups Break with Biden," Politico, June 4, 2020, https://www.politico.com/news/2020/06/04/police-groups-joe-biden-300222.

203 Kamala Harris, *The Truths We Hold: An American Journey* (New York: Penguin, 2019), xvi.

204 Sam Levin and Lois Beckett, "Kamala Harris: Can a 'Top Cop' Win Over Progressives in 2020?," *The Guardian*, January 19, 2019, https://www.theguardian.com/us-news/2019/jan/19/kamala-harris-2020-election-top-cop-prosecutor.

205 Alexander Bolton, "Harris Grapples with Defund the Police Movement amid Veep Talk," *The Hill*, June 11, 2020, https://thehill.com/homenews/campaign/502187-harris-grapples-with-defund-the-police-movement-amid-veep-talk?rl=1.

206 Ronn Blitzer, "Kamala Harris Avoids Question on Whether She Backs 'Defund the Police' Movement," Fox News, June 8, 2020, https://www.foxnews.com/politics/kamala-harris-avoids-question-defund-police-movement.

207 Ruairí Arrieta-Kenna, "The Deep Roots—and New Offshoots—of 'Abolish the Police,'" Politico, June 12, 2020, https://www.politico.com/news/magazine/2020/06/12/abolish-defund-police-explainer-316185.

208 Emma Colton, "NYC First Lady Chirlane McCray Encourages Residents to 'Intervene' in Violent Situations after Calling to Defund the Police," WashingtonExaminer.com, March 8, 2021, https://www.washingtonexaminer.com/news/chirlane-mccray-intervene-violence-defund-police.

209 Tyler Pager, "Biden Starts Staffing a Commission on Supreme Court Reform," Politico, January 27, 2021, https://www.politico.com/news/2021/01/27/biden-supreme-court-reform-463126.

210 Editorial Board, "Biden Commissions the Supreme Court," *Wall Street Journal*, April 9, 2021, https://www.wsj.com/articles/biden-commissions-the-supreme-court-11618008493.

211 Greg Stohr and Jordan Fabian, "Biden Pulled Left in Quest for Judges Outside Corporate Law (1)," BloombergLaw.com, February 12, 2021, https://news.bloomberglaw.com/us-law-week/biden-pulled-left-in-quest-to-seek-judges-outside-corporate-law.

212 Tyler Pager, "Biden Starts Staffing a Commission on Supreme Court Reform," Politico, January 27, 2021, https://www.politico.com/news/2021/01/27/biden-supreme-court-reform-463126.

213 Greg Stohr and Jordan Fabian, "Biden Pulled Left in Quest for Judges Outside Corporate Law (1)," BloombergLaw.com, February 12, 2021, https://news

.bloomberglaw.com/us-law-week/biden-pulled-left-in-quest-to-seek-judges
-outside-corporate-law.

214 Jennifer Bendery, "Biden's Team Tells Senate Democrats to Send Him Judicial
Nominees ASAP," HuffPost, December 30, 2020, https://www.huffpost.com/
entry/joe-biden-courts-progressive-nominees_n_5fecc527c5b6e7974fd18321.

215 Ariane de Vogue, "Get Ready for a Raft of Biden Court Nominees," CNN.com,
March 11, 2021, https://www.cnn.com/2021/03/11/politics/courts-biden
-nominees/index.html.

216 Influence Watch Staff, "Non-Profit: Demand Justice," InfluenceWatch.org,
no date, https://www.influencewatch.org/non-profit/demand-justice/.

217 Dahlia Lithwick, "How to Fight Back against Restrictive Abortion Laws,"
Slate.com, May 31, 2019, https://slate.com/news-and-politics/2019/05/fight
-back-restrictive-abortion-laws-sister-district-project.html.

218 Ed Whelan, "DC Circuit Nominee Cornelia Pillard—Part 5," *National
Review*, July 22, 2013, https://www.nationalreview.com/bench-memos/
dc-circuit-nominee-cornelia-pillard-part-5-ed-whelan/.

219 Nick Howell, "Who Is Zephyr Teachout?," *City & State New York*, May 29,
2014, https://www.cityandstateny.com/articles/politics/campaigns-and
-elections/who-is-zephyr-teachout.html.

220 David Freedlander, "The Woman behind the New York Campaign to Take
Down Trump," Politico, August 17, 2018, https://www.politico.com/magazine/
story/2018/08/17/lock-him-up-donald-trump-zephyr-teachout-219367/.

221 Sherrilyn Ifill, "Tackle Racial Bias in Policing at the Root," *Washington Post*,
September 22, 2016, https://www.washingtonpost.com/opinions/tackle-racial
-bias-in-policing-at-the-root/2016/09/22/4ee3bcba-80e8-11e6-a52d-9a865a0
ed0d4_story.html.

222 Sherrilyn Ifill, *On the Courthouse Lawn: Confronting the Legacy of Lynching in
the 21st Century* (Boston: Beacon Press, 2007), 177.

223 NBC News, "Pamela Karlan Apologizes for Mentioning Barron Trump in
Impeachment Hearing," YouTube.com, December 4, 2019, https://
www.youtube.com/watch?v=wxB5X8jF6KM.

224 Danielle Wallace, "Pamela Karlan Says She Once Crossed the Street to Avoid a
Trump Hotel in DC," Fox News, December 5, 2019, https://www.foxnews.com/
politics/pamela-karlan-trump-hotel-cross-street-impeachment-eric-swalwell
-barron.

225 James Lindsay, "Eight Big Reasons Critical Race Theory Is Terrible for Dealing
with Racism," New Discourses, June 12, 2020, https://newdiscourses.com/
2020/06/reasons-critical-race-theory-terrible-dealing-racism/.

226 LeakSourceArchive, "Economist Thomas Sowell Talks about Harvard Obama
and Derrick Bell," YouTube.com, March 9, 2012, https://www.youtube.com/
watch?v=KDeL-UK1p24.

227 Thomas Sowell, "Racial Quota Fallout," Creators Syndicate, March 14, 2012,
https://www.creators.com/read/thomas-sowell/03/12/racial-quota-fallout.

228 Rudy Takala, "Biden Extends Press Conference to Take Final Question from
Fox News Reporter: 'I Like Him,'" Mediaite, January 25, 2021, https://

www.msn.com/en-us/news/politics/biden-extends-press-conference-to-take
-final-question-from-fox-news-reporter-i-like-him/ar-BB1d5eSj.

229 Thomas Barrabi, "Biden Comment Mocking Trump's Walking Resurfaces after
President Stumbles, Falls Boarding Air Force One," Fox News, March 20, 2021,
https://www.foxnews.com/politics/biden-comment-mocking-trump-walking
-president-stumbles-air-force-one.

230 Brian Flood, "Flashback: Biden Fall Conjures up Memories of Media Hysteria
When Trump Walked Slowly Down a Ramp," Fox News, March 19, 2021,
https://www.foxnews.com/media/flashback-biden-media-went-crazy-trump
-ramp.

231 Joseph Wulfsohn, "Gallup Poll Finds 84% of Americans Say Media to Blame
for US Political Divide," Fox News, August 4, 2020, https://www.foxnews.com/
media/gallup-poll-media-distrust-us-political-divide.

232 Brian Trusdell, "Gallup: People with No Trust in News Media Hits Record,"
Newsmax, December 31, 2020, https://www.newsmax.com/newsfront/gallup
-media-trust-record/2020/12/31/id/1003814/.

233 United States Court of Appeals for the District of Columbia Circuit, Argued
September 14, 2020, Decided March 19, 2021, No. 19-7132, *Christiana Tah
and Randolph Mcclain*, Appellants v. Global Witness Publishing, Inc. and
Global Witness, Appellees, https://www.cadc.uscourts.gov/internet/opinions
.nsf/C5F7840A6FFFCF648525869D004ECAC5/%24file/19-7132-1890626
.pdf (emphasis in original).

234 Alexander Kacala, "Biden Promises Appointees He Will Fire Them 'On the
Spot' If They Disrespect Others," Today.com, January 20, 2021, https://
www.today.com/news/biden-promises-appointees-he-will-fire-them-spot-if
-they-t206392.

235 Erik Wemple, "Opinion: 'I Will Destroy You': The Biden White House's First
Media Scandal," *Washington Post*, February 12, 2021, https://www
.washingtonpost.com/opinions/2021/02/12/i-will-destroy-you-biden-white
-houses-first-media-scandal/; Eve Peyser, "Biden Aide Threatened to 'Destroy'
Reporter Asking about His Girlfriend," *New York Magazine*, February 12, 2021,
https://nymag.com/intelligencer/2021/02/tj-ducklo-threatens-tara-palmeri-over
-alexi-mccammond.html; Tara Palmeri, Eugene Daniels, Rachael Bade, and
Ryan Lizza, "POLITICO Playbook: Trump Compares Impeachment to *The
Apprentice*," Politico.com, February 9, 2021, https://www.politico.com/
newsletters/playbook/2021/02/09/trump-compares-impeachment-to-the
-apprentice-491689.

236 Jen Psaki (@PressSec), Twitter.com, February 12, 2021, https://twitter.com/
presssec/status/1360284947785936899.

237 C-Span, "February 12, 2021 | Clip of White House Daily Briefing," C-Span.org,
February 12, 2021, https://www.c-span.org/video/?c4945703/white-house
-suspends-deputy-press-secretary-heated-conversation-politico-reporter.

238 Rich Noyes, "Special Report: The Eight Worst 'Fake News' Stories of the
Trump Years," NewsBusters.org, May 5, 2020, https://www.newsbusters.org/
blogs/nb/rich-noyes/2020/05/05/special-report-eight-worst-fake-news-stories
-trump-years.

239 Ibid.

240 Ibid.

241 Amy Gardner, "Trump Pressured a Georgia Elections Investigator in a Separate Call Legal Experts Say Could Amount to Obstruction," *Washington Post*, January 9, 2021 (revised and corrected March 11, 2021), https://www.washingtonpost.com/politics/trump-call-georgia-investigator/2021/01/09/7a55c7fa-51cf-11eb-83e3-322644d82356_story.html.

242 Arelis R. Hernández, "Migrants Are Not Overrunning US Border Towns, Despite the Political Rhetoric," *Washington Post*, March 15, 2021, https://www.washingtonpost.com/immigration/migrants-are-not-overrunning-us-border-towns-despite-the-political-rhetoric/2021/03/15/b193f3f2-8345-11eb-ac37-4383f7709abe_story.html.

243 James Dobbins, Simon Romero, and Manny Fernandez, "Border Towns Brace for More Migrants as the Border Slowly Reopens," *New York Times*, March 19, 2021, https://www.nytimes.com/2021/03/19/us/border-migrants-texas.html.

244 Salena Zito, "Democratic Texas Border Mayor Frustrated with Biden Administration as Crisis Heightens," *Washington Examiner*, March 23, 2021, https://www.washingtonexaminer.com/opinion/columnists/democratic-texas-border-mayor-frustrated-with-biden-administration-as-crisis-heightens.

245 Anita Snow, Associated Press, "Arizona Town Calls State of Emergency over Migrant Arrivals," KXAN.com, March 24, 2021, https://www.kxan.com/news/national-news/arizona-town-calls-state-of-emergency-over-migrant-arrivals/.

246 Becket Adams, "Associated Press Denies That Border Crisis Is a Crisis," *Washington Examiner*, March 26, 2021, https://www.washingtonexaminer.com/opinion/associated-press-denies-that-border-crisis-is-a-crisis.

247 Bill D'Agostino, "Let's Compare Coverage of Biden's and Trump's Border Crises," NewsBusters.org, March 23, 2021, https://www.newsbusters.org/blogs/nb/bill-dagostino/2021/03/23/lets-compare-coverage-bidens-and-trumps-border-crises.

248 ABC News, "'This Week' Transcript 3-21-21: Homeland Security Secretary Alejandro Mayorkas, Gov. Doug Ducey, Rep. Michael McCaul, Rep. Judy Chu," ABC News, March 21, 2021, https://abcnews.go.com/Politics/week-transcript-21-21-homeland-security-secretary-alejandro/story?id=76588952.

249 Margaret Sullivan, "Fox News Is a Hazard to Our Democracy. It's Time to Take the Fight to the Murdochs. Here's How," *Washington Post*, January 24, 2021, https://www.washingtonpost.com/lifestyle/media/fox-news-is-a-hazard-to-our-democracy-its-time-to-take-the-fight-to-the-murdochs-heres-how/2021/01/22/1821f186-5cbe-11eb-b8bd-ee36b1cd18bf_story.html.

250 Margaret Sullivan, "Biden's First News Conference Is a Test for Him. But It's a Bigger Test for White House Reporters," *Washington Post*, March 23, 2021, https://www.washingtonpost.com/lifestyle/media/media-biden-news-conference/2021/03/22/c0695328-8b28-11eb-a730-1b4ed9656258_story.html.

251 Mike Allen and Jim VandeHei, "Biden's New Deal: Re-engineering America, Quickly," Axios, March 24, 2021, https://www.axios.com/biden-filibuster-agenda-history-05be3812-6ee0-414b-ae71-b6dfa37d8df4.html; Mike Allen,

"Scoop: Inside Biden's Private Chat with Historians," Axios, March 25, 2021, https://www.axios.com/biden-historians-meeting-filibuster-0a7d726c-4041 -405f-a3ac-c31550c590bc.html.

252 Editors, "H.R.1 Is a Partisan Assault on American Democracy," *National Review*, March 7, 2021, https://www.nationalreview.com/2021/03/h-r-1-is-a-partisan -assault-on-american-democracy/.

253 Ronald Newman, Kate Ruane, and Sonia Gill, "ACLU Letter Opposing H.R.1 (For the People Act of 2019)," ACLU.org, March 6, 2019, https://www.aclu.org/ aclu-letter-opposing-hr-1-people-act-2019.

254 Mike Pence, "Election Integrity Is a National Imperative," *Daily Signal*, March 3, 2021, https://www.dailysignal.com/2021/03/03/election-integrity-is-a -national-imperative/.

255 Jeff Jacoby, "The Constitution Says No to DC Statehood," *Boston Globe*, June 21, 2020, https://www.msn.com/en-us/news/elections-2020/the-constitution -says-no-to-dc-statehood/ar-BB15MkiW.

256 Ayanna Pressley, "Press Release: Rep. Pressley in Oversight Hearing: DC Statehood Is a Racial Justice Issue," Pressley.House.gov, March 23, 2021, https://pressley.house.gov/media/press-releases/rep-pressley-oversight-hearing -dc-statehood-racial-justice-issue.

257 Anna G. Eshoo and Jerry McNerney, "Eshoo-McNerney-TV-Misinfo Letters -2.22.21.pdf," Anna G. Eshoo official website, February 22, 2021, https:// eshoo.house.gov/sites/eshoo.house.gov/files/Eshoo-McNerney-TV-Misinfo %20Letters-2.22.21.pdf.

258 Sara M. Moniuszko, "Chris Cuomo Calls for Police Accountability: 'Too Many See the Protests as the Problem,'" *USA Today*, June 3, 2020, https://www .usatoday.com/story/entertainment/celebrities/2020/06/03/chris-cuomo-calls -police-accountability-defends-protests/3133326001/.

259 Kaiser Family Foundation, "Biden Raises Fears Trump Will Rush Unsafe Vaccine for Political Gain," KHN Morning Briefing, September 17, 2020, https://khn.org/morning-breakout/biden-raises-fears-trump-will-rush-unsafe -vaccine-for-political-gain/.

260 Jacqueline Howard, "The Percentage of Americans Who Say They Would Get a COVID-19 Vaccine Is Falling, CNN Poll Finds," CNN, October 5, 2020, https://www.cnn.com/2020/10/05/health/covid-19-vaccine-willingness-cnn -poll-wellness/index.html.

261 Benjamin Arden, News Release: "FCC Commissioner Carr Responds to Democrats' Efforts to Censor Newsrooms," FCC.gov, February 22, 2021, https://docs.fcc.gov/public/attachments/DOC-370165A1.pdf.

262 *Post* Editorial Board, "Democrats' Sneak Attack on the Free Press," *New York Post*, February 26, 2021, https://nypost.com/2021/02/26/democrats-sneak -attack-on-the-free-press/.

263 Frank Pallone, Jr., "Pallone Opening Statement.CAT_.pdf," Committee on Energy and Commerce Opening Statement, Hearing on "Fanning the Flames: Disinformation and Extremism in the Media," February 24, 2021, https:// energycommerce.house.gov/sites/democrats.energycommerce.house.gov/files/ documents/2021.2.24.%20Pallone%20Opening%20Statement.CAT_.pdf.

264 Matthew S. Schwartz, "Trump Tells Agencies to End Trainings on 'White Privilege' and 'Critical Race Theory,'" NPR.org, September 5, 2020, https://www.npr.org/2020/09/05/910053496/trump-tells-agencies-to-end-trainings-on-white-privilege-and-critical-race-theory.

265 Maureen Callahan, "Peddling the Idea That 'All White People Are Racist' for Profit," *New York Post*, August 6, 2020, https://nypost.com/2020/08/06/peddling-the-idea-that-all-white-people-are-racist-for-profit/.

266 J. C. Pan, "Workplace 'Anti-Racism Trainings' Aren't Helping," *Jacobin magazine*, September 9, 2020, https://www.jacobinmag.com/2020/09/workplace-anti-racism-trainings-trump-corporate-america.

267 Nick Romano, "Amazon No Longer Sells Books 'That Frame LGBTQ + Identity as a Mental Illness,'" *Entertainment Weekly*, March 12, 2021, https://ew.com/books/amazon-doesnt-sell-books-lgbtq-identity-mental-illness/.

268 Ryan T. Anderson, "Amazon Won't Let You Read My Book," *Wall Street Journal*, March 16, 2021, https://www.wsj.com/articles/amazon-wont-let-you-read-my-book-11615934447.

269 Mark Serrels, "Blizzard Pulls Blitzchung from Hearthstone Esports Tournament over Support for Hong Kong Protests," CNet.com, October 8, 2019, https://www.cnet.com/news/blizzard-pulls-blitzchung-from-hearthstone-esports-tournament-over-support-for-hong-kong-protests/.

270 Jamil Smith, "The NBA Chooses China's Money over Hong Kong's Human Rights," *Rolling Stone*, October 7, 2019, https://www.rollingstone.com/politics/politics-news/daryl-morey-nba-hong-kong-houston-rockets-895706/.

271 Maura Moynihan, "Disney's China Problem: West's Elite Covering up CCP's Misdeeds," *Asian Age*, October 21, 2020, https://www.asianage.com/opinion/columnists/211020/maura-moynihan-disneys-china-problem-wests-elite-covering-up-ccps-misdeeds.html.

272 Leslie Stahl, "What Happened in Wuhan? Why Questions Still Linger on the Origin of the Coronavirus," CBS News, *60 Minutes*, March 28, 2021, https://www.cbsnews.com/news/covid-19-wuhan-origins-60-minutes-2021-03-28/.

273 Erin Schumaker and Sony Salzman, "COVID-19 Virus Origin Likely Animal to Human Transmission; Concerns about WHO Report Linger," ABC News, March 30, 2021.

274 Emily Jacobs, "Biden Education Secretary Nominee Added High School Critical Theory Classes," *New York Post*, December 23, 2020, https://nypost.com/2020/12/23/biden-education-secretary-nominee-added-critical-theory-classes/.

275 Ronald Reagan, "January 5, 1967: Inaugural Address," Ronald Reagan Presidential Library and Museum, https://www.reaganlibrary.gov/archives/speech/january-5-1967-inaugural-address-public-ceremony.

Acknowledgments

TO MY FAMILY AND friends. You have always been there for me, through the highs and the lows and I will be forever grateful. God puts many people in our lives and I have truly been blessed with so many people who have enriched my life.

Many thanks to Jim Denney for the passion and time invested in this project. I am so proud of what we accomplished through hours of research, fact checking, and conversations. Thank you for sharing your talents with me. Continued thanks to Katie Armstrong for keeping the trains moving on time both on this project and so much more. My attorney David Limbaugh—you are not only amazing at what you do but are a trusted sounding board and friend.

Mary Glenn and Keith Pfeffer at Humanix who shepherded this project from beginning to end—it is a reality because of your support.

The team at point1: Greg Capelli, Jimmy Keady, Ben Marchi, and Evan Stewart.

The entire team at Newsmax who has given me a platform to raise issues and policies that will impact the future of our families, communities, businesses, and country. The show comes on television (and over the internet) every weeknight because of a talented group of people behind the cameras in Washington, Boca Raton, and New York.

The book and show would not be possible without the vision, support, and friendship of Chris Ruddy. I come to "work" every day excited and grateful for the opportunity Chris has provided me.

Elliot Jacobson and the team that makes *Spicer & Co.* great every night: Amy Mina, Alexa Angelus, Anna Laudiero, Jake Pollack, John Kilbashian, Michelle Lopata, David Wasser, Diego Ciborro, Dave Smolar, and Renee Baldwin.

My co-host Lyndsay Keith. It is an absolute honor and joy to sit next to you every night and put on a great show that informs and transforms. I am blessed and honored to have you as a friend.

And finally a *huge* thank you to the guests, friends, and viewers of *Spicer & Co.* We strive to bring you an amazing hour of lively conversations and outstanding guests every weeknight. Your continued support of the show means more than I can ever express.

Index

About the Author

Sean Spicer served as the 28th White House press secretary and is the author of the bestselling book *The Briefing*. Mr. Spicer is the host of *Spicer & Co.* on Newsmax TV. He is the president of RigWil, LLC, a strategic consulting firm and a partner in Point1, a political mail firm. Mr. Spicer previously served as communications director and chief strategist of the Republican National Committee and worked for several members of Congress. He serves on the Board of Visitors of the U.S. Naval Academy and holds a master's degree from the U.S. Naval War College. Additionally, he was a quarterfinalist on ABC's *Dancing with the Stars* in season 28. Mr. Spicer is a native of Rhode Island and resides in Virginia.

He can be reached at seanspicer.com, found on Instagram @SeanMSpicer or Twitter @SeanSpicer and his show, *Spicer & Co* can be watched weeknights at 6 p.m. ET on Newsmax TV.